This book attempts to show how technological change is generated and the processes by which improved technologies are introduced into economic activity. This is a far more complex process than it is often made out to be, largely because much of the reasoning and modelling of technological change hopelessly oversimplifies its component parts. The process of technological change takes a wide variety of forms so that propositions that might for instance be accurate when referring to the pharmaceutical industry are likely to be totally inappropriate when applied to the aircraft industry or to computers or forest products.

Professor Rosenberg pays particular attention to the nature of the research process out of which new technologies have emerged. A central theme of the book is the idea that technological changes are often "path dependent" in the sense that their form and direction tend to be influenced strongly by the particular sequence of earlier events out of which a new technology has emerged. As a result, attempting to theorize about technologies without taking these factors into account is likely to fail to capture their most essential features.

The book advances our understanding of technological change by explicitly recognizing its essential diversity and path-dependent nature. Individual chapters explore the particular features of new technologies in different historical and sectoral contexts.

Exploring the black box

Exploring the black box

Technology, economics, and history

Nathan Rosenberg
Professor of Economics, Stanford University

CAMBRIDGE
UNIVERSITY PRESS

Published by the Press Syndicate of the University of Cambridge
The Pitt Building, Trumpington Street, Cambridge CB2 1RP
40 West 20th Street, New York, NY 10011-4211, USA
10 Stamford Road, Oakleigh, Melbourne 3166, Australia

First published 1994

Printed in Great Britain at the University Press, Cambridge

A catalogue record for this book is available from the British Library

Library of Congress cataloguing in publication data

Rosenberg, Nathan, 1927–
   Exploring the black box; technology, economics, and history /
Nathan Rosenberg.
      p.   cm.
   ISBN 0 521 45270 8
   1. Technological innovations.   2. Technological innovations–
United States.   3. Technological innovations–Economic aspects.
4. Technological innovations–Economic aspects–United States.
I. Title.
T173.8.R66   1994
609.73–dc20   93-4681   CIP

ISBN 0 521 45270 8 hardback
ISBN 0 521 45955 9 paperback

SE

Contents

List of figures   *page* viii
Preface   ix
Introduction   1

Part I   Dealing with an uncertain future   7

  1 Path-dependent aspects of technological change   9
  2 Charles Babbage: pioneer economist   24
  3 Joseph Schumpeter: radical economist   47
  4 Technological innovation and long waves   62

Part II   Technology in context   85

  5 Economic experiments   87
  6 Why in America?   109
  7 Can Americans learn to become better imitators?   121
  8 Critical issues in science policy research   139

Part III   Sectoral studies in technological change   159

  9 Energy-efficient technologies: past and future
    perspectives   161
  10 Innovation in the chemical processing industries   190
  11 Telecommunications: complex, uncertain, and path
    dependent   203
  12 Understanding the adoption of new technology in
    the forest products industry   232
  13 Scientific instrumentation and university research   250

Index   264

Figures

9.1   Energy consumption per unit of GNP   *page* 167

9.2   Industrial energy intensity by country, all countries   173

9.3   Real prices of energy, 1953 to 1976   178

10.1 Learning curves in innovation   195

12.1 Composition of inventory and harvest of softwood growing stock by size class from 1952 to 1987   237

12.2 Price of Douglas-fir veneer logs in western Washington and Northwest Oregon from 1950 to 1985   237

12.3 Prices of softwood, plywood, and lumber in Douglas-fir region from 1950 to 1985   241

12.4 Price of Douglas-fir veneer compared to price of aspen sawlogs and OSB-waferboard production from 1955 to 1985   242

Preface

I have called this book *Exploring the black box* in order to emphasize its intellectual continuity with an earlier one, *Inside the black box*. In the preface to that book I stated that its purpose was "to break open and to examine the contents of the black box into which technological change has been consigned by economists" (p. vii). That statement of intent would also serve as a useful entry point into what follows. The economics of technological change is a subject that is still seriously befuddled by the failure to come to grips with the immense diversity of the contents of the black box. Readers of the earlier book will find inevitable shifts of priority and direction in this one. Nevertheless, the present work represents a continuation of the intellectual "unpacking" that was central to *Inside the black box*. Although economists are now, happily, devoting considerably more attention to the economic significance of technological phenomena, the marginal returns to further effort of that kind remain extremely high.

My research over the past several years has been generously supported by the Technology and Economic Growth Program of the Stanford Center for Economic Policy Research, for which I am most grateful. Dr. Ralph Landau, the co-director of that program, has been a continuous source of stimulation and encouragement. I have learned a great deal from him about some of the complexities of the interface between technology and economics. I must also express my particular thanks to the indefatigable Scott Stern, who helped in numerous ways in preparing this book for publication.

Introduction

The principal focus of this book is the process by which information – new information as well as old – comes to be embedded in new technologies. The process is not a straightforward matter. Indeed, if it were, most of the chapters of this book would be superfluous. In fact, the main purpose of the book is to provide a better understanding of the diversity of that process, as well as some of the implications of that diversity. Technological change is an extraordinarily complex subject that takes a multiplicity of forms and directions, often requiring different angles of vision for different industries as well as for different periods of history.

Consequently, one recurring focus of interest here is the way in which, and the extent to which, the information necessary for technological improvement can be deduced from existing bodies of theoretical knowledge. Much of the discussion in the following pages differs from other approaches to the economics of technological change by paying explicit attention to the qualitative features of information acquisition. This involves distinguishing between the emergence of theories and concepts, on the one hand, and the often costly empirical experimentation associated with product design in the context of firms pursuing profits in the market place, on the other. While product design and market viability are often informed by theory – for example, a background in chemistry is distinctly helpful in the synthesis of a new molecule – most of the important details need not be a consequence of scientific theory of any sort. Rather, the new product may take its particular shape as a result of certain trade-offs between improved product features and higher cost, the "peculiarities" of consumer tastes in specific markets, or the physical characteristics of complementary technologies. Furthermore, these details and idiosyncratic features will often feed back upon science and powerfully shape the direction taken by scientific research.

Therefore, in order to analyze adequately the determinants and consequences of technological change, these kinds of information interdependencies must be confronted directly. By "getting down into the trenches,"

1

examining the particular sequence of events and institutions within particular industries, one can extract insights into the process by which technological knowledge grows – knowledge of a kind that cannot be deduced from some merely theoretical framework. This is a theme that is developed at greater length in chapter 1, which pays particular attention to the path-dependent nature of technological change. It is also a theme that was well understood by that remarkable nineteenth-century polymath, Charles Babbage, the subject of chapter 2. Babbage cautioned that "the errors which arise from the absence of facts are far more numerous and more durable than those which result from unsound reasoning respecting true data" (*On the Economy of Machinery and Manufactures*, repr. Frank Cass & Co, London, 1963, p. 156).

The reader, I hope, will find that Babbage's admonition has been heeded throughout the book. In fact, the chapters share a deep concern with the consequences of the lack of clear or convincing guidance by scientific or economic theory and the necessity of a central role for historical analysis. There are three particular spheres in which these concerns have directly played a role in the development of these chapters: the determination of optimal product/process design, the inability to foresee the consequences of innovations at the time of invention, and the analysis and criticism of particular assumptions and distinctions within economic theory.

The determination of product and process design

The first set of concerns strikes very deeply at the reasons why technological change is so difficult to analyze. Technological advance, almost by definition, is the result of costly experimentation and the assembly and manipulation of empirical data. While scientific theory sometimes guides the experimentation process, the precise design of an experiment and the mapping of its results into a new product or process are activities that cannot be deduced from theory. This should be apparent from the fact that, for many years, approximately two-thirds of United States research and development (R&D) expenditures have consisted of D, that is, development expenditures. Development expenditures, the realm of engineers and product designers, are activities undertaken by firms in order to acquire information about the physical properties of materials or substances that can guide the design of new products or processes. Science, at best, is of only limited assistance in determining the specificities of such designs.

Thus, in examining the role played by chemical engineers and specialized engineering firms in transforming laboratory curiosities into large-scale continuous-process operations (chapter 10), it is necessary to focus on the costs of scale-up, the role of engineering principles in reducing uncertainty, and the underappreciation of these engineering activities in economists' discussions of technological change. The limited contribution of science to the determination of product design results partly from limitations on the side of science, but also from the fact that many aspects of product design have little, if anything, to do with scientific principles. Successful product design also necessarily reflects important economic and institutional variables, such as the relative scarcities (and therefore prices) of inputs, the availability of complementary technologies, the particular historical sequences in which innovation and adoption have occurred in the past, and the preference structures of firms and consumers. When examining the determinants of technological change within a particular industry or technological system, the chapters in this book attempt to distinguish among the roles played by each of these forces. The underlying premise is that serious analysis of technological change, even in the so-called "high-tech" industries, cannot proceed without an acceptance of the fundamental fact that technological advance is the result of a host of factors, of which guidance from science is only one.

Foreseeing the consequences of innovation

It is easy to conclude that, whatever the difficulties and uncertainties in developing a new product might be, anticipating the subsequent *uses* of the new product, once developed, would be relatively easy. Such a conclusion, however, is not borne out by history. On the contrary, it appears that it has been remarkably difficult to appreciate the potential significance of an invention at the time of its first introduction. Consequently, in examining the multiplicity of ways in which information becomes embedded in technology, several of the chapters focus upon the manner in which the potential applications of new technologies are gradually identified.

The trajectories of telecommunications technologies (chapter 11), for example, provide a rich and diverse history that highlights the vast discrepancies between perceptions of new technologies and their eventual uses. In examining the history of the laser, the telephone, the radio, the computer, the transistor, or most of the other major innovations that have exercised a substantial impact on a telecommunications system, one cannot help being struck by the remarkable inability to foresee the eventual applications of these technologies. Consider the laser which, together with fiber optics, is revolutionizing transmission within the telephone industry. It is reported that patent lawyers at Bell Labs. were initially unwilling to apply for a patent on the laser, on the grounds that optical waves had never played a role in communications and were therefore of no interest to the Bell system.

Similar incidents have occurred in a variety of contexts. The refusal of Western Union to buy out Bell's telephone patent when it was available for a mere $100,000, Marconi's belief that the radio would serve primarily as an instrument for point-to-point communication in situations where communication by wire was not available, and the perception that the computer would be useful only in a few specialized research projects are characteristic of a pervasive inability to predict the consequences of a wide class of innovations. Not all innovations, of course, have been characterized by such huge miscalculations. Instead, innovations that are grossly misjudged at the time of their invention appear to possess one or more of a particular cluster of characteristics. These characteristics, each of which receives attention in the following chapters, can appropriately be considered as constraints on our thinking about the potential uses of new technologies.

1.   New technologies typically come into the world in a very primitive condition. An extensive improvement process, the details of which can hardly be known at the time of invention, vastly expands the practical applications of the technology. The 18,000 vacuum tubes necessary for the functioning of the first electronic digital computer (ENIAC) was a feature of the early machine that led, not surprisingly, to a very conservative estimate of the future demand for computing.

2.   Closely related to (1), the impact of an innovation depends not only on improvements of the invention, but also upon improvements that take place in *complementary* inventions. For laser technologies to become useful in telecommunications, several advances in fiber optics had to be accomplished and the attractive commercial properties of fiber-optics technology had to be recognized. Indeed, telephone transmission today is not being recast by either laser technology or fiber optics in isolation; it is the potential of their *combination* which is exercising such a powerful effect. Further, a range of complementary inventions and technical improvements was involved in applying laser technology to other quite unanticipated uses, including delicate surgery, chemical research, industrial cutting and shaping of materials, high-quality reproduction of sound, and printing the output of computers.

3.   Major technological innovations often constitute entirely new systems. But it appears to be difficult in the extreme to conceptualize an entirely new system. Thus, new technologies are often thought of in limited terms, as mere supplements to a current system. Railroads, electrical generation grids, and the telephone network are all examples of highly complicated systems that were first contemplated as feeders or supplements to already existing systems rather than as new systems that would largely displace the old ones.

4.   Finally, the ultimate impact of some new technological capability is

not just a matter of technical feasibility or improved technical performance; rather, it is a matter of identifying human needs in ways, or in contexts, that have not yet been articulated. What is called for is not just engineering expertise or high-quality professional analysis, but imagination. Sony's Walkman is an excellent example. The design of its component parts required engineering expertise, to be sure. But more impressive was the imaginative leap that identified an important market niche.

The applicability of economic theory

Hence, historical analysis supports the view that technological change often takes place in quite information-poor and uncertain environments. This paucity of information on the part of decision-makers powerfully constrains their ability to assess the consequences of technical advance. However, neoclassical economic models of technological change *assume* very rich information environments, often only restricting the information available to the firm in one or at most two well-defined ways. Instead of proceeding from a natural starting point where firms possess little or no information and acquire information through experience and investment, most economic models of technological change assume that firms are aware of all the technological options available to them (leading to a well-defined production function). In addition, these models assume that firms possess complete information concerning the economic value of the technologies "induced" by expenditures on R&D. With these strong assumptions, it is simple to characterize the linear model of the science/technology/production interface, or to derive comparative statics using the neoclassical growth model. From this point of view, one aim of this book is to persuade the reader that simple linear analysis cannot satisfactorily explore the rich and interrelated terrains of technological change and economic growth.

For example, traditional analysis sharply distinguishes between factor substitution and technical change. Yet, to the extent that firms are not entirely aware of the details of a production process using factor mixes that are technologically distant from the current production process, factor substitution and the growth of technological knowledge are not readily distinguishable. At the very least, much of what is now characterized as R&D (which is often the primary empirical proxy for resources devoted to technological advance) is actually devoted to acquiring information associated with factor substitution rather than technical advance. It is important to recognize that firms have little incentive to be fully aware of technological options which are not going to be used within the present production process. The reason is simple: acquiring new information is costly. Changes in the prices of relevant inputs initiate a process of search and experimentation which yields detailed technical information that has been historically important for long-term economic growth, often in sectors of the economy distant from the initial inquiry. The American experience with energy and forest products (chapters 9 and 12, respectively), the need for greater imitative capabilities by American firms of their Japanese counterparts (chapter 7), and fundamental issues in centralized planning (chapter 5) are all linked by the recognition that producers and innovators only acquire information through experience, experimentation, and invest-ment. But a neoclassical approach, assuming perfect knowledge of the production-possibilities frontier, obscures these issues, thus fundamentally mischaracterizing the content of technical change and factor substitution.

Similarly, as is argued in chapter 8, the determinants of technical change are profoundly underidentified. In order to fill the place of the discredited linear model of innovation, there is an urgent need to explore the landscape of the interactions between science, technology, and institutions so as to guide research and policy in new and fruitful directions. Previous research has focused excessively on the effect of a marginal addition to the total stock of scientific knowledge of technical advance. This focus resulted from the unrealistic assumption that all firms and individuals are already fully cognizant of the existing stock of scientific knowledge. In contrast, the historical record reveals that it is often the rediscovery of old science, or the discovery of an empirical relationship not accounted for by science, that leads to significant technical change. Once we proceed from the assumption that it is quite costly for individuals or firms to acquire scientific knowledge (even old knowledge), then the more complicated interdependencies can be more readily explained.

The book will be successful, at least from my point of view, if it leads to an expanded appreciation of the multiple dimensions of a subject that is, simultaneously, fascinating and challenging in its complexity and full of significance for the human condition.

Part I

Dealing with an uncertain future

1 Path-dependent aspects of technological change

I

It is no longer necessary for an economist to apologize when introducing the subject of technological change. That is, in itself, a (modest) cause for celebration, since the situation was very different as recently as forty years ago. At that time, economics had still not been awakened from its dogmatic slumber on the subject, and was content to treat – or perhaps a more appropriate operational verb would be "to dismiss" – technological change purely as an exogenous variable, one that had economic consequences but no visible economic antecedents. Although sympathetic readers of Marx and Schumpeter had learned to attach great importance to technological change as a major impulse – perhaps *the* major impulse – in generating long-term economic growth, such an awareness had not yet rubbed off on the dominant academic traditions of western economics.

Today, the economic importance of technological change is widely acknowledged. There cannot be many economists who would dissent from the view that the growth of technological knowledge is fundamental to the improvement of economic performance. In addition, it is widely accepted that, in advanced industrial economies, the growth in technological knowledge relies increasingly, although in ways that are never clearly specified, on science.[1]

I have had valuable discussions of the issues treated in this chapter with Stanley Engerman, William Parker, and Scott Stern. I owe a particular debt to Paul David for his gentle but persistent encouragement in formulating my thoughts about path-dependent phenomena. The chapter draws, occasionally, upon two earlier papers: "How Exogenous is Science?", chapter 7 of Nathan Rosenberg, *Inside the Black Box*, Cambridge University Press, Cambridge, 1982, and Nathan Rosenberg, "The Commercialization of Science by American Industry," in Kim Clark, Robert H. Hayes, and Christopher Lorenz (eds.), *The Uneasy Alliance*, Harvard Business School Press, Boston (MA), 1985.

[1] An interesting index of this lack of clarity is that, for many years, the most valuable single source of quantitative information on technological matters was (and still is) the National Science Foundation's biennial publication, *Science Indicators*. Only since the publication of the 1987 issue was it finally acknowledged in the title that the volume is at least equally concerned with matters pertaining to technology. Since that year it has borne the title *Science and Engineering Indicators*.

Thus, it seems reasonable to pose two questions: what can be said about the manner in which the stock of technological knowledge grows over time? And, to what factors is it responsive, and in what ways?

In dealing with these questions I will argue that the main features of the stock of technological knowledge available at any given time can only be understood by a systematic examination of the earlier history out of which it emerged. There is, as I intend to show, a strong degree of path dependence,[2] in the sense that one cannot demonstrate the direction or path in the growth of technological knowledge merely by reference to certain initial conditions. Rather, the most probable directions for future growth in knowledge can only be understood within the context of the particular sequence of events which constitutes the history of the system.

Further, although I believe that economic factors have powerfully shaped the growth of that knowledge, I also believe that there is no prospect of adequately accounting for the *content* of that knowledge by any economic model. In this respect economic theory is not, and never can be, a *substitute* for history, although it is obviously an invaluable complement. Economic forces powerfully influence the decision to undertake a search process, but they do so in ways that do not predetermine the nature and the shape of the things that are *found*. The findings of scientific research, and their economic consequences, remain shrouded in uncertainty. They reflect certain properties of the physical universe that are uncovered by the search, and not the economic goals that were in the mind of decision-makers who allocated resources to the research process in the first place.[3]

---

[2] The most rigorous formulation of path-dependent phenomena in terms of their relevance for history is by Paul David. See, in particular, "Path Dependence: Putting the Past Into the Future of Economics," unpublished manuscript, Stanford University, July 1988. Elsewhere David has stated: "[I]t is sometimes not possible to uncover the logic (or illogic) of the world around us except by understanding how it got that way. A *path-dependent* sequence of economic changes is one in which important influences upon the eventual outcome can be exerted by temporally remote events, including happenings dominated by chance elements rather than systematic forces. Stochastic processes like that do not converge automatically to a fixed-point distribution of outcomes, and are called *non-ergodic*. In such circumstances 'historical accidents' can neither be ignored, nor neatly quarantined for the purposes of economic analysis; the dynamic process itself takes on an *essentially historical* character." Paul David, "Understanding the Economics of QWERTY: The Necessity of History," in William N. Parker (ed.), *Economic History and the Modern Economist*, Basil Blackwell, Oxford, 1986, p. 30. See also Brian Arthur, "Competing Technologies, Increasing Returns, and Lock-In by Historical Small Events," *Economic Journal*, 99 (1989), pp. 116–131.

[3] As Arrow once succinctly put it: "European desire for spices in the fifteenth century may have had a good deal to do with motivating Columbus' voyages, but the brute, though unknown, facts of geography determined what in fact was their economic results." Kenneth Arrow, "Classificatory Notes on the Production and Transmission of Technological Knowledge," *American Economic Review Papers and Proceedings* (May 1969), p. 35.

II

Of course, it would not be quite correct to say that economic analysis has ever totally ignored the subject of technology. Rather, an explicit examination of technology and knowledge about technology has simply been suppressed by introducing certain assumptions, often only implicit, into the theory of the firm. Central to that theory, and therefore at the foundation of modern microeconomics, has been the assumption of a given set of tastes and some given stock of technological knowledge. This technological knowledge is (somehow) embedded in a set of production possibilities, a collection of known alternative combinations of factor inputs that may be employed in producing a given volume of output. *Given* this knowledge of tastes and technology, the firm then determines its optimal behavior, including the choice of technique, through the explicit consideration of factor prices. The implications for resource allocation of *changes* in technology or in factor prices can then be readily examined within this static equilibrium framework.

For many purposes this would seem to be quite enough to get the analytical ball rolling.[4] If one is interested only in exploring the implications of maximizing behavior, one is surely entitled to say that it is not a matter of primary concern to that analysis to know how any particular state of the world came to be that way. And exploring the implications of maximizing behavior subject to certain constraints is, obviously, a legitimate intellectual exercise.

I want to suggest that, even at this level, serious problems arise – not, of course, as a matter of pure logic, but as a matter of the potential explanatory usefulness of an analysis built on such premises. Moreover, the problems are not "merely" epistemological, but are central to the question of how to understand the level of technological competence that prevails in an economy at any particular time.

Why, to begin with, is it plausible to assume that a firm would *know* a range of technical options that are located far from the one that is presently employed? Once it is recognized that the acquisition of new technological knowledge is a costly process, why should resources be expended in acquiring knowledge that is not – or is not expected to be – economically useful?

One answer would rely on drawing a sharp distinction between the state of scientific knowledge and the state of technological knowledge. Such an answer might argue that a given level of scientific knowledge will always

---

[4] Not for the purposes of Joseph Schumpeter, though. For a discussion of Schumpeter's criticism of neoclassical economics, see chapter 3 of this book pp. 47–61.

illuminate a wide spectrum of technological options, and that these are precisely the options represented on a production isoquant; that is, the production isoquant simply identifies the technological options that are made available by the existing stock of scientific knowledge. This is essentially the position that was argued by W.E.G. Salter in his valuable book, *Productivity and Technical Change*.

At one level this position is totally plausible. However difficult it may be to speak of the state of scientific knowledge as if it were some quantifiable magnitude, surely it is meaningful to say that the body of presently available scientific knowledge imposes certain *constraints* on what is technologically possible and also, by the same token, permits a range of technological alternatives to be taken up within the frontiers imposed by that knowledge.[5] As a statement about the scientific and technological realms, this is obviously useful. As a statement that has relevance for the *economic realm*, however, it is distinctly problematical.

Perhaps it is helpful to invoke a distinction that Boswell offered to his readers in his *Life of Johnson*: "Knowledge," he said, "is of two kinds. We know a subject ourselves, or we know where we can find information upon it." Precisely. Science will often provide the capability to acquire information about technological alternatives that we do not presently possess, but *science does not make the acquisition of this information costless*. Indeed, it may for certain purposes be useful to think of science as a guide for exploring the technological realm, and it is also plausible to believe that, *ceteris paribus*, the greater the stock of scientific knowledge, the lower will be the cost of acquiring necessary, but presently unavailable, information concerning technological alternatives. But I suggest that the starting point for serious thinking about technological knowledge is the recognition that one cannot move *costlessly* to new points on the production isoquant, especially points that are a great technological distance from the present location of productive activities. There are, I believe, distinct limits to the usefulness of the notion of technological alternatives being "on-the-shelf." Although we may indeed, as Boswell suggested, know where we can find information on the subject at hand, *acquiring* the information, in the detailed sense of being able to base productive activities upon it, may be, and surely often is, a very expensive activity.[6] And one need not belabor the

---

[5] I put aside here the important consideration that technological progress can – and does – often go *beyond* the frontiers of what is understood in a scientific sense. The limited scientific understanding of the combustion process has not prevented the operation of blast furnaces or coal-fired electric power generating plants, and the absence of a theory of turbulence has not posed an impossible barrier to the design of reliable aircraft.

[6] Even when certain blueprints are literally on the shelf, the technology may not be as "freely" available as might be assumed. Ken Arrow pointed out a number of years ago that "when the British in World War II supplied us with the plans for the jet engine, it took ten months to redraw them to conform to American usage." Arrow, "Classificatory Notes," p. 34.

point that the cost of alternative courses of action is precisely what economic analysis is all about.

One valuable perspective on the cost of acquiring information is offered by the available data on R&D expenditures. These data are additionally valuable in showing the extent to which the generation and diffusion of knowledge has become an endogenous economic activity. In the year 1991, according to *Science and Engineering Indicators*, total R&D spending in the United States was estimated to amount to $152 billion, of which private industry financed almost 56 percent. Of particular importance for present purposes is the fact that the great bulk of total R&D spending is for Development activities, not for Basic or Applied Research. Development expenditures accounted for approximately 67 percent of total R&D spending. These figures, at the very least, suggest great skepticism about the view that the state of *scientific* knowledge at any time illuminates a wide range of alternative techniques from which the firm may make cost-less, off-the-shelf selections. It thereby also encourages skepticism toward the notion that is so deeply embedded in the neoclassical theory of the firm, that one can draw a sharp and well-delineated distinction between technological change and factor substitution. Although it is essential to the argument of this paper that the D of R&D encompasses a wide range of diverse, information-acquiring activities, it also includes many expenditures that are essential to make possible what economists have in mind when speaking of factor substitution.[7]

The extent to which total R&D spending is dominated by the Development component calls attention to some critical aspects of the manner in which technological knowledge grows. At least in respect of "high-technology" products, it is misleading to speak of some as-yet-untried but on-the-shelf technologies as "known." It is of the essence of these technologies that their designs need to undergo protracted periods of testing, redesign and modification, and retesting before their performance characteristics are well enough understood for them to be produced and sold in reasonable confidence.[8] Although these expensive and time-consuming Development activities are typically not of great interest for their specific scientific content, the information so acquired is absolutely essential from an economic point of view. Performance characteristics of high-technology products simply cannot be accurately predicted without extensive testing. A new jet-engine design, or airplane wing, or weapons system, or electronic switching system, or synthetic-fuel plant, or pharmaceutical product, may

---

[7] This argument is pursued further in chapter 6 of this book, which argues that the relative abundance of natural resources within the United States (in addition to a host of other variables) affected the direction of American technological change throughout the first half of the nineteenth century.

[8] Some of these issues are examined in Rosenberg, "Learning by Using," *Inside the Black Box*, chapter 6.

require an enormous amount of testing before its performance characteristics can be understood with a high enough degree of accuracy and reliability to warrant commercial introduction. A large part of the D of R&D is devoted precisely to acquiring such information.[9] It cannot be overemphasized that such information typically cannot be *deduced* from scientific principles.[10]

It is curious that whereas so much attention in the last few decades has been properly devoted to incorporating the effects of uncertainty into economic analysis, these effects should have been totally neglected in this particular realm – the determination of optimal design of specific products. Such uncertainties are of very limited interest from the point of view of academic science. But the essential economic point is that these uncertainties are extremely costly to reduce or resolve. When considering the possibility of technological alternatives that are so far only on the shelf, the reduction of design, cost, and performance uncertainties is of absolutely central economic importance. In fact, workable technological knowledge in highly industrialized societies today is, in considerable measure, the (eventual) product of Development activities. Much of the Development effort is, in effect, directed toward the progressive reduction of cost and performance uncertainties in product (and process) design.

This observation concerning the importance of Development activities highlights an additional feature of the growth of technological knowledge. That is, most Development activities at any time are not devoted to the introduction of entirely new products, but rather to the improvement and modification of existing products. Although it is difficult to draw precise boundaries among the separate components of Development activities, undoubtedly the bulk of such activities, at any time, is devoted to efforts to improve existing products rather than to the introduction of entirely new products. In this respect, present activities are powerfully shaped by technological knowledge inherited from the past. Existing technologies commonly throw off signals and focusing devices indicating specific directions in which technological efforts can be usefully exercised. These internally generated pressures and compulsions play a large role in shaping day-to-day Development activities.[11] Such activities involve endless minor

---

[9] The means of acquiring this information are themselves being transformed by new technologies. New aircraft designs are increasingly "tested" on supercomputers rather than in more traditional wind tunnels. Nevertheless, simulated testing, or other forms of laboratory testing, is often still very remote from actual operating conditions, and therefore of limited reliability.

[10] For a full documentation of this point in the context of aeronautical engineering, see Walter Vincenti, *What Engineers Know and How They Know It*, The Johns Hopkins University Press, Baltimore (MD), 1991.

[11] For further discussion of these themes, see Nathan Rosenberg, "The Direction of Technological Change: Inducement Mechanisms and Focusing Devices," in Nathan Rosenberg, *Perspectives on Technology*, Cambridge University Press, Cambridge, 1976,

modifications and improvements in existing products, each of which is of small significance but which, cumulatively, are of major significance. Once the basic technology of generating electric power through the burning of fossil fuels had been introduced at the beginning of the twentieth century, it set the stage for several decades of minor plant improvements. This included a steady rise in operating temperatures and pressures, new alloys, modification of boiler design, etc. Although only specialists would be able to identify even a few of the associated improvements, the amount of coal required to generate a kilowatt-hour of electricity fell by almost an order of magnitude in the course of the following decades. More recently, by focusing upon a succession of individually small improvements, the semi-conductor industry was able to move from products incorporating a single transistor on a chip to products incorporating more than a million such components. Similarly, in the computer industry the speed of computational capability has been increased, again by individually small increments, by *many* orders of magnitude.

III

The instances of the electric power plant, the transistor, and the computer may be useful as a way of defining a major innovation. A major innovation is one that provides a framework for a large number of subsequent innovations, each of which is dependent upon, or complementary to, the original one. We can readily think of the framework established by the invention of the steam engine, machine tools, the internal combustion engine, electric power, or the vacuum tube in this context. But another way of expressing these connections is that each constitutes the initiation of a long sequence of path-dependent activities, typically extending over several decades, in which later developments cannot be understood except as part of a historical sequence.

There is commonly a certain logic in the sequence of some technological developments, a kind of, at least, "soft determinism," in which one historical event did not rigidly prescribe certain subsequent technological developments, but at least made sequences of technological improvements in one direction easier – and hence both cheaper and more probable – than improvements in other directions. Technological knowledge is by nature cumulative: major innovations constitute new building blocks which provide a basis for subsequent technologies, but do so selectively and not randomly. The ability to generate and transmit electric power certainly did not make the invention of the vacuum tube inevitable, but it is difficult to

chapter 6. See also Paul A. David, *Technical Choice, Innovation and Economic Growth*, Cambridge University Press, Cambridge, 1975, introduction and chapter 1, for an illuminating analysis of the learning issues underlying the process of technological change.

think of the vacuum tube, and the transistor, without the prior development of some sort of electric-power generating capability. Again, sequences matter. Technological knowledge grows in distinctly path-dependent ways.

In all these ways, then, ongoing technological research is shaped by what has gone before. There is always a huge overhang of technological inheritance which exercises a powerful influence upon present and future technological possibilities. Much technological progress at any given time, therefore, has to be understood as the attempt to extend and further exploit certain trajectories of improvement that are made possible by the existing stock of technological knowledge. There are continuities of potential improvements which are generally well understood by engineers and product designers. Expert knowledge of the workings of the vacuum tube did not provide an adequate basis for a "discontinuous leap" to the transistor. However, once the transistor was invented, it created a set of opportunities for further improvement by pursuing a trajectory of miniaturization of components (including integrated circuitry) which has occupied the attention of technical personnel for nearly half a century.

So far the discussion of path dependence has been confined to its functioning within certain restricted technological spheres. However, it has also been important, historically, between fields that stood in some sort of complementary relationship to one another, and even between the realms of technology and science.

Scientific knowledge has been closely dependent upon progress within the technological realm. It would not be difficult to show, by drawing upon the long history of the microscope (starting from the simple screw-barrel type in the eighteenth century and proceeding through the compound microscope of the nineteenth century to the electron microscope of the twentieth century), the telescope (including the more recent radio telescope), and the recent histories of x-ray crystallography, the ultracentrifuge, the cyclotron, the various spectroscopies, chromatography, and the computer, how instrumentation possibilities have selectively distributed opportunities in ways that have pervasively affected both the rate and the direction of scientific progress.[12] At the same time, to leave the discussion at that level would constitute a rather crude sort of technological determinism. In fact, the relationship between technology and science is far more interactive (and dialectical) than such a determinism would imply. For the decision to push hard in the improvement of one specific class of instruments will often reflect a determination to advance a particular field of science as well as an expectation that the relevant instrumentation is ripe for improvement. Furthermore, instrumentation technologies differ enor-

---

[12] An extended discussion of this phenomenon is taken up in the final chapter in this book.

mously in the range of their scientific impact. The linear accelerator and the ultracentrifuge are each relevant to a much narrower portion of the scientific spectrum than, say, the computer. The computer, in fact, has turned out to be a general-purpose research instrument, although it was certainly not visualized in that way by the scientists who invented it. Thus, different instruments may differ enormously in the specificity or generality of their impact upon fields of science. And, consequently, the rate and direction of progress in science is likely to be powerfully shaped by the peculiar characteristics of prior progress in scientific instruments.

At the same time, improvements in observational capabilities were, by themselves, of limited significance until concepts were developed and hypotheses formulated that imparted potential meaning to the observations offered by new instruments. The microscope had existed for over 200 years and many generations of curious observers had called attention to strange homunculi under the lens before Pasteur finally formulated a bacterial theory of disease, and the modern science of bacteriology, in the last third of the nineteenth century. The expansion of observational capability had to be complemented, in turn, by the formulation of meaningful interpretive concepts and testable hypotheses before the microscope could make large contributions to scientific progress. Thus, path dependence was critical in the sense that a particular body of science, bacteriology, had to await progress in an observational technology. But such progress was, of course, not sufficient for the scientific advance, only necessary.

IV

It is possible to accept everything that has been said so far but to argue that it is nevertheless restricted in significance. After all, much of what has been said can be captured within the summary observation that the technological trajectories that have been traversed in the past leave a profound imprint upon the present, and that they do so in a variety of ways. They serve to define technological possibilities by facilitating further progress in some directions but not in others. On the other hand, one might respond that the occurrence of major new scientific breakthroughs in effect opens up entirely new technological territories for exploration, thus *liberating* the economy from the constraints of the past.

There is undoubtedly some truth in this observation. It can be argued that precisely because new scientific knowledge opens up new paths, such knowledge creates discontinuities that loosen the influence of the otherwise heavy hand of the past. In this sense, scientific research is a disrupter of technologically generated, path-dependent phenomena.

I believe that this is, at best, only partially true. The possibility of important new scientific findings does not eliminate the impact of path-dependent forces of the kind that have been emphasized so far. In particular, it by no means eliminates the influence of inherited technological capabilities in shaping the future performance of the economy.

This is because the ability to *exploit* new scientific knowledge in a commercial context will depend directly and heavily upon the technological capabilities that are available within an economy. Consider the great excitement all over the world concerning the recent remarkable breakthroughs in superconductivity. As a purely scientific breakthrough, the excitement is well justified. Nevertheless, it may be decades before this is actually translated into better computers, magnetically levitated trains, the transmission of electricity without loss, or the storage of electricity. Achieving these outcomes is not primarily a matter of scientific research, although progress toward their achievement may draw very heavily upon scientific knowledge. Designing new products that exploit the knowledge of high-temperature superconductors, and then designing and making the technology that can produce these new products, are activities that draw primarily upon existing technological capabilities.

This brings us back again to the D of R&D: developing new product concepts, casting them in specific design forms, testing new prototypes, redesigning them, devising new manufacturing technologies that make it possible to achieve drastic reductions in cost, etc. In fact, one of the most forceful economic lessons of the post Second World War period – although there were ample prewar antecedents for those who were interested – is that the ability to achieve the commercial exploitation of new scientific knowledge is heavily dependent upon social capabilities that are remote from the realm of science. These capabilities involve skills in organization, management, and marketing in addition to those of a technological sort. But, in the context of the issues addressed in this chapter, it is inherited, path-dependent technological capabilities that have dominated the eventual commercial exploitation of new technologies whose underlying technological feasibility has been made possible by the advancement of science.

Thus, economic and technological considerations remain powerfully and inextricably involved in converting new scientific research findings into tangible human benefits. In some cases the new scientific understanding has been so limited, or so remote from a capability for exploiting it in an economically meaningful way, that an entirely new discipline had to be created to bring this about. Such was the case toward the end of the nineteenth century in chemistry, and the result was the development of the new discipline of chemical engineering early in the twentieth century.[13] At

---

[13] For a discussion of the contemporary situation, see chapter 10 below.

about the same time, the achievement of heavier-than-air flight at the beginning of the twentieth century gave rise to the entirely new discipline of aeronautical engineering. Aeronautical engineering, as a discipline, had far less of a scientific base to draw upon than did chemical engineering. Indeed, to this day, aircraft design remains an activity that is less guided by a systematic scientific base and is therefore compelled to rely much more heavily upon experimentation and testing of prototypes.

I conclude that there are sharply defined limits to the extent to which new scientific knowledge can liberate an economy's performance from the technological capabilities inherited from the particular path that it has traversed in arriving at its present state.

V

There are other ways in which prior developments in technology have shaped the progress of science and the economic consequences of science. A major development of the twentieth century is that the changing needs of the technological sphere have come to play a major role in shaping the agenda of science. In this sense, as well, scientific research itself has become increasingly dependent upon the path of technological change. Thus, I suggest that the formulation of the research agenda itself cannot be understood without paying attention to prior developments in the realm of technology.

This kind of dependence is not, of course, a uniquely twentieth century phenomenon. It can be seen in the spectacular developments in the iron-and-steel industry that began in the 1850s. In the cases of the three great innovations in the second half of the nineteenth century – the Bessemer converter, Siemens' open-hearth furnace, and the Gilchrist–Thomas basic lining that made possible the exploitation of high phosphorus ores – none of them drew upon chemical knowledge that was *less* than half a century old. However, adoption of these innovations dramatically raised the payoffs resulting from acquisition of new scientific knowledge concerning the properties of steel.

The very success of the Bessemer process in lowering the price of steel and in introducing steel to a rapidly expanding array of new uses made it necessary to subject the inputs of the process to quantitative chemical analysis. This was because, as was quickly discovered, the quality of the output, and its structural integrity, was highly sensitive to even minute variations in the composition of the inputs. Sulfur and phosphorus content had an immediate and very deleterious effect upon the quality of the final product. The addition of even minute quantities of nitrogen from the air during the course of the Bessemer blast led eventually to serious and unexpected deterioration in the performance of the metal, although this causal relationship was not established until many years later. Indeed, it is fair to say that the modern science of metallurgy had its origins in the need to solve practical problems that were associated with the emergence of the modern steel industry.

I suggest that, even well into the twentieth century, metallurgy can be characterized as a sector in which the technologist typically "got there first," that is, developed powerful technologies, or alloys, *in advance of* systematized guidance by science. The scientist was commonly confronted by the technologist with certain properties or performance characteristics that demanded a scientific explanation. A particularly fruitful area of research lay in trying to account for specific properties produced by certain technologies or exploiting particular inputs. Such phenomena as deterioration with age or the brittleness of metals made with a particular fuel were intriguing to scientifically trained people. At the same time, the economic payoff to the solution of such problems had become very high.

The increasing extent to which science became influenced by technology was, of course, greatly reinforced by one of the most important institutional innovations of the twentieth century: the emergence of a large number of industrial research laboratories – almost 12,000 in 1992. Research at these laboratories was obviously strongly shaped by the desire to improve the effectiveness of the technology upon which the firm depended. As these laboratories have matured, the best of them have not only applied scientific knowledge to industrial purposes; they have also been generating much of that knowledge. The recent award of Nobel Prizes to scientists working at IBM in Europe, and to scientists at Bell Labs. in the United States, is an index of the quality of at least the best scientific research work that is conducted in industrial contexts where the research agenda is clearly shaped by a concern with specific advanced technological systems. The problems encountered by sophisticated industrial technologies, and the anomalous observations and unexpected difficulties that they have produced, have served as powerful stimuli to much fruitful scientific research, in the academic community as well as the industrial research laboratory. In these ways the responsiveness of scientific research to economic needs and technological opportunities has been powerfully reinforced.[14]

How else can one account for the fact that solid-state physics, presently the largest subdiscipline of physics, attracted the attention of only a few physicists before the advent of the transistor in 1948?[15] In fact, at that time there were many universities that did not even teach the subject. It was the

---

[14] For further discussion, see Rosenberg, "How Exogenous is Science?", in *Inside the Black Box*, chapter 7.

[15] An extended discussion of the development of the transistor can be found in chapter 11 below.

development of the transistor that transformed that situation by dramatically upgrading the payoff to research in solid-state physics. Moreover, it is important to emphasize that the rapid mobilization of intellectual resources in research on the solid state occurred in the university as well as in private industry immediately after the momentous findings that were announced in 1948. The sequence of events is essential to my argument: transistor technology was not building upon a vast *earlier* commitment of resources to solid-state physics. Rather, it was the initial breakthrough of the transistor that gave rise to a *subsequent* large-scale commitment of scientific resources. Similarly, surface chemistry has become much more important for the same reason. More recently, and to oversimplify somewhat, the development of laser technology suggested the feasibility of using optical fibers for transmission purposes. This possibility naturally pointed to the field of optics, where advances in scientific knowledge could now be expected to have potentially high payoffs. As a result, optics as a field of scientific research has experienced a great resurgence in recent years. It has been converted by changed expectations, based upon past and prospective technological innovations, from a relatively quiet intellectual backwater of science to a burgeoning field of research. Under modern industrial conditions, therefore, technology shapes science in the most powerful of ways: it plays a major role in determining the research agenda of science.

One could examine these relationships in much finer detail by showing how, throughout the high technology sectors of the economy, shifts in the needs of industry have brought with them associated shifts in emphasis in scientific research. When the semiconductor industry moved from a reliance upon discrete circuits (transistors) to integrated circuits, there was also a shift from mechanical to chemical methods of fabrication. That shift brought with it an identifiable increase in chemical science and in the volume of resources devoted to that subject.

Although the technological realm plays a role of growing importance in identifying research problems, the places where the eventual findings of science will have useful applications remain full of uncertainty. Consider information theory, a powerful intellectual tool developed since the Second World War. That this methodology should have been developed in the telephone industry, where channel capacity has been perhaps the most fundamental single constraint on the provision of the industry's service, is hardly surprising.[16] Shannon's analysis of how to determine the transmission capacity of a communication channel offered insights of critical importance to engineering design within the telephone system, where channel capacity is, of course, a dominating constraint. But, as is often the

[16] Claude Shannon, "A Mathematical Theory of Communications," *Bell System Technical Journal* (July 1948).

case, a methodology that had been developed within a very specific context turned out to be capable of providing illuminating insights far from its place of origin. It has shaped the design of hardware and software in other communications media, including radio and television, as well as in data-processing technologies generally. But its uses have not been confined to the realm of engineering or the physical sciences; information theory has also been extensively employed in cryptography, linguistics, psychology, and economics.

Here again there have been highly important historical sequences that cannot, at least in any obvious way, be explained by recourse to economic (or other) logic. The specific needs of a particular technology – the telephone system – gave rise to a body of abstract theory that, in turn, had beneficial applications in numerous and remote contexts. Thus, although it can be explained why a telephone company was willing to support research in a particular direction (possible enlargement of channel capacity) economic factors are of little help in grasping the distinctive characteristics of what was learned as a result of the research.

VI

The purpose of this chapter has been to describe the manner in which technological knowledge grows over time, and some of the determinants and consequences of this growth. A main aim has been to emphasize the extent to which technological change and scientific knowledge are responsive to underlying economic variables. This should not be too surprising, in view of the fact that the financing of R&D is generally undertaken with some explicit economic goal in mind. However, the peculiar nature of the information-acquisition process, especially the uncertainty of what will be found once a search has been undertaken, argues against adherence to a belief in a strict economic determinism. Even if one believes that technical change is propelled by economic forces, it does not follow that some simple functional form exists to describe the relationship between economic incentives and the qualitative nature of technical change. It is true that the transistor was the result of a search process that was set in motion for good economic reasons, that is, to reduce AT&T's costly reliance on vacuum tubes for Long Lines switching. However, the disparate nature of the technological spillovers and social benefits that emerged from Bell Labs.' research effort is quite difficult to analyze without an appreciation of the sequence of events that transpired after the invention of the transistor. Ex ante analysis could not have predicted the transistor's definitive role in reducing the cost of numerical calculation by many orders of magnitude through its central role in computer architecture. It is not simply that an appropriate probability distribution of the transistor's social benefits would be analytically daunting. The deeper point is that, at the point of invention, a well-defined and even marginally informative probability distribution simply could not be constructed.

Although modern economic analysis has, in recent years, paid some explicit attention to technological change, it has not dealt, in any depth, with its particular characteristics. The misreading of technological change, when viewed from a neoclassical perspective, should be apparent from the historical analysis offered in this chapter. Additional knowledge of new production possibilities is not costless, nor is the rate and direction of technological change exogenous.

Consequently, understanding the particular sequence of events that has shaped the knowledge of the technological frontier is crucial, not only to the historian, but to the economist as well. Technology and science, which are now generally acknowledged to be central to the achievement of economic growth, need to be understood as path-dependent phenomena. Indeed, it follows that economic growth itself needs to be understood in terms of path dependence. An economy's history has left a large deposit of technological capabilities and possibilities on the shelf. The cost of taking items off that shelf is never known with any precision. Historical analysis, however, can allow us at least to narrow our estimates and thus to concentrate resources in directions that are more likely to have useful payoffs.

2 Charles Babbage: pioneer economist

> ... the arrangements which ought to regulate the interior economy of a
> manufactory, are founded on principles of deeper root than may have
> been supposed, and are capable of being usefully employed in preparing
> the road to some of the sublimest investigations of the human mind.[1]

Charles Babbage has recently been rediscovered as the "pioneer of the
computer."[2] He needs to be rediscovered a second time for his contribution
to the understanding of economics, especially for his penetrating and
original insights into the economic role played by technological change in
the course of industrial development. Indeed, it is fair to say that it was
Babbage's book which first introduced the factory into the realm of
economic analysis.

Babbage has lived a furtive, almost fugitive existence in the literature of
economics. Joseph Schumpeter, in his magisterial *History of Economic
Analysis*, refers to Babbage's book, *On the Economy of Machinery and
Manufactures*, as "a remarkable performance of a remarkable man."[3]
Nevertheless, although Schumpeter's well-known book is more than 1,200

This chapter first appeared in Herbert Hax, Nathan Rosenberg, and Karl Steinbuch, *Charles Babbage, Ein Pionier der Industriellen Organisation*, Verlag Wirtschaft und Finanzen GmbH, Dusseldorf, 1992. The author wishes to acknowledge the able assistance of Scott Stern in the preparation of this paper, and to thank Stanley Engerman for his customarily astute comments and suggestions. The Technology and Economic Growth Program of the Center for Economic Policy Research at Stanford University provided financial support for the research upon which the paper is based.

[1] Charles Babbage, *On the Economy of Machinery and Manufactures*, fourth edition, 1835; reprinted by Frank Cass & Co., London, 1963, p. 191. All further references to *On the Economy of Machinery and Manufactures* will mention only the page number of the 1963 edition.

[2] See the valuable biography by Anthony Hyman, *Charles Babbage: Pioneer of the Computer*, Princeton University Press, Princeton (NJ), 1982.

[3] Joseph Schumpeter, *History of Economic Analysis*, Oxford University Press, New York, 1954, p. 541.

dense pages long, the treatment of Babbage is confined to a single footnote. Mark Blaug, in his *Economic Theory in Retrospect*, uses the same adjective as Schumpeter. He cites Babbage's book only to point out its influence on John Stuart Mill's discussion of increasing returns to scale in chapter 9 of book I of Mill's *Principles of Political Economy*. Mill's treatment of that subject, Blaug states, "is heavily indebted to a remarkable book, *On the Economy of Machinery and Manufactures* (1833) by Charles Babbage."[4]

Babbage the economist deserves far better treatment than this. His book contains important contributions to economics which have received unduly short shrift. A book that, at the time of its publication, provided a considerable improvement upon a topic as seminal as Adam Smith's treatment of the division of labor and, at the same time, offered the first systematic analysis of the economies associated with increasing returns to scale, surely deserves to be rescued from the comparative obscurity of footnotes and parenthetic references.

I

Babbage's purpose in writing *On the Economy of Machinery and Manufactures* was to examine "the mechanical principles which regulate the application of machinery to arts and manufactures" (p. iii). The book is, in fact, invaluable for its detailed, nontechnical descriptions of the manufacturing technologies that were employed in English workshops at the beginning of the 1830s. Babbage had, himself, travelled extensively through the industrial districts of England as well as continental Europe. And he was, as we know from his other remarkable accomplishments, no casual observer. On the contrary, he saw everything through the inquiring eyes of someone searching for more general underlying principles, categories, or commonalities. He sought, continuously, for some basis for classification and meaningful comparison. In brief, he wanted to illuminate his subject matter by rendering it subject to quantification and calculation.

In fact, the relationship of Babbage the economist to Babbage the inventor is a close one. That is to say, the book is, in an important sense, a by-product of Babbage's lifelong preoccupation with the development of a calculating machine. Indeed, the opening sentence of the preface to the first edition of the book states that: "The present volume may be considered as one of the consequences that have resulted from the Calculating-Engine, the construction of which I have been so long superintending." Thus, the book shares a common provenance with the calculating engine. The power of systematic reasoning that Babbage invested in his attempt to develop

---

[4] Mark Blaug, *Economic Theory in Retrospect*, Cambridge University Press, Cambridge, third edition, 1978, p. 198.

such a machine is abundantly evident in the ways in which he organizes and classifies his data on the English industrial establishment in this book.[5]

This is particularly evident in chapter 11, "Of Copying," by far the longest chapter in the book. Babbage brings together in this chapter a wide array of industrial processes involving specific applications of printing, casting, moulding, engraving, stamping, punching, etc. The cheapness of machine operations in such processes turns upon the skill devoted to some original instrument or tool that subsequently may become the basis for many thousands of copies. The situation – involving the common denominator of a large fixed cost that lays the basis for cheap per-unit costs – is typical of the mass production technologies that were just beginning to emerge in Babbage's time.[6]

Babbage's travels through the manufacturing workshops of England were largely a consequence of the difficulties that he encountered in his own construction problems and his determination to become better informed concerning his technological options. Babbage's observations and descriptions are so informative that his book is well worth reading today just for its contribution to the history of technology, even if it were totally devoid of any other merit. Babbage even provides the reader with a guide for extracting useful and reliable information concerning productivity from factory visits.[7] The guide includes a suggested set of structured questions as well as some discreet methods of verifying the accuracy of responses by checking for the internal consistency of answers. He also offers suggestions when reliable information on factory output is not available:

When this cannot be ascertained, the number of operations performed in a given time may frequently be counted when the workman is quite unconscious that any person is observing him. Thus the sound made by the motion of a loom may enable the observer to count the number of strokes per minute, even though he is outside the building in which it is contained. (p. 117)

Babbage would certainly have made a good industrial spy!

If Babbage at times seems to be writing with an excessively didactic hand, it is partly because he believes that greater attention to the empirical world, and especially the activities inside a factory, would significantly elevate the quality of economic analysis and reasoning generally.

---

[5] For further discussion of the context in which Babbage came to write this book, see Hyman, *Charles Babbage*, chapter 8.

[6] See Babbage's discussion of the Navy Board's contract to make iron tanks for ships. Maudslay at first was reluctant to take the contract because it was "out of his line of business" but also because the holes for the large number of rivets ordinarily involved an expensive hand-punching process. The Navy Board subsequently offered a larger contract which Maudslay accepted because it then became worthwhile to introduce specialized tools. "The magnitude of the order made it worth his while to commence *manufacturer*, and to make tools for the express business" (p. 121). Babbage's italics.

[7] See chapter 12, "On the Method of Observing Manufactories."

Political economists have been reproached with too small a use of facts, and too large an employment of theory. If facts are wanting, let it be remembered that the closet-philosopher is unfortunately too little acquainted with the admirable arrangements of the factory; and that no class of persons can supply so readily, and with so little sacrifice of time, the data on which all the reasonings of political economists are founded, as the merchants and manufacturer; and, unquestionably, to no class are the deductions to which they give rise so important. Nor let it be feared that erroneous deductions may be made from such recorded facts: the errors which arise from the absence of facts are far more numerous and more durable than those which result from unsound reasoning respecting true data. (p. 156)

A person who could pen these words – especially the last sentence – obviously has something of importance to say to the present generation of economists![8]

II

Babbage's distinctly economic contribution is taken up in section II, the largest portion of the book, where he considers the "economic principles which regulate the application of machinery," after the purely "mechanical principles" that were the focus of section I. The central point is that, as soon as one undertakes to produce a product in large volume, to become a "manufacturer" rather than a "maker," it becomes necessary to devote careful and explicit attention to the organization of production, to "the whole system" (p. 121) of the factory. Moreover, a manufacturer must be prepared to utilize, and perhaps to design, tools made expressly for a specialized purpose. One needs to consider, in other words, the division of labor.

Babbage begins his critical chapter 19, "On the Division of Labour," by asserting that "Perhaps the most important principle on which the economy of a manufacture depends, is the *division of labour* [Babbage's *italics*] amongst the persons who perform the work" (p. 169).Babbage's most distinctive contributions to the discipline of economics are generally regarded as his contributions to this subject. That view will not be challenged. However, I will suggest that his analysis of the division of labor constitutes an advance upon the classic treatment of the subject of much greater dimensions than has yet been recognized. Indeed, Babbage himself, a man who did not suffer from excessive modesty, also understated the extent of his own improvement upon Adam Smith.

---

[8] At the same time, Babbage urged the undertaking of statistical estimation in order to improve decision-making within the business community: "The importance of collecting data, for the purpose of enabling the manufacturer to ascertain how many additional customers he will acquire by a given reduction in the price of the article he makes, cannot be too strongly pressed upon the attention of those who employ themselves in statistical inquiries" (p. 120). Babbage was the founder of the London Statistical Society.

As Babbage reminds his readers, Smith attributed the increased productivity flowing from the division of labor to "three different circumstances: first, to the increase of dexterity in every particular workman; secondly, to the saving of time, which is commonly lost in passing from one species of work to another; and, lastly, to the invention of a great number of machines which facilitate and abridge labour, and enable one man to do the work of many" (p. 175). Babbage goes on to assert that Smith has overlooked a key advantage that flows from the analysis of the *Wealth of Nations*, and that the analysis is therefore seriously incomplete.

When there is only a limited division of labor, each worker is required to perform a number of tasks, involving a variety of skills and physical capabilities. The supply of such skills and capabilities varies considerably, for reasons having to do with length of training, previous experience, and natural differences in physical endowment. Accordingly, the remuneration received by workers who supply different skills will also vary considerably.

However, when there is a limited division of labor the employer is required, in effect, to purchase "bundles" of labor. Consequently, a workman who is capable of performing highly skilled work will need to receive a wage appropriate to these high skill levels, even though he will spend much, perhaps most, of his time performing work of lower skill, and pay, levels.

Seen from this perspective, the great virtue of the division of labor is that it permits an "unbundling" of labor skills, and allows the employer to pay for each separate labor process no more than the market value of the lower capabilities commensurate with such work. Under an extensive division of labor, the employer is no longer confronted with the necessity of purchasing labor corresponding to higher skill levels than those required for the specific project at hand.

In Babbage's own words,

the master manufacturer, by dividing the work to be executed into different processes, each requiring different degrees of skill or of force, can purchase exactly that precise quantity of both which is necessary for each process; whereas, if the whole work were executed by one workman, that person must possess sufficient skill to perform the most difficult, and sufficient strength to execute the most laborious, of the operations into which the art is divided. (pp. 175–176; emphasis Babbage's)

In elaborating his analysis of this point, and examining its implications, Babbage reverts to Adam Smith's time-honored example of the division of labor in a pin factory. He presents a detailed enumeration of the sequence of steps involved in the English manufacture of pins – wire-drawing, wire-straightening, pointing, twisting, and cutting the heads, heading, tinning, and papering. For each separate step in the sequence, he identifies those who supply the labor – man, woman, boy, girl – and their rate of remuneration for each step. The wage rates of these separate labor inputs vary all the way from 4.5 pence per day up to 6 shillings per day (see table, p. 184). Taking into account the amount of time required for each step, and assuming that the highest-paid worker, the pin whitener (who earned 6 shillings a day at his specialty), could carry out each of the steps in pinmaking in the same amount of time as the individuals who perform each step under the prevailing division of labor, Babbage concludes that pins would cost 3.75 times as much as they actually did (p. 186). He then draws the generalization: "The higher the skill required of the workman in any one process of a manufacture, and the smaller the time during which it is employed, so much the greater will be the advantage of separating that process from the rest, and devoting one person's attention entirely to it" (pp. 168–187).

Years later, Babbage cogently restated his central point as follows:

The most effective cause of the cheapness produced by the division of labour is this:

By dividing the work to be executed into different processes, each requiring different degrees of skill, or of force, the master manufacturer can purchase exactly that precise quantity of both which is necessary for each process. Whereas if the whole work were executed by one workman, that person must possess sufficient skill to perform the most difficult, and sufficient strength to execute the most laborious, of those operations into which the art is divided.

Needle-making is perhaps the best illustration of the overpowering effect of this cause. The operatives in this manufacture consist of children, women, and men, earning wages varying from three or four shillings up to five pounds per week. Those who point the needles gain about two pounds. The man who hardens and tempers the needles earns from five to six pounds per week. It ought also to be observed that one man is sufficient to temper the needles for a large factory; consequently the time spent on each needle by the most expensive operative is excessively small.

But if a manufacturer insist on employing one man to make the whole needle, he must pay at the rate of five pounds a week for every portion of the labour bestowed upon it.[9]

This analysis of the benefits of an extensive division of labor was highly original. It did indeed constitute a major addition to Adam Smith's formulation, and it was precisely this point that exercised a heavy influence upon later economists, most especially, as we will see later, Marx. Nevertheless, Babbage also improved upon the formulation of Smith and others in several additional important respects that have not been widely recognized. This involved not only points of clarification but also points of analytical rigor.

Babbage observes that a more extensive division of labor leads to a

---

[9] Charles Babbage, *Passages from the Life of a Philosopher*, volume XI in *The Works of Charles Babbage* William Pickering, London, 1989, p. 328.

reduction in the time required for learning, and therefore to a shortening of the time period during which a new labor force entrant is employed in a relatively unproductive and unremunerative way (p. 170). Then he makes the important observation, not to be found in Adam Smith, that the conventional apprenticeship of five to seven years' duration was necessary in the past, not merely to allow the young man to acquire the requisite skills, but also "to enable him to repay by his labour, during the latter portion of his time, the expense incurred by his master at its commencement" (p. 170). If a new labor force entrant is required to learn only a single operation instead of many, he will much more quickly arrive at the stage where his employment generates a profit to his employer. If a competitive situation prevails among the masters, "the apprentice will be able to make better terms, and diminish the period of his servitude" (p. 170). Thus, the length of apprenticeship needs to be understood as determined not just by the time necessary to acquire a skill, but also by the time necessary for the master to reap a normal rate of return upon his investment in the human capital of his apprentice (p. 170). One does not need to interpret Babbage's analysis here with excessive generosity in order to see it as a tantalizing precursor of the contemporary work of Gary Becker and Jacob Mincer on learning-by-doing.[10]

Babbage also makes an extremely significant qualification to Adam Smith's central point that specialization leads to increased dexterity and therefore greater speed on the part of the workman who is no longer required to perform a number of separate operations. Babbage refers to Smith's example of nail-making. Smith had claimed that a smith, who was accustomed to make nails, but who was not solely occupied as a nailer, could only make 800 to 1,000 per day, "whilst a lad who had never exercised any other trade, can make upwards of two thousand three hundred a day" (p. 173). In the case of the boys in his example, Smith had added the (perhaps not insignificant) qualification, "when they exerted themselves."[11] Moreover, Smith, as reported in his lectures, had used the lower figure of two thousand, although he also added "and those incomparably better."[12]

Babbage believed that the case of nail-making is "rather an extreme one" (p. 173). Moreover, factories with an extensive division of labor tend also to pay on the basis of piecework, which renders comparisons of labor productivity more difficult, since this mode of payment provides stronger

---

[10] Babbage also adds, as a separate point, that greater division of labor will lead to reduced waste of materials in the learning process, and a consequent reduction in the cost and the price of the product (p. 171).

[11] Adam Smith, *Wealth of Nations*, 1776; Modern Library Reprint, New York, 1937, p. 8.

[12] Adam Smith, *Lectures on Justice, Police, Revenue and Arms*, reprinted by Kelley & Millman, New York, 1963, p. 166.

incentives to increase output. But he had a much more fundamental qualification to append to Smith's emphasis upon the greater dexterity acquired by the workman who continuously performs the same process. These advantages to repetition, he states, are merely ephemeral. Under stable conditions, less specialized workers will move more slowly down the relevant learning curves, but they will eventually approach, even if they never entirely attain, some lower labor cost asymptote. Thus, the gain from the constant repetition of a process "is not a permanent source of advantage; for, though it acts at the commencement of an establishment, yet every month adds to the skill of the workmen; and at the end of three or four years they will not be very far behind those who have never practiced any other branch of their art" (p. 173). Here, as elsewhere, Babbage makes skillful use of a primitive sort of time-period analysis, which enables him to distinguish between immediate and longer-term consequences.[13] Thus, even though Babbage makes these points in a context where he is ostensibly recounting what was, when he wrote, merely conventional wisdom, he in fact ended up providing a fresh and quite powerful new insight.

III

Adam Smith's third advantage of the division of labor was that it gave rise to inventions. Smith's treatment of the determinants of inventive activity is extremely sparse; the textual treatment of the subject in chapter 1 of the *Wealth of Nations* occupied not much more than a single page. In Smith's view, in the earlier stages of industrial development, most inventions were the work of the users, that is, workmen whose attention was increasingly fixed upon a single object. Eventually, however, when the division of labor gives rise to specialized makers of machinery, the ingenuity of these machine makers comes to play an increasingly important role; and finally, a more prominent role comes to be played by those to whom Smith refers as "philosophers or men of speculation, whose trade it is not to do any thing, but to observe every thing; and who, upon that account, are often capable of combining together the powers of the most distant and dissimilar objects."[14]

Babbage's discussion of the determinants of invention is far richer than that of Smith, and there is of course a perfectly straightforward reason. Smith, writing in the late 1760s and 1770s, was writing about, and

---

[13] See, in particular, Babbage's analysis of the impact of the introduction of machinery upon employment in chapter 32, "On the Effect of Machinery in Reducing the Demand for Labour."

[14] Smith, *Wealth of Nations*, p. 10. For a more extensive treatment of Smith's views on this subject, see Nathan Rosenberg, "Adam Smith and the Division of Labor: Two Views or One?" *Economica*, 57, no. 3 (May 1965).

commenting upon, a society that was still essentially pre-industrial. Babbage, on the other hand, wrote his book some sixty years later. The interval between the writing of the two books constituted the heyday of the British industrial revolution. Babbage is therefore analyzing a society where the division of labor had been carried to far greater lengths than the society that was known to Adam Smith. Indeed, very little of the descriptive accounts in Babbage's book, aside from the examples that Babbage deliberately chose from Smith's own book, dealt with machinery that would have been recognizable to the author of the *Wealth of Nations*.

A central point for Babbage is that an extensive division of labor is itself an essential prerequisite to technical change. This is so for two related reasons. First of all, technical improvements are not generally dependent upon a few rarely gifted individuals, although the more "beautiful combinations" are indeed the work of the occasional genius (p. 260). Rather, and secondly, inventive activity needs to be seen as a consequence as well as a cause of the division of labor. This is so because "The arts of contriving, of drawing, and of executing, do not usually reside in their greatest perfection in one individual; and in this, as in other arts, the *division of labor* must be applied" (p. 266; emphasis Babbage's).

It is also worth noting that Babbage shows an acute awareness of the economic forces that drive inventive capability in specific directions and that influence the timing of inventive effort. In fact, his observations deserve to be regarded as possibly the earliest treatment of the economic determinants of inventive activity. Technological change is not, for him, some totally exogenous phenomenon. On the contrary, he clearly sees the direction of technological improvements as responding to the relative prices of factor inputs, and the commitment of resources to the improvements of machinery as directly connected to the state of demand for the final product that the machines produce. In urging the importance of careful cost accounting, Babbage points out that one of its main advantages "is the indication which it would furnish of the course in which improvement should be directed" (pp. 203–204); a firm would invest in those technological improvement activities that offered the highest payoff in terms of cost reduction, but only if it had a close understanding of those costs. On the demand side, he observes that: "The inducement to contrive machines for any process of manufacture increases with the demand for the article" (p. 213). And he also observes that "overmanufacturing" is likely to lead to efforts to reduce costs through machinery improvement or the reorganization of the factory (p. 233). Babbage also suggests a highly valuable research project on the relationship between gluts and technological improvements. "It would be highly interesting, if we could trace, even approximately, through the history of any great manufacture, the effects of gluts in producing improvements in machinery, or in methods of working; and if we could shew what addition to the annual quantity of goods previously manufactured, was produced by each alteration." He then adds the conjecture: "It would probably be found, that *the increased quantity manufactured by the same capital, when worked with the new improvement, would produce nearly the same rate of profit as other modes of investment.*"[15]

It seems to be a reasonable claim that Babbage is the first observer of the events of the industrial revolution to call attention in an explicit way to the causal links between economic forces and inventive activity.

IV

Chapter 27 of Babbage's book, "On Contriving Machinery," provides valuable insights into the difficulties associated with the innovation process in the period when Britain was attaining to the status of "Workshop of the World."

Babbage expresses great concern over the difficulties of executing a new machine design and putting it into operating form in close accordance with the specifications of the inventor. This chapter clearly bears the painful imprint of the author's numerous frustrating experiences in designing highly complex machines in an age when machine making was still a relatively primitive art. This was a period when precision in the design and execution of new machinery was only just coming of age, but when the establishment of a new production facility was still attended by innumerable uncertainties with respect to the cost and performance of machinery of novel design. To be sure, the master machine-tool designer and builder, Henry Maudslay, inventor of the slide rest, makes an appearance in the pages of Babbage's book, but his contributions represented only the beginning of a long process of learning to work metals with higher degrees of precision. Indeed, Babbage thought it appropriate to include a separate chapter enumerating precisely these difficulties, in which he placed particular emphasis upon the problems involved in calculating the cost of new machines.[16]

Babbage stresses in several places the importance of accuracy in the actual paper design of a new machine. "It can never," he states, "be too strongly impressed upon the minds of those who are devising new machines, that to make the most perfect drawings of every part tends

[15] Pp. 233–234. Babbage's italics. See also pp. 158–159.
[16] Chapter 35, "Inquiries Previous to Commencing Any Manufactory."

essentially both to the success of the trial, and to economy in arriving at the result" (p. 262). It is clear from his admonitions on this matter that high-quality draughtsmanship could by no means be taken for granted. Nevertheless, "if the exertion of moderate power is the end of the mechanism to be contrived, it is possible to construct the whole machine upon paper" (p. 261).

However, for more complex machinery where performance will depend heavily upon "physical or chemical properties" (p. 261), optimum design cannot be determined on paper alone, and testing and experimentation ("direct trial") will be unavoidable. One can piece together, from various chapters of the book, a vivid account of the difficulties confronting would-be innovators during a period characterized by rapid technical change, particularly in the realm of machine making itself.

Chapter 29, "On the Duration of Machinery," deals with what a later generation would call "technological obsolescence," especially as the problem applies to capital goods with long useful lives, "such as wind-mills, water-mills, and steam-engines" (p. 283). Babbage introduces a table (p. 284) of the average annual duty performed by steam engines in Cornwall over the period 1813–1833, as well as the "average duty of the best engines." These engines, which were employed in Cornwall's extensive mining operations, provide impressive evidence of improvements in the construction and management of such engines. One wishes one had more information concerning their operation; nevertheless, on the face of it, they show a strong upward trend in performance. For the 21-year period as a whole the average duty of the *best* engines more than triples, from 26,400,000 in 1813 to 83,306,092 in 1833. Over the same period the average duty of all the engines rose from 19,456,000 to 46,000,000.

In such an environment, technological obsolescence is a dominating commercial consideration, and the physical life of a capital good becomes of secondary importance. Babbage here offers a powerful insight that, it seems fair to say, is still not fully absorbed today.

Machinery for producing any commodity in great demand, seldom actually wears out; new improvements, by which the same operations can be executed either more quickly or better, generally superseding it long before that period arrives: indeed, to make such an improved machine profitable, it is usually reckoned that in five years it ought to have paid itself, and in ten to be superseded by a better." (p. 285)

The effect of such obsolescence was a rapid downward revaluation of the market price for older machinery, which indeed is soon rendered commercially worthless. Babbage cites technological improvements in frames for making patent-net "not long ago." As a result, a machine that had cost £1200 and was still "in good repair" a few years later, sold for a mere £60.

But even more extreme evidence of the impact of rapid ongoing technological improvements in that trade was the decision to abandon the construction of unfinished machines "because new improvements had superseded their utility."[17]

Babbage ends this chapter by pointing out that the effect of competition with respect to durable goods had been to render them even less durable. When manufactured articles are transported a considerable distance, it is not uncommon for broken articles to be deemed unworthy of the cost of repair if the price of labor is higher than in its original place of manufacture. It is cheaper to purchase a new article (p. 292). This appears to be a practice of recent vintage when Babbage wrote.

V

In examining the innovation process specifically from the point of view of the developer of a potential new machine, rather than its possible user, Babbage warns his readers of the peculiar uncertainties of the technical problems involved. In situations that require testing what we would today call a prototype, the outcome of the tests may be especially sensitive to the quality of workmanship that was employed in producing the contrivance. Otherwise "an imperfect trial may cause an idea to be given up, which better workmanship might have proved to be practicable" (p. 264).

But there is another reason why the outcome of such a test may be inconclusive. The "art of making machinery" was undergoing such improvement "that many inventions which have been tried, and given up in one state of art, have at another period been eminently successful" (p. 264). This statement might serve as a remarkably appropriate epitaph to the author's own celebrated technical accomplishments. Indeed, one may read his conclusion as both an astute observation on the uncertainties associated with the innovative process during his own lifetime, and also as a personal and correct premonition concerning his own ambitious technical enterprise. "These considerations prove the propriety of repeating, at the termination of intervals during which the art of making machinery has received any great improvement, the trials of methods which, although founded upon just principles, had previously failed" (p. 265).

For the subset of inventions that survives the rigors and uncertainties of this experimental period, the commercial risks may prove to be as hazardous as the purely technical risks that had been overcome. The reason is

[17] P. 286. For a discussion of the complexity of the decision-making process when technological change is not only rapid, but is anticipated to continue to be rapid in the future, see Nathan Rosenberg, "On Technological Expectations," *Economic Journal* (September 1976); reprinted as chapter 5 in Rosenberg, *Inside the Black Box.*

simplicity itself. The machine may work perfectly well but produce its output "at a greater expense than that at which it can be made by other methods" (p. 265). Babbage at several points in the book had urged his readers to pay the most careful attention to *all* the costs that would be incurred in some prospective new machine, while at the same time admitting the difficulties of arriving at accurate estimates.

But there is still a further and final irony concerning the plight of the would-be innovator. Assuming that all previous hurdles and initial "teething troubles" had been overcome, subsequent units of the product could be produced far more cheaply than the first. Babbage clearly identifies what later generations would refer to as a "learning curve." His words deserve to be quoted in full:

It has been estimated roughly, that the first individual of any newly-invented machine, will cost about five times as much as the construction of the second, an estimate which is, perhaps, sufficiently near the truth. If the second machine is to be precisely like the first, the same drawings, and the same patterns will answer for it; but if, as usually happens, some improvements have been suggested by the experience of the first, these must be more or less altered. When, however, two or three machines have been completed, and many more are wanted, they can usually be produced at much less than one-fifth of the expense of the original invention. (p. 266)

But the subsequent financial fortunes of such an innovator are by no means assured. Much would depend not only upon the subsequent demand for the innovation but upon the ability of the innovator to control and capture the flow of profits generated by the innovation. In a highly competitive environment of the sort described by Babbage, the profits might well be captured by others unless the innovator had some specific means that allowed him to appropriate the benefits – patents, secrecy, tacit knowledge, access to scarce skills, etc.

Babbage's analysis here takes on additional importance because it powerfully influenced Marx, who quoted Babbage's estimate approvingly.[18] In this particular context Marx was anxious to emphasize how the technological improvements in a machine shortened its life expectancy and thereby intensified the forces making for the prolongation of the working day on the part of the capitalists anxious to recoup their large investments as quickly as possible.[19] On the other hand, in volume III of *Capital* Marx, again drawing upon Babbage's treatment, called attention to "the far greater cost of operating an establishment based on a new invention as compared to later establishments, arising *ex suis ossibus*. This is so very true

[18] Karl Marx, *Capital*, vol. I, Foreign Languages Publishing House, Moscow, 1961, p. 405, footnote 1.   [19] *Ibid.*, especially footnote 2.

that the trail-blazers generally go bankrupt, and only those who later buy the buildings, machinery, etc., at a cheaper price make money out of it."[20] This is an intriguing statement on Marx's part, insofar as it portrays the capitalist, or at least the innovating capitalist, in a distinctly sympathetic way. But, more importantly, it would be essential to know how "generally" such bankruptcy occurs. Moreover, if this *were* generally the case, and if technological change were as central to long-term capitalist growth as Marx consistently asserted, it would constitute a powerful argument for the social necessity of high profits in order to compensate the occasional successful innovator for undertaking such great risks. Not surprisingly, Marx does not draw this implication.

VI

Babbage's concern with the division of labor as it relates to technological improvements leads him to a significant extension of his analysis into the field of international trade. His main concern was with a special issue: the restrictions that had recently been imposed by parliament upon the export of certain classes of machinery. Such restrictions, in his view, represented a needless and, indeed, counterproductive pandering to the interests of the users of machinery, who feared the prospect of commercial competition from foreigners equipped with the latest machinery. But Babbage perceives[21] that Britain was already well on the way to developing a dynamic comparative advantage in the making of machinery. In his view, if the country could maintain its superiority in the manufacture of machinery, it would have little to fear from the acquisition of high-quality machinery by overseas competitors.

Babbage distinguishes sharply between the ability to contrive new machines and the ability to manufacture them. Even if the ability to contrive were equally distributed among countries, "the means of execution" are nevertheless different (p. 365). These means of execution obviously include the highly skilled makers of machinery, a class of workers who are "as a body, far more intelligent that those who only use it" (p. 364). In a regime of rapid technological change, the country with a higher skill capability will continue to have much speedier access to the best machinery. By allowing domestic manufacturers the opportunity to sell their products abroad, the country will in fact solidify its superiority in machine making (pp. 370–373). It will enrich itself by enlarging the class of machine makers. Such workmen

---

[20] *Ibid.*, vol. III, Foreign Languages Publishing House, Moscow, 1959, p. 103. See also chapter 5 below, pp. 95–97.   [21] Chapter 34, "On the Exportation of Machinery."

possess much more skill, and are paid much more highly than that class who merely *use* it; and, if a free exportation were allowed, the more valuable class would, undoubtedly, be greatly increased; for, notwithstanding the high rate of wages, there is no country in which it can at this moment be made, either so well or so cheaply as in England. We might, therefore, supply the whole world with machinery, at an evident advantage, both to ourselves and our customers. (p.372; emphasis Babbage's)

The separate strands of Babbage's argument in this chapter are not entirely distinct. On the one hand, he asserts that, in the absence of trade restrictions, English machine users will always have the advantage of prior access to the best machines. On the other hand, he also asserts that such access is not a sufficient condition for commercial success. Even if foreign competitors have equal access to the best technology, they will not compete successfully so long as they fail to achieve the admirable organizational adaptations of the industrial economy that have already been achieved in England. Here Babbage seems to have come full circle, to the overarching theme of the book: the advantages accruing to a society that manages to organize its economic life in close accordance with the dictates of the division of labor.

This seems to be the spirit of his response to the charge that the elimination of restrictions on machinery exports will provide foreigners with machinery that will threaten England's competitive advantage.

It is contended that by admitting the exportation of machinery, foreign manufacturers will be supplied with machines equal to our own. The first answer which presents itself to this argument is supplied by almost the whole of the present volume; *That in order to succeed in a manufacture, it is necessary not merely to possess good machinery, but that the domestic economy of the factory should be most carefully regulated.*[22]

Of course, for the larger economy outside the "domestic economy of the factory," appropriate regulation should be understood to include the force of competition: "it is only in countries which have attained a high degree of civilization, and in articles in which there is a great competition amongst the producers, that the most perfect system of the division of labour is to be observed" (p. 169). And countries that can maintain a more advanced division of labor, in this enlarged sense, than their foreign competitors, need not be excessively concerned over their prospective competitiveness.

---

[22] P. 376. Babbage's italics. Substantially the same point is made several pages later. "The fact that England can, notwithstanding her taxation and her high rate of wages, actually undersell other nations, seems to be well established: and it appears to depend on the superior goodness and cheapness of those raw materials of machinery the metals, – on the excellence of the tools, – and on the admirable arrangements of the domestic economy of our factories" (p. 374).

VII

Chapter 20, "On the Division of Mental Labours," is a fascinating chapter for several reasons. It involves, to begin with, a direct application of Babbage's reasoning on the division of labour in the previous chapter, to the specific realm of the activities of the human mind. Second, it contains an extensive discussion of Babbage's own work on a "calculating engine," placed in the larger context of his analysis of the application of machine methods to industrial production. And, third, it provides an absorbing historical account of the project that culminated in Babbage's own efforts to develop a calculating-engine.

Starting with this third point, these efforts had their origin, remarkably enough, in the accidental perusal of Smith's *Wealth of Nations* by a French government official who happened upon the volume in a bookstore. A Monsieur Prony had been charged by the French government with the Herculean task of superintending the production of a series of logarithmic and trigonometric tables that would facilitate the transition to the recently adopted decimal system.[23]

The tables that M. Prony was to calculate were to occupy no less than seventeen large folio volumes.

Il fut aisé à M. de Prony de s'assurer que même en s'associant trois ou quatre habiles co-operateurs, la plus grande durée presumable de sa vie, ne lui suffirai pas pour remplir ses engagements. Il était occupé de cette fâcheuse pensée lorsque, se trouvant devant la boutique d'un marchand de livres, il apperçut la belle edition Anglaise de Smith, donnée a Londres en 1776; il ouvrit le livre au hazard, et tomba sur le premier chapitre, qui traite de *la division du travail*, et où la fabrication des épingles est citée pour exemple. A peine avait-il parcouru les premières pages, que, par une espèce d'inspiration, il conçut l'expédient de mettre ses logarithmes en *manufacture* comme les épingles. (p. 193; emphasis Babbage's)

M. Prony then proceeded with a threefold division of labor including (1) "five or six of the most eminent mathematicians in France," (2) seven or eight persons, not eminent mathematicians, but persons possessed of a "considerable acquaintance with mathematics," and (3) a group whose number varied between sixty and eighty, who generated the final tables "using nothing more than simple addition and subtraction" (p. 194)

---

[23] The decimal system was, of course, adopted in France but not in England. Babbage points out the advantages of the decimal system in facilitating monetary calculations, and observes that "it becomes an interesting question to consider whether our own currency might not be converted into one decimally divided. The great step, that of abolishing the guinea, has already been taken without any inconvenience, and but little is now required to render the change complete" (p. 124). Babbage's countrymen were, of course, to wait for more than a century before acquiring the conveniences of this conversion. For other purposes, such as measurement of length and weight, they are still waiting.

M. Prony's procedure, Babbage astutely observes, "much resembles that of a skillful person about to construct a cotton or silk-mill, or any similar establishment" (p. 195). None of the well-educated groups involved in the project played any role in the "dog-work" of actual calculation. It was, of course, Babbage's intention that his calculating engine would provide a machine substitute for all of the work performed by the third group.

Babbage completes the specification of the neat parallelism of the division of labor between the mechanical and mental domains:

We have seen, then, that the effect of the *division of labour*, both in mechanical and in mental operations, is, that it enables us to purchase and apply to each process precisely that quantity of skill and knowledge which is required for it: we avoid employing any part of the time of a man who can get eight or ten shillings a day by his skill in tempering needles, in turning a wheel, which can be done for sixpence a day; and we equally avoid the loss arising from the employment of an accomplished mathematician in performing the lowest processes of arithmetic. (p 201)

But the improvements in the cost of calculation which are now on the horizon, and which are the offspring of the division of labor, are by no means exhausted by purely financial considerations. For, in Babbage's view, as a country progresses in its arts and manufactures, continued progress comes to depend increasingly upon a growing intimacy between science and industry. In the final chapter of the book (chapter 35), "On the Future Prospects of Manufactures as Connected with Science," Babbage argues that science itself is becoming subject to the same law of the division of labor that is the central theme of the book. Science needs to be cultivated as a full-time, specialized activity by those with the "natural capacity and acquired habits" (p. 379). Such specialization is unavoidable because "the discovery of the great principles of nature demands a mind almost exclusively devoted to such investigations; and these, in the present state of science, frequently require costly apparatus, and exact an expense of time quite incompatible with professional avocations" (p. 380). Babbage's reference to "costly apparatus" is especially apposite. One of the most costly of all research instruments today is a large Cray computer!

Babbage closes a long apotheosis to science by pointing out that the progress of science itself will be increasingly governed by progress in the ability to calculate: "It is the science of *calculation*, – which becomes continually more necessary at each step of our progress, and which must ultimately govern the whole of the applications of science to the arts of life."[24]

[24] Pp. 387–388. Babbage's italics. It is interesting to note that, in the very next paragraph, Babbage anticipates precisely the question that so troubled Jevons several decades later in his book, *The Coal Question*, Macmillan and Co., London, 1865. Babbage recognizes the threat posed to a society increasingly dependent upon the power of steam, that "the coal-

In short, it is Babbage's view that mankind's future prospects will be dominated by the fact that "machinery has been taught arithmetic" (p. 390). Babbage was of course remarkably prescient, but the possibility of teaching machinery arithmetic would have to await the age of electronics.

VIII

Thus, Babbage's analysis involves a long chain of reasoning that has its origin in the division of labor; from there, Babbage spells out what he perceives as its far-reaching implications through the realms of technology and then even science. But one further feature, of great significance, has so far been neglected. The extension of the division of labor can and was necessarily leading to the establishment of large factories.[25] Indeed, Babbage provides the first extended discussion in the literature of economics of an issue of immense future significance: the economies associated with large-scale production. The chapter devoted to this topic, chapter 22, "On the Causes and Consequences of Large Factories," in turn powerfully influenced the treatment of this topic by two of the most influential, perhaps *the* two most influential economists of the nineteenth century, John Stuart Mill and Karl Marx.

Babbage had shown in chapter 19, "On the Division of Labour," that a critical advantage of that division was that it enabled the employer to purchase only the precise amount of each higher skill category, and no more, that was required by the different processes under his roof. Ideally, although the ideal was hardly ever fully achieved, no worker was ever paid at a rate that was higher than that appropriate to his assigned activity. But in chapter 22 he specifies an important implication of such an arrangement. In order to produce at minimum cost, it will be necessary to expand the factory by some multiple whose size will depend upon the specific labor requirements imposed by the division of labor. It follows from the principle of the division of labor that "*When the number of processes into which it is most advantageous to divide it, and the number of individuals to be employed by it are ascertained, then all factories which do not employ a direct multiple of this latter number, will produce the article at a greater cost*" (p. 212; emphasis Babbage's).

mines of the world may ultimately be exhausted." Nevertheless, with the growth of knowledge he appears to be confident that substitute sources of power will be found. He identifies one possibility upon which research is presently being conducted in the United Kingdom: tidal power. "(T)he sea itself offers a perennial source of power hitherto almost unapplied. The tides, twice in each day, raise a vast mass of water, which might be made available for driving machinery" (p. 388).

[25] The importance of this insight cannot be overstated, for the rise of the large manufacturing enterprise is central to the arguments of both Marx and Schumpeter. For a further discussion, see chapters 3 and 5 below.

Babbage adds a variety of other circumstances that, he believes, will offer advantages to manufacturing establishments of great size. The most common denominator involves the indivisibility of certain valuable inputs which fail to be fully utilized in smaller establishments. These would include the availability of higher-wage workmen who are skilled in adjusting or repairing machines;[26] a small factory with few machines could not fully utilize such a highly skilled worker. Similarly, the introduction of lighting for night work, or an accounting department, involve sizable fixed costs that are also under-utilized at low levels of output. The possibilities for effectively utilizing waste materials are greater in a larger plant, and this is sometimes further facilitated by "the union of the trades in one factory, which otherwise might have been separated" (p. 217) Agents who are employed by large factories frequently provide services that cost little more than those provided to smaller establishments, even though the benefits of the service to the large factory are far more valuable.

Finally, Babbage quotes approvingly a Report of the Committee of the House of Commons on the Wool Trade (1806) which asserts that large factories can afford the risks and experiments to generate technological change that are not feasible for the "little master manufacturers."

it is obvious, that the little master manufacturers cannot afford, like the man who possesses considerable capital, to try the experiments which are requisite, and incur the risks, and even losses, which almost always occur, in inventing and perfecting new articles of manufacture, or in carrying to a state of greater perfection articles already established ... The owner of a factory ... being commonly possessed of a large capital, and having all his workmen employed under his own immediate superintendence, may make experiments, hazard speculation, invent shorter or better modes of performing old processes, may introduce new articles, and improve and perfect old ones, thus giving the range to his tastes and fancy, and, thereby alone enabling our manufacturers to stand the competition with their commercial rivals in other countries. (p. 223)

IX

Babbage's treatment, although obviously of limited scope, was nevertheless a pioneering first effort to identify the economic advantages of bigness on which first John Stuart Mill and later Karl Marx drew extensively.[27] It has

---

[26] Although Babbage does not make it clear why such a worker needs to be in constant attendance so long as the machines are above some minimal threshold of reliability.

[27] Mill's treatment of the specific issue of the division of labor, although coming almost three-quarters of a century after Adam Smith, constituted no substantial improvement over Smith's treatment. As Blaug observes of Mill's *Principles of Political Economy*: "Book 1, chapter 8, on the division of labor, adds little to Adam Smith's treatment and may be passed over without loss." Blaug, *Economic Theory in Retrospect*, p. 198.

often been asserted that Marx was the first economist to identify the sources making for a tendency for firms to expand in size. But that priority, if denied to Babbage, certainly belongs to Mill, whose analysis well preceded that of Marx. Chapter 9, book I, of Mill's hugely successful *Principles of Political Economy* (1848), titled "Of Production on a Large, and Production on a Small Scale," is the first systematic treatment of increasing returns to large-scale production. Mill acknowledges his debt to Babbage in the opening paragraph of this chapter. He points out that there are advantages to large-scale enterprise

when the nature of the employment allows, and the extent of the possible market encourages, a considerable division of labour. The larger the enterprise, the farther the division of labour may be carried. This is one of the principle causes of large manufactories. Even when no additional subdivision of the work would follow an enlargement of the operations, there will be good economy in enlarging them to the point at which every person to whom it is convenient to assign a special occupation, will have full employment in that occupation.[28]

Mill illustrates this statement by an extensive quotation from Babbage's chapter "On the Causes and Consequences of Large Factories." The extract covered most of the points that we have just discussed and it amounted to two full pages of Babbage's original text. Mill included an even more extensive extract from Babbage on the optimal payment arrangements for workers in the first (1848) and second (1849) editions of his *Principles*.

Marx's intellectual indebtedness to Babbage on the matter of increasing returns to large-scale production appears to be at least as extensive as Mill's and is amply acknowledged, especially by the use of numerous citations and quotations. But Babbage's influence on Marx is even more pervasive, as would be revealed by a close textual comparison of Babbage's treatment of the causes and consequences of the division of labor with that of Marx in the two central chapters of volume I of *Capital*: chapter 14 on "Division of Labour and Manufacture," and chapter 15 on "Machinery and Modern Industry." It would take us much too far afield to explore this relationship in detail. The essential point is that Marx's most fundamental criticisms of capitalism as a social and economic system turn upon its peculiar division of labor. The degradation of the worker under advanced capitalism, especially the dehumanizing effects of specialization, and the systematic tendency to deprive the worker of skills and to incorporate those skills into the machine, are all consequences of the division of labor as treated by Babbage.

Marx even takes his definition of a machine from Babbage. According to

[28] Mill, *Principles*, p. 132.

Marx, "The machine, which is the starting-point of the industrial revolution, supersedes the workman, who handles a single tool, by a mechanism operating with a number of similar tools, and set in motion by a single motive power, whatever the form of that power may be."[29] Marx here cites as his authority Babbage's statement from his chapter (19) on the division of labor: "The union of all these simple instruments, set in motion by a single motor, constitutes a machine."[30]

Much of Marx's critique of capitalism flows from examining exactly those characteristics of the division of labor that Babbage had identified as sources of improved efficiency in the factory. However, Marx considers them from a very different perspective: specifically, from the point of view of the welfare of the worker. From Babbage's perspective, "One great advantage which we may derive from machinery is from the check which it affords against the inattention, the idleness, or the dishonesty of human agents" (p. 54). Putting aside the matter of dishonesty, Marx sees the introduction of machinery as introducing an entirely new form of oppression and loss of the worker's essential humanity.

In handicrafts and manufacture, the workman makes use of a tool, in the factory, the machine makes use of him. There the movements of the instrument of labour proceed from him, here it is the movements of the machine that he must follow. In manufacture the workmen are parts of a living mechanism. In the factory we have a lifeless mechanism independent of the workman, who becomes its mere living appendage. (Marx, *Capital*, p. 422)

Additionally, of the system of manufacture, Marx states: "It converts the labourer into a crippled monstrosity, by forcing his detail dexterity at the expense of a world of productive capabilities and instincts; just as in the States of La Plata they butcher a whole beast for the sake of his hide or his tallow" (*ibid.*, p. 360). The freedom of the capitalist, under the division of labor, to purchase labor of lower skills, translates into "deskilling" from the laborer's point of view. Babbage's continuous citation of the "advantages" of the division of labor in making it possible to insert women, boys, and girls at very low pay into jobs formerly performed by men readily translates into Marx's searing indictment of capitalism precisely *because* of its intensive exploitation of the division of labor.

Within the capitalist system all methods for raising the social productiveness of labour are brought about at the cost of the individual labourer; all means for the development of production transform themselves into means of domination over, and exploitation of, the producers; they mutilate the labourer into a fragment of a

---

[29] Marx, *Capital*, p. 376.
[30] See also Babbage, *Economy of Machinery*, p. 12, and Karl Marx, *The Poverty of Philosophy*, Foreign Languages Publishing House, Moscow, pp. 132–133.

man, degrade him to the level of an appendage of a machine, destroy every remnant of charm in his work and turn it into a hated toil; they estrange from him the intellectual potentialities of the labour-process in the same proportion as science is incorporated in it as an independent power; they distort the conditions under which he works, subject him during the labour-process to a despotism the more hateful for its meanness; they transform his life-time into working-time, and drag his wife and child beneath the wheels of the Juggernaut of capital. (Marx, *Capital*, p. 645)

It is tempting to conclude that Marx's analysis of the division of labor and its consequences is the same as that of Babbage, only considered dialectically!

I have attempted to show why Babbage continues to be deserving of our attention, not only as the pioneer of the computer, but as an original contributor to the development of economic ideas. Moreover, these two roles were, as we have seen, closely connected by Babbage's own personal experiences. His prolonged frustrations over the attempt to construct a working computer led him to many of the profound and precocious insights that are developed in his book. The book has much to offer to any reader today who wishes to understand the difficulties confronting the innovative impulse in the early days of industrialization. Babbage's difficulties were, of course, far greater than those of most innovators because the goal he had set for himself was so breathtakingly ambitious. In confronting his own difficulties as a computer pioneer more than a century ahead of its time, Babbage in fact became, however reluctantly, a pioneer economist.

If the world has eventually beaten a path back to Babbage's door as a result of the computer revolution, a strong case can now be made that a second path to that door remains to be beaten. For Babbage, as we have seen, also pioneered in the analysis of technological change. The subject suffered a long neglect when the main thrust of economic analysis came to be dominated by the neoclassical analysis of comparative statics in the late nineteenth century. With only a few notable exceptions, including the seminal work of Schumpeter and Kuznets, economists devoted little attention to either the causes or consequences of technological change until the 1950s.

The revival doubtless owed a great deal to the reawakening of interest in problems of long-term economic growth in less-developed countries as well as in the industrialized west. The renewed interest was reinforced, within the economics profession, by the researches of Jacob Schmookler, Moses Abramovitz, Robert Solow, and others, which pointed forcefully to two things: (1) the existence of economic forces that powerfully shape both the rate and the direction of inventive activity; and (2) the prominent role played by technological change in generating long-term economic growth.

Babbage's book, *On the Economy of Machinery and Manufactures*, continues to have much to say to readers who are concerned with the causes as well as the consequences of technological change. But it can, of course, equally well be read for the sheer intellectual excitement it provides in following a first-class mind as it attempts to comprehend, and to impose order upon, newly emerging forms of economic activity and organization.

3   Joseph Schumpeter: radical economist

I

This chapter will deal with Schumpeter's book, *Capitalism, Socialism and Democracy*, as the mature statement of the most radical scholar in the discipline of economics in the twentieth century.

Of course, I do not mean to suggest that Joseph Schumpeter held views on the organization of the economy, or society generally, that make it appropriate to label him as a radical in the political sense. In his social and political views Schumpeter was anything but radical. In fact, one could make a case – although I do not propose to do so – that Schumpeter was not merely conservative in his social views, but reactionary. In his most private thoughts, as suggested by a recent biography, he seemed to possess an insatiable longing for the glorious later days of the Hapsburg monarchy. Moreover, the most charitable characterization of his attitude toward Nazi Germany in the darkest days of the 1930s and the Second World War is that he was ambivalent.

The reason I propose to call Schumpeter a radical is that he urged the rejection of the most central and precious tenets of neo-classical theory. Indeed, I want to insist that very little of the complex edifice of neo-classical economics, as it existed in the late 1930s and 1940s, survives the sweep of Schumpeter's devastating assaults. But in examining Schumpeter's criticisms, it is not my primary intention to enlist his authority in an attack upon neo-classical economics. Rather, I propose to show that the quintessential, later Schumpeter, the author of *Capitalism, Socialism and Democracy*, held views that were not only genuinely radical, but that are deserving of far more serious attention than they receive today, even, or perhaps especially,

This chapter was first presented at the meetings of the Schumpeter Society in Kyoto, in August, 1992. That meeting marked the fiftieth anniversary of the publication of *Capitalism, Socialism, and Democracy*.

from scholars who think of themselves as working within the Schumpeter-ian tradition. While this chapter focuses on *Capitalism, Socialism, and Democracy*, I draw upon Schumpeter's other writings to round out the argument and interpretation that I am proposing.

II

I begin by quoting from Schumpeter's preface to the Japanese edition of *The Theory of Economic Development*, for in that preface Schumpeter sketches out what is probably the most precise and succinct statement of his own intellectual agenda that he ever committed to print. That agenda focuses not only upon the understanding of how the economic system generates economic change, but also upon how that change occurs as a result of the working out of purely endogenous forces:

If my Japanese readers asked me before opening the book what it is that I was aiming at when I wrote it, more than a quarter of a century ago, I would answer that I was trying to construct a theoretic model of the process of economic change in time, or perhaps more clearly, to answer the question how the economic system generates the force which incessantly transforms it ... I felt very strongly that ... there was a source of energy within the economic system which would of itself disrupt any equilibrium that might be attained. If this is so, then there must be a purely economic theory of economic change which does not merely rely on external factors propelling the economic system from one equilibrium to another. It is such a theory that I have tried to build.[1]

It should be noted that these words were published in 1937, when Schumpeter was, as we know, already at work on *Capitalism, Socialism and Democracy*. In fact, I regard *Capitalism, Socialism and Democracy* as the fulfillment of precisely the intellectual agenda that Schumpeter articulated in the passage to his Japanese readers that I have just quoted.

Of course, an account of how and why economic change took place was precisely something that could not be provided within the "rigorously static" framework of neo-classical equilibrium analysis, as Schumpeter referred to it. Schumpeter also observed that it was Walras' view that economic theory was only capable of examining a "stationary process," that is, "a process which actually does not change of its own initiative, but merely produces constant rates of real income as it flows along in time." As Schumpeter interprets Walras:

---

[1] Joseph Schumpeter, Preface to Japanese edition of *Theorie Der Wirtschaftlichen Entwick-lung*, as translated by I. Nakayama and S. Tobata, Tokyo, Iwanami Shoten, 1937. As reprinted in *Essays of J.A. Schumpeter*, ed. Richard V. Clemence, Addison-Wesley, Cambridge (MA), 1951, p. 158.

He would have said (and, as a matter of fact, he did say it to me the only time that I had the opportunity to converse with him) that of course economic life is essentially passive and merely adapts itself to the natural and social influences which may be acting on it, so that the theory of a stationary process constitutes really the whole of theoretical economics and that as economic theorists we cannot say much about the factors that account for historical change, but must simply register them.[2]

The critical point here is that Schumpeter directly rejects the view of Walras that economic theory must be confined to the study of the stationary process, and that it cannot go farther than demonstrating how departures from equilibrium, such as might be generated by a growth in population or in savings, merely set into motion forces that restore the system to an equilibrium path. In proposing to develop a theory showing how a stationary process can be disturbed by internal as well as external forces, Schumpeter is suggesting that the essence of capitalism lies not in equilibrating forces but in the inevitable tendency of that system to *depart* from equilibrium – in a word, to disequilibrate. Equilibrium analysis fails to capture the essence of capitalist reality. Lest there should be any doubt about Schumpeter's position on this critical matter, we cite his own forceful formulation: "Whereas a stationary feudal economy would still be a feudal economy, and a stationary socialist economy would still be a socialist economy, stationary capitalism is a contradiction in terms."[3]

Although Schumpeter did in fact make important use of Walrasian general equilibrium in his analysis of the circular flow in a stationary state, he used the concept precisely as a means of demonstrating how capitalist economies would behave *if they were deprived of their essential feature*: that is, innovative activities that are the primary generator of economic change.

It is important to understand this methodological use that Schumpeter makes of the neo-classical analysis of a stationary economic process. As Schumpeter stated: "In appraising the performance of competitive enterprise, the question whether it would or would not tend to maximize production in a perfectly equilibrated stationary condition of the economic process is ... almost, though not quite, irrelevant."[4]

The reason it is not completely irrelevant is that the model of a stationary competitive process helps us to understand the behavior of an economy that possesses no internal forces generating economic change. Thus, the model of a Walrasian circular flow constitutes Schumpeter's starting point in understanding the essential elements of capitalist reality because it shows

---

[2] *Ibid.*, pp. 2–3.

[3] Joseph Schumpeter, "Capitalism in the Postwar World," in *Essays of J.A. Schumpeter*, ed. Clemence, p. 174.

[4] Joseph Schumpeter, *Capitalism, Socialism and Democracy*, second edition, George Allen & Unwin, Ltd., London, 1943, p. 77.

how that system would behave in the absence of its most distinctive feature – innovation. It is an invaluable abstraction precisely because it makes it possible to trace out with greater precision the impact of innovative activity. This is the role served by the Walrasian conception of the circular flow in Schumpeter's analysis of business cycles as well as growth.

Of course, one can always adopt the position that Schumpeter and neo-classical economics address very different questions, and that the theoretical analysis of each is valid in its particular intellectual context. Newton's law of gravity, after all, was not invalidated by Mendeleev's periodic table of the elements. Each theory was devised to account for different classes of phenomena. They do not contradict each other and they may, therefore, be simultaneously valid – or invalid.

I believe that there is something to be said in support of such a position. But I am not at all confident that the Schumpeter of part II of *Capitalism, Socialism and Democracy* would have been satisfied with it. Schumpeter's position seems to be that, if you want to understand what capitalism is all about as an economic system, the fundamental question is how it generates economic change rather than how it restores stability. Not all theoretical frameworks are equally useful in analyzing the essential feature of modern capitalism. And again, the essential feature, in Schumpeter's view, is economic change. This is because the capitalist form of economic organiza-tion has a built-in logic that dominates the behavior of that economic system. Thus, economists who purport to have something to say that is pertinent to the contemporary operation of capitalism have the obligation to deal with certain distinctive patterns of capitalist behavior and to explain their consequences. The behavior of capitalism is totally dominated by the continual working out of its inner logic, the essence of which is economic change resulting from the impact of the innovation process.

Equilibrium analysis, on the other hand, focuses upon adjustment mechanisms that are only peripheral, and not central, to the logic of capitalist organization and incentives. Therefore a theoretical approach that neglects persistent disequilibrium, instability and growth is an approach that deals with processes that are, at best, phenomena of secondary importance, or only mere epiphenomena.[5]

III

I do not propose to examine in any detail Schumpeter's views on inno-vation, or the breadth of his definition of innovation, since these are

[5] For a perceptive examination of the limits of equilibrium analysis in the context of innovation studies, see Richard R. Nelson, "Schumpeter and Contemporary Research on the Economics of Innovation," unpublished manuscript, Columbia University, February 1992.

familiar to all readers of his major works. I do, however, propose to underline the rather radical implications that Schumpeter himself drew from the primacy that he attached to innovation – implications that have received little attention. The dynamic forces that are inherent in the capitalist structure lead Schumpeter to treat capitalism as a system whose essential feature is an evolutionary process and not the mechanisms that force the system to revert to an equilibrium after some external force has produced a small departure from that equilibrium. For those who find the term "disequilibrium analysis" too paradoxical to be useful as a description of Schumpeter's mode of economic analysis, I suggest the propriety of the term "evolutionary." My justification is a simple one: it is Schumpeter's own frequently used term in *Capitalism, Socialism and Democracy*:

The essential point to grasp is that in dealing with capitalism we are dealing with an evolutionary process ... Capitalism ... is by nature a form or method of economic change and not only never is but never can be stationary. And this evolutionary character of the capitalist process is not merely due to the fact that economic life goes on in a social and natural environment which changes and by its changes alters the data of economic action; this fact is important and these changes (wars, revolutions and so on) often condition industrial change, but they are not its prime movers. Nor is this evolutionary character due to a quasi-automatic increase in population and capital or to the vagaries of monetary systems of which exactly the same thing holds true.[6]

I ask readers of *Capitalism, Socialism and Democracy* to ponder the far-reaching implications of this statement. For it involves not only the recognition of the inherently dynamic nature of capitalism. It involves also nothing less than the rejection of the competitive ideal itself, as that ideal is enshrined not only in economists' models but also in decades of government regulation and, in the United States, in a full century of anti-trust legislation. In this view, textbook competition is not an ideal state to be pursued. The welfare implications of the competitive ideal reflect a mistaken preoccupation with the distinctly secondary issue of how the economy allocates an existing stock of resources; whereas the far more significant concern for Schumpeter is how successful an economic system is at generating growth – growth in a qualitative as well as a quantitative sense. In my own reading, this deserves to be regarded as the central message of *Capitalism, Socialism and Democracy*. Capitalists survive, if they survive at all, by learning to live in, and to participate in, a "perennial gale of creative destruction ... the problem that is usually being visualized is how capitalism administers existing structures, whereas the relevant problem is how it creates and destroys them."[7] I call attention to the

---

[6] Schumpeter, *Capitalism, Socialism and Democracy*, p. 82. See also *ibid.*, p. 58.
[7] *Ibid.*, p. 84.

significant fact that Schumpeter attached so much importance to this last observation that he repeated it, almost verbatim, in the preface to the second edition of *Capitalism, Socialism and Democracy*.[8]

In my view, if one is looking for a distinctively "Schumpeterian hypothesis," it lies in this definition of the essential nature of the competitive process. Perhaps this should not be regarded as a hypothesis, since it is difficult to reduce it to a testable, potentially refutable form. It is more in the nature of a conception or, better, to use a favorite Schumpeterian term, a "vision" of the essential nature of capitalism. It is a vision in which it is a mistake to reduce monopoly to the purely restrictive and anti-social consequences that are normally ascribed to it, since monopoly power is often a temporary adjunct of the process of creative destruction. The Schumpeter of *Capitalism, Socialism and Democracy* does indeed attach considerable significance to the growth in the absolute size of the firm in the course of the twentieth century. At the same time, I would like to insist that a "Schumpeterian hypothesis," which postulates a strong association between market power and innovation, is an extreme oversimplification of a much more sophisticated – and much more radical – view of the meaning of competition.[9]

Thus, Schumpeter is involved in an explicit rejection of the central neo-classical notion that atomistic competition offers unique welfare advantages. In *Capitalism, Socialism and Democracy* he posits a novel conception of competition based upon innovation as a central element in a disequilibrium process that leads the economy to higher levels of income, output, and, presumably, well-being. In the course of the twentieth century the large-scale firm, with its internal research capabilities, has become the dominant engine of technical progress. This is a main theme of *Capitalism, Socialism and Democracy*, as opposed to his earlier book, *The Theory of Economic Development*. Schumpeter's argument is certainly closely tied to bigness and to the dismissal of the virtues of perfect competition. It recognizes some degree of monopoly power as a passing phase of the innovation process. But rejecting the virtues of perfect competition is not the same thing as saying that monopoly power is inherently favorable to innovation.

Thus it is not sufficient to argue that because perfect competition is impossible under modern industrial conditions – or because it always has been impossible – the large-scale establishment or unit of control must be accepted as a necessary evil inseparable from the economic progress which it is prevented from sabotaging by the forces inherent in its productive apparatus. What we have got to accept is that it

---

[8] *Ibid.*, p. x.
[9] See Nelson, "Schumpeter and Contemporary Research on the Economics of Innovation," for an illuminating discussion of this issue.

has come to be the most powerful engine of that progress and in particular of the long-run expansion of total output not only in spite of, but to a considerable extend through, this strategy which looks so restrictive when viewed in the individual case and from the individual point of time. In this respect, perfect competition is not only impossible but inferior, and has no title to being set up as a model of ideal efficiency.[10]

Indeed, the perennial gale of creative destruction is continually sweeping away entrenched monopoly power that appeared so secure until a new innovation consigned it to the scrapheap of history. That is precisely why the perennial gale is such a critically important economic force.

IV

But there is much more to Schumpeter the radical anti-neo-classicist than has been suggested so far. This becomes apparent as soon as it is recognized that innovation, the central feature of capitalist reality, is not a product of a decision-making process that can be described or analyzed as "rational":

the assumption that business behaviour is ideally rational and prompt, and also that in principle it is the same with all firms, works tolerably well only within the precincts of tried experience and familiar motive. It breaks down as soon as we leave those precincts and allow the business community under study to be faced by – not simply new situations, which also occur as soon as external factors unexpectedly intrude but by – new possibilities of business action which are as yet untried and about which the most complete command of routine teaches nothing. Those differences in the behaviour of different people which within those precincts account for secondary phenomena only, become essential in the sense that they now account for the outstanding features of reality and that a picture drawn on the Walras-Marshallian lines ceases to be true – even in the qualified sense in which it is true of stationary and growing processes: it misses those features, and becomes wrong in the endeavour to account by means of its own analysis for phenomena which the assumptions of that analysis exclude.[11]

It is, of course, difficult to imagine a more profound rejection of neo-classical economics than is embodied in Schumpeter's forceful assertion that the most important feature of capitalist reality – innovation – is one to which rational decision-making has no direct application. The nature of the innovation process, the drastic departure from existing routines, is inherently one that cannot be reduced to mere calculation, although subsequent imitation of the innovation, once accomplished, can be so reduced. Innovation is the creation of knowledge that cannot, and therefore should

[10] Schumpeter, *Capitalism, Socialism and Democracy*, p. 106.
[11] Joseph Schumpeter, *Business Cycles*, 2 vols., McGraw-Hill Book Company, New York, 1939, vol. I, pp. 98–99.

not, be "anticipated" by the theorist in a purely formal manner, as is done in the theory of decision-making under uncertainty. In Schumpeter's view, it would be entirely meaningless to speak of "the future state of the world," as that state is not merely unknown, but also indefinable in empirical and historical terms. Serious doubt is thus cast on what meaning, if any, can be possessed by intertemporal models of equilibrium under uncertainty, in which the essential nature of innovation is systematically neglected.

Thus, if rationality is reduced in the neo-classical world more and more to the tautology that people do the best they can, given the whole gamut of constraints they face – among the most important of which is the informational constraint – then accepting Schumpeter's concept of innovation means that human actions are always second best in a way that ultimately cannot be subjected to further analysis. For rational behavior, in Schumpeter's view, is most significant in a world of routine and repetition of similar events. (Needless to say, the modern literature on rational expectations does not overcome Schumpeter's strictures here. The "rationality" of rational expectations is limited by currently available information, and thus the inherent uncertainty concerning the future is not eliminated).

But this is not the end of Schumpeter's rather complex treatment of the role of rationality. If one considers rationality in the long historical context, Schumpeter mounts an argument in *Capitalism, Socialism and Democracy* the essential element of which is that capitalism, considered as a civilization, has continuously enlarged the social space within which rationalistic attitudes and habits of thought come to prevail.[12] In chapter 11, "The Civilization of Capitalism," Schumpeter argues that capitalism has expanded the sphere within which "rational cost-profit calculations" could be carried out. Moreover,

primarily a product of the evolution of economic rationality, the cost-profit calculus in turn reacts upon that rationality; by crystallizing and defining numerically, it powerfully propels the logic of enterprise. And thus defined and quantified for the economic sector, this type of logic or attitude or method then starts upon its conqueror's career, subjugating – rationalizing – man's tools and philosophies, his medical practice, his picture of the cosmos, his outlook on life, everything in fact including his concepts of beauty and justice and his spiritual ambitions.[13]

This aspect of Schumpeter's argument – what he himself might have described as his own "economic sociology" – is, in my opinion, analytically brilliant, breathtaking in its sweep and, historically, substantially correct. I regret that it is impossible here to examine his argument in detail. I remind

---

[12] Contrast this view with Babbage's treatment of rationality and the "Mental Division of Labour" in the previous chapter.

[13] Schumpeter, *Capitalism, Socialism and Democracy*, pp. 123–124.

you of it now because it is the linch pin of Schumpeter's argument that
capitalism will eventually "self-destruct." The self-destruction is inevitable
because, in his view, the historical expansion of rationality brings in its
wake two crucial consequences.

The first is that rationality challenges and unfrocks beliefs and institutions that cannot survive the searching and corrosive glare of a (presumably
narrow) rationality: "When the habit of rational analysis of, and rational
behavior in, the daily tasks of life has gone far enough, it turns back upon
the mass of collective ideas and criticizes and to some extent 'rationalizes'
them by way of such questions as why there should be kings and popes or
subordination or tithes or property."[14]

The second consequence is that, as capitalism expands the sphere to
which rationality applies, it learns eventually how to supplant the entrepreneur, the human "carrier" of innovation, with institutions that do away
with the social leadership of the entrepreneur himself. The entrepreneurial
function itself becomes rationalized – or bureaucratized – with the growth
of the large firm. "For . . . it is now much easier than it has been in the past to
do things that lie outside familiar routine – innovation itself has been
reduced to routine. Technological progress is increasingly becoming the
business of teams of trained specialists who turn out what is required and
make it work in predictable ways."[15]

Of course, the growth of large-scale enterprise and the "obsolescence of
the entrepreneurial function" led Schumpeter, through the rich argument
of his economic and political sociology, to his conclusion that capitalism
cannot survive. The ideology and social myths that once sustained it cannot
survive its tendency to "automatize progress"[16] and thus to reveal its new-
found ability to do without the leadership and vitality once provided by the
entrepreneur and the bourgeoisie.

My own view – with the easy wisdom of fifty years of retrospection – is
that Schumpeter much overstated the extent to which technological
progress would become automatized. I believe that this, in turn, is partly
due to his intensive focus upon the earliest stages in the innovation process,
and to his failure to consider the degree to which commercial success is
dependent upon subsequent stages in the carrying out of an innovation.
But, regrettably, these issues cannot be explored here. What is essential to
my examination of Schumpeter the radical is the observation that, both in
the past and in the future, it is Schumpeter's view that a rational approach
to the innovation process is incompatible with capitalist institutions. So
long as the function was carried out by the individual entrepreneur, it was
an act based upon intuition and charismatic leadership; when capitalist

[14] *Ibid.*, p. 122.   [15] *Ibid.*, p. 132.   [16] *Ibid.*, p. 134.

institutions eventually, at some future date, succeed in subjecting inno-vation to a rationalized routine, those institutions will, *ipso facto*, lose their lustre and social justification, and be replaced by a socialized state.

Thus, in a world where capitalist institutions continue to prevail, innovation calls upon a decision-making process that goes beyond rational calculation. When capitalist development eventually leads to the institutio-nalization of innovation, the organizational basis of the economy will, Schumpeter believes, be transformed into some form of socialism. In neither case, ironically, does Schumpeter concede a significant role for the neo-classical analysis of rational behavior.

V

Schumpeter's radical anti-neo-classical stance extends even to the issue of what it is that constitutes the *explicanda* of economic analysis. It is normal practice for neo-classical economists to take tastes and technology as exogenously given, and to seek to examine issues of resource allocation by explicit reference to changes in incomes and relative prices.[17]

Thus, Schumpeter's assault upon neo-classical economics includes even his deliberate violation of the *sanctum sanctorum* of the neo-classical citadel: the commitments to the exogeneity of consumer preferences and the associated virtues of consumer sovereignty. His belief that the central problem of the economist is to account for economic change over time undoubtedly played an important role in sharpening his perception of the forces influencing consumer preferences:

Innovations in the economic system do not as a rule take place in such a way that first new wants arise spontaneously in consumers and then the productive apparatus swings round through their pressure. We do not deny the presence of this nexus. It is, however, the producer who as a rule initiates economic change, and consumers are educated by him if necessary; they are, as it were, taught to want new things, or things which differ in some respect or other from those which they have been in the habit of using. Therefore, while it is permissible and even necessary to consider consumers' wants as an independent and indeed the fundamental force in a theory of the circular flow, we must take a different attitude as soon as we analyse *change*.[18]

Schumpeter made the same essential point later on in *Business Cycles*:

We will, throughout, act on the assumption that consumers' initiative in changing their tastes – i.e., in changing that set of our data which general theory comprises in

---

[17] See George Stigler and Gary Becker, "De Gustibus non est Disputandum," *American Economic Review*, 67 (1977), pp. 76–90.

[18] Joseph Schumpeter, *The Theory of Economic Development*, Harvard University Press, Cambridge (MA), 1949, p. 65 Schumpeter's italics. (first published in German in 1911).

the concepts of "utility functions" or "indifference varieties" – is negligible and that all change in consumers' tastes is incident to, and brought about by, producers' actions. This requires both justification and qualification.

The fact on which we stand is, of course, common knowledge. Railroads have not emerged because any consumers took the initiative in displaying an effective demand for their service in preference to the services of mail coaches. Nor did the consumers display any such initiative wish to have electric lamps or rayon stockings, or to travel by motorcar or airplane, or to listen to radios, or to chew gum. There is obviously no lack of realism in the proposition that the great majority of changes in commodities consumed has been forced by producers on consumers who, more often than not, have resisted the change and have had to be educated up by elaborate psychotechnics of advertising.[19]

Although modern economists have, of course, investigated the consequences of endogenous preferences for welfare judgments, most have considered it better, for reasons of division of labor with other disciplines, in particular psychology, to neglect the investigation of why and how tastes change.[20] But Schumpeter asserted that innovation, the fundamental driving force of the historical evolution of capitalism, would mould tastes as well as technology in unexpected ways. The implications, both for the development of the economic and social systems, as well as for microeconomic welfare judgments were, as Schumpeter recognized, potentially radical. Just before his death in 1950 he severely criticized economists for the uncritical belief that so many seem to harbor in the virtues of consumers' choice:

First of all, whether we like it or not, we are witnessing a momentous experiment in malleability of tastes – is not this worth analyzing? Second, ever since the physiocrats (and before), economists have professed unbounded respect for the consumers' choice – is it not time to investigate what the bases for this respect are and how far the traditional and, in part, advertisement-shaped tastes of people are subject to the qualification that they might prefer other things than those which they want at present as soon as they have acquired familiarity with these other things? In matters of education, health, and housing there is already practical unanimity about this – but might the principle not be carried much further? Third, economic theory accepts existing tastes as data, no matter whether it postulates utility functions or indifference varieties or simply preference directions, and these data are made the starting point of price theory. Hence, they must be considered as independent of prices. But considerable and persistent changes in prices obviously do react upon tastes. *What, then, is to become of our theory and the whole of microeconomics?* It is investigations of this kind, that might break new ground, which I miss.[21]

---

[19] Schumpeter, *Business Cycles*, vol. I, p. 73.
[20] See, for example, Milton Friedman, *Price Theory*, Aldine Publishing Company, New York, 1976, p. 13.
[21] Joseph Schumpeter, "English Economists and the State-Managed Economy," *Journal of Political Economy* (1949), pp. 380–381. Schumpeter's italics.

The earlier discussion of Schumpeter's analysis of innovation has already anticipated his unwillingness to treat technological change, as well as consumers' tastes, as an exogenous phenomenon. But it is necessary to distinguish between the earlier Schumpeter of *The Theory of Economic Development* (1911) and the later Schumpeter of *Capitalism, Socialism and Democracy* (1942). In his earlier book, Schumpeter looked upon invention as an exogenous activity and upon innovation as endogenous. Whereas inventors conducted their activities off the economic stage and contributed their artifacts to a pool of invention, the timing of the entrepreneurial decision to draw from this pool was decisively shaped by economic forces. But the later Schumpeter saw both invention and innovation as generated by economic forces inside the large firm with its own internal research capabilities. The reason for the change in Schumpeter's views during this period is not far to seek: the economic world, the object of Schumpeter's studies, had changed substantially during the period between the publication of the two books. Schumpeter's altered views were an acknowledgment of empirical changes that had occurred during his own professional lifetime.

Schumpeter's insistence upon the role of endogenous forces applies, not only to technology, but also to science itself. The rationalizing influence of the capitalistic mentality and institutions created "the growth of rational science" as well as its "long list of applications."[22] Significantly, Schumpeter cites as examples not only "Airplanes, refrigerators, television and that sort of thing ..." but also the "modern hospital." Although one might be surprised at the appearance here of an institution that is not commonly operated on a profitmaking basis, Schumpeter's explanation is illuminating. It is

fundamentally because capitalist rationality supplied the habits of mind that evolved the methods used in these hospitals. And the victories, not yet completely won but in the offing, over cancer, syphilis and tuberculosis will be as much capitalist achievements as motorcars or pipe lines or Bessemer steel have been. In the case of medicine, there is a capitalist profession behind the methods, capitalist both because to a large extent it works in a business spirit and because it is an emulsion of the industrial and commercial bourgeoisie. But even if that were not so, modern medicine and hygiene would still be by-products of the capitalist process just as is modern education.[23]

Thus, Schumpeter insisted that both science and technology, normally so far from the world of phenomena examined by neo-classical economics, are in reality highly endogenous to the economic world, subject to the gravitational pull of economic forces. In one of the last articles published during his own lifetime, Schumpeter identified his views with those of Marx

---

[22] Schumpeter, *Capitalism, Socialism and Democracy*, p. 125.   [23] *Ibid.*, pp. 125–126.

on the role played by western capitalism in accounting for progress in both science and technology. Schumpeter observed that Marx had, in the *Communist Manifesto*, "launched out on a panegyric upon bourgeois achievement that has no equal in economic literature." After quoting a relevant portion of the text, he says:

No reputable "bourgeois" economist of that or any other time – certainly not A. Smith or J.S. Mill – ever said as much as this. Observe, in particular, the emphasis upon the creative role of the business class that the majority of the most "bourgeois" economists so persistently overlooked and of the business class as such, whereas most of us would, on the one hand, also insert into the picture non-bourgeois contributions to the bourgeois success – the contributions of non-bourgeois bureaucracies, for instance – and, on the other hand, commit the mistake (for such I believe it is) to list as independent factors science and technology, whereas Marx's sociology enabled him to see that these as well as "progress" in such fields as education and hygiene were just as much the products of the bourgeois culture – hence, ultimately, of the business class – as was the business performance itself.[24]

Did Schumpeter then believe, along with Marx, in the economic interpretation of history? I suggest that he did, with certain qualifications. However, the qualifications that Schumpeter imposed upon the economic interpretation of history were of a sort that, if anything, actually strengthened its usefulness as a device for explaining economic change. It is important here to recall that the first four chapters of *Capitalism, Socialism and Democracy* are devoted entirely to an examination of Marx's views on a range of subjects. Schumpeter offered a sympathetic and approving treatment of the economic interpretation of history; moreover, almost all of his own writing fits conveniently into that interpretation. But Schumpeter also compresses the economic interpretation into just two propositions:

1. The forms or conditions of production are the fundamental determinants of social structures which in turn breed attitudes, actions and civilizations.
2. The forms of production themselves have a logic of their own; that is to say, they change according to necessities inherent in them so as to produce their successors merely by their own working.[25]

Schumpeter asserts that "Both propositions undoubtedly contain a large amount of truth and are, as we shall find at several turns of our way, invaluable working hypotheses."[26] His main qualification, if that is what it really is, is his insistence upon the importance of lags, that is, social forms that persist after they have lost their economic rationale. It is far from clear that Marx would have disagreed with such a qualification, since Marx was much too sophisticated a historian to believe that economic changes

[24] Joseph Schumpeter, "The Communist Manifesto in Sociology and Economics," *Journal of Political Economy* (1949), p. 293. See also *Capitalism, Socialism and Democracy*, chapter 1.
[25] Schumpeter, *Capitalism, Socialism and Democracy*, pp. 11–12.   [26] *Ibid.*, p. 12.

generated the "appropriate" social changes instantaneously. Schumpeter, in making the qualification about lags, adds that Marx, although perhaps not fully appreciating their implications, would not have taken the simplistic position involved in denying them a role:

Social structures, types and attitudes are coins that do not readily melt. Once they are formed they persist, possibly for centuries, and since different structures and types display different degrees of this ability to survive, we almost always find that actual group and national behaviour more or less departs from what we should expect it to be if we tried to infer it from the dominant forms of the productive process. Though this applies quite generally, it is most clearly seen when a highly durable structure transfers itself bodily from one country to another. The social situation created in Sicily by the Norman conquest will illustrate my meaning. Such facts Marx did not overlook but he hardly realized all their implications.[27]

VI

Whether or not one concludes, as I do, that Schumpeter believed in a form of the economic interpretation of history, he clearly was strongly committed to the view that economic phenomena, in order to be meaningfully examined, must be studied in an historical context. Since I have spent a significant portion of my own professional life studying economic behavior in historical contexts, I am naturally pleased to be able to invoke the authority of Schumpeter in support of such an approach. At the same time, I believe that this interpretation of Schumpeter is more than a merely self-serving exercise on my part.

The fact is that most of what Schumpeter wrote qualifies as history, both economic and intellectual. Not only *Capitalism, Socialism and Democracy* but, in addition, *Business Cycles* and his posthumous *History of Economic Analysis* are historical works. His commitment to the historical approach was deeply rooted in his thought. Schumpeter had a profound appreciation of the path-dependent nature of economic phenomena and therefore of economic analysis itself.[28] More than this. The very subject matter of economics, in Schumpeter's view, *is* history. Economics is about economic change as it has occurred over historical time. That is why he insists upon the importance of studying capitalism as an evolutionary process. It is also why he assigns such a limited importance to the study of stationary economic processes. And these things have a great deal to do with Schumpeter's highest regard for some of Marx's contributions to economic analysis:

[27] *Ibid.*, pp. 12–13.
[28] For a more precise definition of path dependence and further analysis of the relationship between modern economic theory and historical analysis, see chapter 1 in this book.

There is . . . one thing of fundamental importance for the methodology of economics which he actually achieved. Economists always have either themselves done work in economic history or else used the historical work of others. But the facts of economic history were assigned to a separate compartment. They entered theory, if at all, merely in the role of illustrations, or possibly of verifications of results. They mixed with it only mechanically. Now Marx's mixture is a chemical one; that is to say, he introduced them into the very argument that produces the results. He was the first economist of top rank to see and to teach systematically how economic theory may be turned into historical analysis and how the historical narrative may be turned into *histoire raisonnée*.[29]

This passage, it seems to me, is also the best explanation for Schumpeter's frequent expression of admiration for, and intellectual indebtedness to Marx.

I can think of no better way of closing this chapter than by reminding you of certain views that Schumpeter expressed in chapter 2 of his *History of Economic Analysis*. After stating that a "scientific" economist is to be identified by the demonstrated command over three techniques – history, statistics, and theory – he goes on to say:

Of these fundamental fields, economic history – which issues into and includes present-day facts – is by far the most important. I wish to state right now that if, starting my work in economics afresh, I were told that I could study only one of the three but could have my choice, it would be economic history that I should choose. And this on three grounds. First, the subject matter of economics is essentially a unique process in historic time. Nobody can hope to understand the economic phenomena of any, including the present, epoch who has not an adequate command of historical facts and an adequate amount of historical sense or of what may be described as *historical experience*. Second, the historical report cannot be purely economic but must inevitably reflect also "institutional" facts that are not purely economic; therefore it affords the best method for understanding how economic and non-economic facts *are* related to one another and how the various social sciences *should* be related to one another. Third, it is, I believe, the fact that most of the fundamental errors currently committed in economic analysis are due to a lack of historical experience more often than to any other shortcoming of the economist's equipment.[30]

It is sad to have to conclude with the observation that some knowledge of history is still not regarded as essential to competent economic analysis. Indeed, judging by the curricula of the graduate programs in American universities today, the very idea would appear to be distinctly perverse and alien. In this, as in so many other respects, Schumpeter the radical economist still has a great deal to teach us.

[29] *Ibid.*, p. 44.
[30] Joseph Schumpeter, *History of Economic Analysis*, Oxford University Press, New York, 1954, pp. 12–13. Schumpeter's italics.

4 Technological innovation and long waves

NATHAN ROSENBERG AND CLAUDIO FRISCHTAK

This chapter is about the existence of long cycles or long waves of economic growth. No one who has examined the dynamics of capitalist economies over long historical periods can doubt that they experience significant long-term variations in their aggregate performance. The question is whether these long-term variations are more than the outcome of a summation of random events and, further, whether they exhibit recurrent temporal regularities that are sufficiently well-behaved to call them "long waves." In recent years there has been a strong resurgence of interest in such long-term movements, since their existence could provide a coherent explanation for the poor performance of capitalist economies over the past decade.[1] This renewed interest also reflects a search for alternative ways of explaining the unbalanced nature of the growth processes of mature capitalist economies that go uncaptured by the Solow–Swan paradigm, in its concern with equilibrium dynamics and steady states of one, two, or multisector representations of the economy.

The study of price and output swings of extended duration has a long tradition, having initially drawn the interest of both Marxist and non-Marxist writers around the turn of the century.[2] Yet, it was the work of

This chapter is reprinted from *Cambridge Journal of Economics*, Spring 1984. An earlier version appeared in Christopher Freeman (ed.), *Design, Innovation, and Long Cycles in Economic Development*, The Thetford Press, Thetford, Norfolk, 1984. A much-condensed version of this paper was published in the *American Economic Review, Papers and Proceedings*, May 1983. The authors wish to thank Moses Abramovitz, Paul David, Albert Fishlow, Donald Harris, and Sidney Winter for their helpful comments and criticisms of earlier drafts. We are also grateful to an anonymous referee of the *Cambridge Journal of Economics* for valuable suggestions.

[1] It is interesting to note, however, that the poor economic performance in the past decade or so has not been confined to capitalist economies, although it has certainly been pervasive among them. Indeed, the socialist bloc countries of eastern Europe shared the abysmal economic performance of capitalist countries.

[2] Among those who expressed some belief in the existence of long waves are W.S. Jevons, *Investigations in Currency and Finance*, Macmillan, London, 1884; W. Wicksell, *Geldszins und Guterpreise*, G. Fischer, Jena, 1898 (an English translation appears as *Interest and*

Kondratiev in 1925 which constituted the first systematic attempt to confirm such movements with data that included not only prices, interest rates, and wage series, but foreign trade, industrial production, and consumption for France, Britain, and (to a lesser extent) the United States. Kondratiev concluded that the data suggested the existence of long cycles with an average length of fifty years, and going back to the end of the eighteenth century. However, in formulating the possibility of long cycles, Kondratiev expressed himself with great caution, calling attention to the fact that the available historical evidence dealt with fewer than three full cycles as well as to the poor quality of production time series before 1850.[3]

Kondratiev's hypothesis gave rise to two distinct lines of historical research, one centered around the notion of a price (or interest-rate) cycle, and another focusing on long waves as a phenomenon in real quantities. Taken as price cycles, long waves have been alternatively interpreted as the outcome of real and monetary forces, whereas taken as fluctuations in real quantities, long waves have been understood as ultimately driven either by the process of capital accumulation, as in Kondratiev,[4] or by that of technological innovation, as in the Schumpeterian tradition.

This paper is not an attempt to examine the historical evidence for long cycles. We have in fact examined this evidence and we find it unconvincing. Although historical data might conceivably lend some plausibility to the

Prices: A Study of the Causes Regulating the Value of Money, Augustus Kelley, New York, 1965); A. Helphand (Parvus), *Die Handelskrise und die Gewerkschaften*, M. Ernst, Munich, 1901; G. Cassel, *Theoretische Sozialökonomie*, C.F. Winter, Leipzig, 1918 (an English translation appeared as *The Theory of Social Economy*, Harcourt, Brace, and Co., New York, 1983); J. van Gelderen, "Springvloed-Beschovwingen over industrieele ontwikkeling en prijsbewegigng," *Die Nieuwe Tijd*, 18 (April, May, and June 1913); and S. de Wolff, "Prosperitats-und Depressionperioden", in O. Jensen (ed.), *Der lebendige Marxismus: Festgabe zum 70 Geburtstage von Karl Kautsky*, Thuringer Verlagsanstalt, Jena, 1924. For an excellent annotated bibliography on long waves, see K. Barr, "Long Waves: A Selective Annotated Bibliography", *Review*, 4 (Spring 1974).

3 N.D. Kondratiev, "The Long Waves in Economic Life," *Review*, 4 (Spring 1979), p. 520 (a complete translation of *The Major Economic Cycles*, Voprosy Koniunktury, Moscow, 1925, vol. I).

4 As Kondratiev noted, when discussing causality of such long-term movements, "the material basis of the long cycles is the wearing out, replacement and expansion of fixed capital goods which require a long period of time and enormous expenditures to produce. The replacement and expansion of these goods does not proceed smoothly, but in spurts, another expression of which are the long waves of the conjuncture ... The period of increased production of these capital goods corresponds to the upswing ... conversely, the slowing down of this process causes a movement of economic elements toward the equilibrium level and below it. It must be stressed that the equilibrium level itself changes, in the process of cyclical fluctuations, and shifts, as a rule, to a higher level" (N.D. Kondratiev and E.I. Oparin, *The Major Economic Cycles*, Krasma Presma, Moscow, 1928, pp. 60–61 as quoted by R. Day, "The Theory of the Long Cycle: Kondratiev, Trotsky, Mandel," *New Left Review* (September–October 1976), p. 76 and G. Garvy, "Kondratieff's Theory of Long Cycles," *Review of Economics and Statistics*, 25 (November 1943), p. 208.

notion of long cycles in prices, we remain, at present, skeptical of the case that has so far been made for their presence in real phenomena, that is, in aggregate output or employment (moreover, even with respect to prices, it is very unlikely that there have been long waves during the upward drift in absolute prices of the last half century, although there have certainly been drastic changes in the terms of trade between industrial goods and primary commodities).[5]

What we offer here, instead, and consistent with our present skepticism, is an attempt to examine the economic logic of long waves. More specifically, we ask: what conditions would need to be fulfilled in order for technological innovation to generate long cycles in economic growth of the periodicity postulated by Kondratiev and his disciples? Surprisingly, in view of the amount of current interest in the subject, this question is hardly ever addressed by advocates of long waves with sufficient analytical rigor. In fact, an adequate or even plausible theory of long cycles, based primarily upon technological determinants, does not presently exist, although *belief* in such long waves is now widespread.[6] It is our view that such a theory, which might account for the presence of long cycles in some real economic variable, would have to fulfill a set of logically interdependent requirements. We discuss these requirements under the four categories of causality, timing, economy-wide repercussions, and recurrence.

Causality

The first of the requirements for a technological theory of long cycles is a clear specification of causality among the factors associated with this

[5] P. David and P. Solar, "A Bicentenary Contribution to the History of the Cost-of-Living in America," in P. Uselding (ed.), *Research in Economic History*, vol. II, JAI Press, Greenwich (CT), 1977, in their careful review of the changes in the cost-of-living in the United States for the 200-year period (1774–1974) do, in fact, identify long cycles in the rate of change of consumer prices lying in the range between thirty-six and sixty years. However, they find no counterpart in real phenomena for these long cycles which they attribute to wars and gold discoveries. Similarly C. van Ewijk "A Spectral Analysis of the Kondratieff Cycle," *Kyklos*, 35 (3) (1982), after employing a spectral analytic test of price and volume series for Great Britain, France, Germany, and the United States, confirms only the existence of long cycles in prices, but not in output. An earlier work of van Ewijk ("The Long Wave – A Real Phenomenon?" *De Economist*, 129 (3) (1981) also presents a reasonably strong case against long waves as a phenomenon in "real" variables. For the most carefully articulated empirical case for the existence of long waves in output, see J.J. van Duijn, *The Long Wave in Economic Life*, George Allen and Unwin, London 1983.

[6] See for example, C. Freeman, J. Clark, and L. Soete, *Unemployment and Technical Innovation: A Study of Long Waves and Economic Development*, Frances Pinter, London, 1982, which is among the best of the contemporaneous statements on long waves; J.J. van Duijn, "Fluctuations in Innovations over Time," *Futures*, 13 (August 1981), and his *The Long Wave in Economic Life*; and G. Mensch, *Stalemate in Technology: Innovations Overcome the Depression*, Ballinger, Cambridge (MA), 1979 (originally published in German in 1975, under the title *Das technologische Patt*).

phenomenon. Kondratiev was insistent that capitalism had its own internal regulating mechanisms, and he regarded the pace or rhythm of the long cycle as an expression of these internal forces. Long cycles, as Kondratiev put it, "arise out of causes which are inherent in the essence of the capitalist economy."[7] The cyclical behavior of the capitalist economy in turn shapes the conditions that are favorable to technological innovation. In this specific sense, therefore, technological activities stand in the position of dependent variables whose volume and timing are determined by those deeper-rooted forces that shape the rhythm of capitalist development.[8]

Furthermore, Kondratiev sees an unusually wide range of economic and social phenomena as being endogenously shaped – not only technological innovation but also wars, gold discoveries, and the entry of new geographic regions into the nexus of market relationships with capitalist economies. It remains true, of course, that Kondratiev views technological change as exercising an important influence on the course of capitalist development; yet the essential point is that these technological changes are viewed as occurring in response to endogenous forces within capitalism.[9]

[7] Kondratiev, "The Long Waves in Economic Life," p. 543.

[8] Kondratiev's main academic critic was D.I. Oparin, yet it was Trotsky who set the tone for much of the Russian debate on the "prospects of the world economy." Trotsky asserted as early as 1923 that "for those long (50 year) intervals of the capitalist curve, which Professor Kondratiev hastily proposes also to call *cycles*, their character and duration is determined not by the internal play of capitalist forces, but by the external conditions in which capitalist development occurs. The absorption by capitalism of new continents and countries, the discovery of new natural resources and, in addition, significant factors of a 'superstructural' order, such as wars and revolutions, determine the character and alteration of expansive, stagnating or declining epochs in capitalist development" (cited by Day, "The Theory of the Long Cycle," p. 71).

Implicit here is the idea that distinct growth-generating factors are associated with different phases of capitalism. Thus the long waves, if observable, would either by driven by extra-economic phenomena, or by unsystematic (or non-recurrent) economic impulses. This conception seems to have been at the root of much of the criticism directed at Kondratiev by his Russian colleagues, who shared the belief that the Marxist notion of evolution precluded the continual reproduction of a mode of production without its qualitative transformation over time. The gist of their argument can be summarized by stating that the qualitative dimension *dominates* the quantitative one, a proposition which would entail looking at waves in their singularity, which would be clearly at odds with the idea of a long-wave pattern.

[9] It may be added that, in spite of substantial differences among them, some present-day advocates of long cycles – W.W. Rostow, "Kondratieff, Schumpter, and Kuznets: Trend periods Revisited," *Journal of Economic History*, 35 (December 1975) and his *The World Economy: History and Prospect*, University of Texas Press, Austin, 1978; E. Mandel, *Late Capitalism*, New Left Books, London, 1975, and his "Explaining Long Waves of Capitalist Development," *Futures*, 13 (August 1981); and J. Forrester, "Growth Cycles," *De Economist*, 125, no. 4 (1977) and his "Innovation and Economic Change," *Futures*, 13 (August 1981) – seem to share the Kondratiev view that innovations are, somehow, disciplined and structured, and have their timing determined by, such long-term movements. As Forrester has put it: "I believe that the long wave strongly influences the climate for innovation ... but I do not see innovation as causing the long wave ... instead I see the long wave as compressing technological change into certain time intervals and as altering

Schumpeter was, of course, the foremost and most influential articulator of the opposite view – that long cycles are caused by, and are an incident of, the innovation process. Indeed, Kondratiev's ideas were first brought to the attention of English-speaking economists through Schumpeter's treatise on business cycles, in spite of the fact that Schumpeter urged a causality that was sharply in contrast with Kondratiev's. Moreover, it is the Schumpeterian variant of the long-cycles hypothesis, stressing the initiating role of innovations, that commands the widest attention today.

In Schumpeter's view, technological innovation is at the center of both cyclical instability and economic growth, with the direction of causality moving clearly from the fluctuations in innovation to fluctuations in investment and from that to cycles in economic growth.[10] Moreover, Schumpeter sees innovations as clustering around certain points in time – periods that he refers to as "neighborhoods of equilibrium," when entrepreneurial perception of risk and returns warranted innovative commitments.[11] These clusterings, in turn, lead to long cycles by generating

the opportunities for innovation" (Innovation and Economic Change," p. 338). Similarly, Mandel also denies that "innovations create more or less automatically an expansionary long wave" (*ibid.*, p. 334). Although regularly using terms like "Kondratievs" and "Long Cycles," Rostow is not primarily concerned with aggregates or overall movements. His focus is consistently sectoral, especially the changing sectoral composition of investment. His main emphasis is sectoral shifts in *relative* prices (terms of trade) between agriculture and raw materials, on the one hand, and industrial output on the other, which have assumed a long-wave pattern. These relative price shifts have, of course, influenced profit rates by sector and, in turn, have accounted for changing patterns in the allocation of capital. In addition, Rostow rejects the emphasis on innovation as the main determinant of overall and sectoral price swings. Note in this connection that W.A. Lewis, *Growth and Fluctuations, 1870–1913*, George Allen and Unwin, London, 1978, is more restrictive in his argument for the existence of price swings, insofar as he is looking only at the period 1870–1913. Further, in Lewis (as opposed to Rostow), the Kondratiev cycle was primarily in *absolute* price levels, which was "accompanied by" changes in the terms of trade between agriculture and industry (p. 27).

[10] Of course, Schumpeter's definition of innovation was much broader than the mere technological component, but this issue is not explored here for the reason that his long-wave hypothesis is grounded upon the technological aspect of the innovation process. We also ignore the considerable shift in emphasis that appeared in Schumpeter's *Capitalism, Socialism and Democracy* (Harper & Row, New York, 1942), which tended to see technological innovation itself as much more endogenous than the view expressed in his *Business Cycles, A Theoretical, Historical and Statistical Analysis of the Capitalist Process*, McGraw-Hill, New York, 1939.

[11] The extent to which innovation can be reduced to rational calculation, based upon observable market conditions, is of course, a complex question. Schumpeter was fond of emphasizing the social leadership role of the entrepreneur, especially his willingness to take bold leaps into the unknown, and to undertake commitments that cannot possibly be subjected to the ordinary calculus of business decision-making. Thus, for Schumpeter, America's vast western railroad construction meant "building ahead of demand in the boldest acceptance of the phrase and everyone understood them to mean that. Operating deficits for a period which it was impossible to estimate with any accuracy were part of the data of the problem" (Schumpeter, *Business Cycles*, vol. I, p. 328). This view has been

periods of acceleration (and eventual deceleration) in aggregate growth rates.[12] *Why* clustering should occur is obviously crucial to a theory of long cycles and we will therefore return to this question shortly. But it is essential to stress that an exponent of the view that technological changes is at the root of the long cycle needs to demonstrate:

a. that changes in the rate of innovation govern changes in the rate of new investment, and

b. that the combined impact of innovation clusters takes the form of fluctuations in aggregate output or employment.

Such causal links are not demonstrated in the neo-Schumpeterian literature. Consider Freeman, Clark, and Soete, *Unemployment and Technical Innovation* (1982), which we regard as the best statement on long waves from this perspective. The conditions which set in motion the diffusion and clustering of basic and related innovations and which would stand behind the upswing of a long wave are only loosely specified. The authors variously stress the "role of advances in basic sciences, and social, managerial and organizational changes in triggering and facilitating clusters of basic inventions and innovations" (p. x), "the phase of the long wave, particular breakthroughs in technology" and their "natural trajectories" as influences in the clustering process (p. 64), "the scientific, technical, and economic links" among constellations of widely adaptable innovations (p. 64), and "a social change which permits a market to grow rapidly or large amounts of capital to be raised or invested" (p. 65).

In spite of this long listing of possible influences, we are left without a precise knowledge of what are the necessary and sufficient changes in the environment which, even conceptually, can bring out a bandwagon-like diffusion of some number of basic innovations. In other words, there is no well-specified set of elements that effectively links and elucidates the

challenged by Albert Fishlow, who argued that the pattern of railroad expansion into the midwest during the *ante bellum* period is best understood in terms of a response to existing and not long-deferred and uncertain profit opportunities – a view that is borne out by the fact that railway enterprises earned profits from the start which were fully comparable to profits earned elsewhere in the economy. Fishlow carefully examines the pattern and sequence of roadbuilding on a state-by-state basis, and demonstrates that they were profitable from the beginning (see A. Fishlow, *American Railroads and the Transformation of the Ante-Bellum Economy*, Harvard University Press, Cambridge (MA), 1965, chapter 4).

[12] Note that in Schumpeter's complex treatment of Kondratievs, the links between innovation clusters and the phases of the cycle are mediated by the varying degrees of "roundaboutness" of the methods of production (time being essential to build new plant and equipment), and by gestation and absorption lags involved in the introduction of innovations into the economic system. Further, Schumpeter's schema implies that output of consumer goods increases most in recessions and revivals whereas output of producer goods increases most in revivals and prosperity, so that total output increases through all the phases of the cycle. In contrast, the price level rises in the prosperity phase, and it falls in the recession phase.

direction of causality between the basic innovations, the "general level of profitability and business expectations," and their diffusion in the form of a swarm of new products and processes. More generally, nowhere in the literature is there to be found an unambiguous treatment of causality within a neo-Schumpeterian framework, which establishes the precedence of innovation clusters over investment outlays and aggregate movements in the economy.

Timing

The process of technological innovation involves extremely complex relations among a set of key variables – inventions, innovations, diffusion paths, and investment activity. The impact of technological innovation on aggregate output is mediated through a succession of relationships that have yet to be explored systematically in the context of long waves. Specifically, the manner in which various economic and technological forces may influence the lag between invention and innovation, as well as the speed of the diffusion process and the impact on output growth, is insufficiently appreciated.[13] A technological theory of long cycles needs to demonstrate that these variables interact in a manner that is compatible with the peculiar timing requirements of such cycles.[14]

It is not enough to argue that the introduction of new technologies generates cyclical instability. It is necessary to demonstrate why technological innovation leads to cycles of four-and-a-half to six decades in length, with long periods of expansion giving way to similarly extended periods of stagnation.[15] Of course the burden of establishing such a connection lies with proponents of the long-cycle theory. We therefore offer a brief inventory of strategic factors that may be expected to determine the length of the time period required for the introduction of new technologies and the realization of their full impact upon aggregate output. In particular, long waves involve a diffusion period of appropriate length, the spacing (non-

---

[13] Partly for this reason, too much importance is commonly attached to specifying the year in which an invention may be said to have occurred. Some of these issues are treated in Rosenberg, *Perspectives on Technology*, Cambridge University Press, Cambridge, 1976, chapter 2.

[14] It is interesting to note that, although Schumpeter popularized the notion of long cycles, or Kondratievs, in his three-cycle schema, he was nevertheless careful to assert that his own innovation theory of business cycles did not require cycles of the length postulated by Kondratiev. "It cannot be emphasized too strongly that the 3-cycle schema does not follow from our model – although multiplicity of cycles does – and that approval of it or objection to it does not add to or detract from the value or otherwise of our fundamental idea, which would work equally well or ill with many other schemata of this kind" (Schumpeter, *Business Cycles*, pp. 169–170).

[15] In this discussion we are examining the case of a closed economy and we are therefore ignoring the additional complexities that would arise from the international transmission of long cycles.

overlapping) of substitute technologies, and the clustering of those which are of complementary and unrelated natures.

New inventions are typically very primitive at the time of their birth. Their performance is usually poor, compared to existing (alternative) technologies as well as to their future performance. Moreover, the cost of production, at this initial stage, is likely to be very high – indeed, in some cases a production technology may simply not yet exist, as is often observed in major chemical inventions (e.g. nylon, rayon). Thus, the speed with which inventions are transformed into innovations, and consequently diffused, will depend upon the actual *and* expected trajectory of performance improvement and cost reduction.

This process is rendered more complex, first, by the fact that in the early stages, when performance is still very modest and production costs are high, improvements leading even to significant cost reductions may have no sizable effect upon rates of adoption. When, on the other hand, the new product attains cost levels roughly equivalent to those prevailing under the older technology, even *small* further cost reductions may lead to widespread adoption. Or, alternatively, at this point relatively small changes in factor prices may shift the balance sharply in favor of the innovation, depending upon the nature of its factor-saving bias. Thus there may be a highly non-linear relationship between rates of improvement in a new product and rates of adoption. Further, there is often a long gestation period in the development of a new technology during which gradual improvements are not exploited because the costs of the new technology are still substantially in excess of the old. However, as the threshold level is approached and pierced, adoption rates of the new technology become increasingly sensitive to further improvements.

Second, since innovation and investment decisions are future-oriented and therefore inevitably involve a high degree of uncertainty, adoption and diffusion rates are also powerfully shaped by expectation patterns. In certain cases, these expectation patterns may lead to a prolonged delay in the introduction of potentially superior new technologies by adversely affecting their expected profitability. This could be the result of uncertainty regarding the timing and significance of future improvements in the technology being considered for adoption; of the expected availability of substitute innovations; and of the expected and actual improvements along the old trajectory.[16] Indeed, it has been very common for competitive

---

[16] See N. Rosenberg, *Inside the Black Box: Technology and Economics*, Cambridge University Press, Cambridge, 1982, chapter 5. For an analysis of the impact of technological uncertainties upon investment activity, see K. Moene, "Timing of Indivisible and Irreversible Projects: Micro Considerations Related to the Instability of Investment Activity," *Research Papers in Economics of Factor Markets*, 38, Stanford Univesity, 1982, pp. 38–43.

pressures generated by a new technology to lead to substantial improvements in the old technology, so that the new one establishes its superiority more slowly than would otherwise have been the case.

Note in this respect that major improvements in productivity, as well as output growth, may be stretched out over very long time periods, as a product goes through innumerable minor modifications and alterations in design. The camera, a mid-nineteenth-century innovation, experienced remarkably rapid diffusion in the post Second World War years. The Fourdrinier papermaking machine was patented in England and France in 1799; the first machine was made in 1803. In spite of innumerable modifications, its basic principles of operation remain the same, and the machine continues, more than one-and-three-quarter centuries later, as the dominant technology in the manufacture of paper. Substantial productivity improvements continue to be developed within this technological framework. More widely used products like a steam engine, electric motor, or machine tool have experienced a proliferation of changes, as they are adapted to the diversity of needs of numerous ultimate users. To the extent that major innovations vary relative to the time period for which they remain important, in part because substantial improvements will often take place long after the initial introduction of the innovation, it renders highly problematical the whole exercise of inferring a Kondratiev long cycle from a particular innovation. How does one date the long cycle associated with the steam engine? Beginning with Watt's seminal inventions in the 1770s? What we know about the slow pace of its adoption in the late eighteenth century renders this extremely doubtful. But, in addition, the improvements associated with the compound engine brought huge productivity improvements, sufficient to introduce the steam engine to important new uses – and this came a full century after Watt's major contribution. How does one date the impact of the airplane? It was about thirty years after the first successful achievement of the Wright Brothers at Kitty Hawk that the airplane had a significant commercial impact – with the introduction of the DC-3 in the mid 1930s. But with the subsequent innovation of the jet engine, fully half a century after the first achievement of heavier-than-air flight, the commercial impact of the aircraft increased by at least an order of magnitude.

One may say, of course, that the compound engine and the jet engine each deserve to be treated as separate innovations in themselves, with contributions to separate long cycles. There is nothing objectionable, in principle, about such a procedure, if it can indeed be employed to provide a convincing account of historical change involving long waves.[17] For the

---

[17] It does involve recognizing that, if we insist upon employing biological analogies, such as life-cycle models, in economics, we need to recognize the possibility of rejuvenation of

present we only wish to assert that such an accounting remains to be presented by advocates of technologically determined long waves.

Third, the adoption of a new technology is often critically dependent upon the availability of complementary inputs or, in some cases, upon an entire supporting infrastructure. Cars required extensive networks of roads, petrol stations, and repair facilities. The electric lamp required an extensive system for the generation and distribution of electric power. Seldom do new products fit into the existing social system without some intervening period of accommodation during which these complementary considerations are arranged. Not only does this signify a heavy commitment to an established technology, and a further reason for a *slow* initial shift to a best-practice frontier but, in addition, the time period required for such accommodations may vary greatly from one innovation to another.

Even if major innovations experience appropriately long and logistically shaped diffusion paths, with technologies going through phases of accelerated growth and eventually petering out, it does not necessarily imply that the slack in the declining phase of an individual innovation cycle might not be taken up by other technological innovations, thus eliminating the impact of a long phase of "sectoral" retardation upon the aggregate performance of the economy. What would still be needed for a wave-like pattern of growth is that other major substitute innovations were excluded until the original one had run its course. Without such a *spacing* mechanism, partially overlapping innovations might otherwise generate steady rates of growth rather than cycles.

What technological forces might impose cyclical behaviour rather than some sort of relative stability of economic activity along any given path traced out by a sequence of major substitute innovations? We have already suggested three such forces which might delay the introduction and widespread adoption of a new substitute technology; namely, a production cost differential that may still persist between the old and new technologies; certain expectational patterns held in common by entrepreneurs regarding improvements in both technologies; and the costs associated with scrapping and replacing the infrastructure committed to the old one. An additional possibility is that major innovations may establish certain trajectories of readily available performance improvements and cost reduction (more circuits on a chip, fewer pounds of coal per kilowatt-hour of electricity). Engineers and technically trained personnel often work with such implicit notions. Thus, the awareness of these trajectories may serve as focusing devices that fix the attention of engineers upon teasing out the further improvements that are understood to be available from the existing

mature or senescent industries – whatever the plausibility of such a notion in the biological realm.

technological framework, rather than searching for entirely new technologies. In this sense, the commitment of large amounts of resources to the exploitation of electric power may have been retarded as long as there seemed to be high payoffs available from further improvements in the technology of steam power, just as the nuclear power option may have been seriously explored only when there was a growing sense that further improvements in fossil-fuel-burning installations were approaching exhaustion. Similarly, the search process that culminated in the invention of the transistor was initiated by increasing dissatisfaction with performance limitations of the widely used vacuum tube.

In addition, these trajectories may be expected to shape the educational system and the training of engineers and other technical personnel. The inertial forces here may strengthen the commitment to an existing technology and render more difficult the exploration of new realms of technical possibilities. Whether such trajectories in fact played an important role in the spacing of technological innovations is an interesting hypothesis on which there is, at present, little evidence. Proponents of long cycles might find it worth exploring, because it may serve as an important support of the long-cycle hypothesis.

The reasons so far invoked for lengthy delays in the adoption of new technologies, of a kind that might produce extended periods of industry-wide stagnation, were discussed earlier in connection with major *substitute* innovations. Should similar considerations of spacing be extended to cases of *unrelated* or *complementary* technologies unfolding along many different trajectories?

In the case of unrelated technologies, the answer, prima facie, would be no. Here it is important to distinguish between the impact of innovations that compete with existing technologies in a given industry or sector, and those that do not. Even if one argued that there were forces leading to the spacing of innovations in the same industrial sector, in the sense that the arrival of a new technology had to wait until the benefits of moving along the previous technological trajectory had been largely exhausted, this would be of limited relevance for major innovations in *other* industries. The fact that we are still on a highly productive portion of the steam trajectory might conceivably tell us something about the timing of substitute innovations such as electric motors, but little, if anything, about the timing of unrelated innovations and their subsequent diffusion in electronics, synthetic fibres, or pharmaceuticals.

Yet the long-cycle hypothesis might be considerably strengthened if a large number of unrelated innovations had the main phases of their life-cycles synchronized by macroeconomic conditions. Indeed, the simultaneous diffusion of a large number of unrelated innovations might be regulated by general conditions in financial, factor, and product markets. If favorable, they might lead to a "bandwagon effect" along a number of separate industry trajectories, followed by a slowdown.[18] The result would be an innovation cluster of type "M," the vertical summation of sectoral logistics. Its impact would take the form of a period of fast and then slow growth rates, but now in many different trajectories simultaneously.

In the case of related technologies, an additional reason can be invoked for the synchronization of separate diffusion paths: they may be linked by a system of technologically-connected "families" of innovations, made up of complementary, induced, and closely related ones.[19] This would come about because the interactions of a few basic technologies would provide the essential foundations for other technological changes in a series of ever-widening concentric circles. A technological cluster, or a cluster of type "T," arises therefore when one (or a small number of) major related innovations provides the basis around which a large number of further cumulative improvements is positioned. Let us look in more detail for the *technological* reasons why innovations come in clusters, and not in a continuous stream.

a. Innovations breed other innovations because one innovation may raise sharply the economic payoff to the introduction of another, bringing those which are known to be technically feasible but so far economically unattractive to the point of adoption. Moreover, there are internal pressures within a technological system which serve to provide inducement mechanisms of a dynamic sort. The attention and effort of skilled engineering personnel are forcefully focused upon specific problems by the shifting succession of bottlenecks which emerge as output expands. More generally, an innovation leads to further innovations to the extent that it provides a *framework* which makes it possible to conceptualize, design, and work on a number of complementary and related technologies.[20]

b. Innovations breed investment insofar as new products and processes call for new vintages of machinery and equipment and, as we previously mentioned, the availability of a complementary infrastructure. Yet the reverse is also true: investment stimulates inventive and innovative activity. It is an incentive for inventions, if they are understood as an economic response to shifting financial payoffs to their different categories.[21] Perhaps more important, infrastructure investment, once in place, serves as an inducement to the introduction and adoption of

---

[18] The "bandwagon effect," according to Schumpeter, is observed "because first some, and then most, firms follow in the wake of a successful innovation" (*Business Cycles*, p. 100).
[19] See Freeman, Clark, and Soete, *Unemployment and Technical Innovation*, chapter 4.
[20] See S. Kuznets, "Innovations and Adjustments in Economic Growth," *Swedish Journal of Economics*, 74 (November 1972), pp. 437–438.
[21] See J. Schmookler, *Inventions and Economic Growth*, Harvard University Press, Cambridge (MA), 1966.

innovations which plug in to the already existing supportive apparatus. Once an extensive electric-power distribution system has been installed to meet the requirements of residential lighting, the time required to achieve high rates of adoption for a variety of other electricity-using consumer durables is considerably reduced.

The technological clustering of innovations around different diffusion paths should therefore be taken as a corollary of the fact that certain innovations bring other innovations *directly*, by providing a working frame within which further innovations become possible, and *indirectly*, either through their forward investment links, or their backward connections with inventive activity.

We have shown so far that:

a. Technological forces exist which may lead to cyclical behaviour in certain industries, where major innovations come to substitute for one another sequentially in time.

b. There also appear to be technological reasons for industries which stand in a complementary relationship to each other to experience common fluctuations in economic activity (beyond the more obvious technical complementarities in production).

c. There are macroeconomic reasons for apparently unrelated industries to have the pace of their economic activity synchronized over time.

Yet, the basic question persists: is spacing within and synchronization among different diffusion paths, for both technological and macroeconomic reasons, sufficient to provide a long-wave pattern of aggregative growth? And if so, how?

It is our present, tentative assessment that modes of argument at the technological level, while potentially interesting and well worth further exploration, will be of only limited usefulness in providing a convincing account of the generation of long waves. The mechanisms within the purely technological realm appear to be insufficiently robust for this purpose. Technologically driven long waves can be made to appear plausible only if macroeconomic factors can be shown to play a dominant role in shaping and disciplining the timing of the introduction of innovations. The beginning of an upswing would therefore be characterized by a sufficiently large stimulus from the "M" clustering process upon the previously positioned "T" cluster. In other words, at the initial phase of industry life cycles, the state of the economy (or "market conditions") regulates, to a large extent, demand conditions in most sectors, so that the introduction of new products and processes tends not to occur unless the economic environment is conducive to increases in consumer spending and investment activity. On the other hand, once activated by the macroeconomic environment, the technological long cycle is required to detach itself from swings in demand which closely track short-run changes in macroeconomic conditions and instead follow the internal dynamics of technological factors. Such autonomy might indeed be observed once the new industries have surpassed their initial (experimental) phase and before they have reached maturity (when output changes are again in line with aggregate demand changes in the economy). At that point, the dissemination of new products and processes would present self-sustaining mechanisms, not only to the extent that such innovations tend to cluster in a pattern of mutual feedback and reinforcement, but also because they actively substitute and displace older products and processes. In sum, they create a market for themselves in direct relation to their scope for substituting for mature commodities and complementing new ones.

The outcome of this non-trivial interaction between factors which belong to the technological realms and those which are responsible for decisions to carry out substitution in consumption and production may lead, in a manner which we have previously discussed, to extended periods of multisectoral growth and retardation, although there is no reason to believe that they will add up to cycles of 45- to 60-year duration. What has not been shown so far is the connection between such factors and the derived and induced demands for capital and consumer goods which would account for the economy-wide impact of innovation clusters.

Therefore, to argue effectively for a technologically driven long cycle, an additional requirement has to be met: the cluster of innovations must occupy a strategic position in the economy in terms of backward and forward links, the subject of the next section.

Economy-wide repercussions

An essential step in a technological theory of long cycles is the demonstration of the mechanisms through which particular changes in technology exercise *sizable* changes in the performance of the macroeconomy. Much of the present literature on long cycles cites specific innovations in association with specific historical long cycles, but without even attempting to demonstrate how these innovations, or innovation clusters, might be expected to exercise macroeffects of the size required by a long-cycle model. Precise quantification is admittedly an impossible task partly, as we will see, because of the elusive nature of the relationships, but also because of the data requirements that such an exercise would involve. Nevertheless, to be persuasive, or even plausible, some estimates of at least the orders of magnitude involved are indispensable.

The economy-wide impact of technological innovations needs to be understood not only in terms of the direct impact of cost reductions and the release of resources to alternative uses, but of the strength of their backward and forward linkages.[22]

a. They should be strongly linked backwards in terms of expenditures for buildings, machinery, equipment, and raw materials, such that the initial innovation and investment requirements lead to further investment decisions in the production-goods sector. Historically, this second wave of investment has often bred a second wave of innovations, more explicitly "process" oriented, and concentrated in the production-goods sector. It should be particularly noted that this last set of innovations has frequently had the effect of increasing the productivity of the economy at locations far from the specific sector that originally gave rise to the innovative activity.

b. The impact of innovations will also depend upon the strength of their forward linkages. These might take the form of a reduction in the price of the products into which the innovation enters as an input, leading to an expansion in the size of their market, and therefore also to an expansion in the rate of capital accumulation, output growth, and technical progress in these industries. These induced responses would depend upon the number of industries into which the innovation enters as an input, its substitutability for other inputs, the proportion of total costs it accounts for, and the extent of cost reductions it imposes upon the product.[23] More important, innovations may induce the creation and diffusion of *new* products and processes that, in their turn, would bring about the widespread adoption of the original innovation (the microchip is a compelling recent example). Alternatively, the impact will depend upon the extent to which the initial innovation proves to be at the core of "major natural trajectories" (such as the electric motor in relation to the process of electrification) or, more generally, in key sectors of the economy, such as energy and transport.

It is, therefore, the strategic location that innovations occupy within the economy, in terms of generating both investment and further technological change, which may tell us a great deal about their ability to generate a long-cycle growth pattern.[24] Yet this is particularly difficult to assess, as it is

[22] For the sake of completeness, mention should also be made of the so-called "lateral effects" arising out of major innovations and their corresponding leading sectors. These effects, not detailed here, would take the form of "urban overhead capital; institutions of banking and commerce; and the construction and service industries required to meet the needs of those who manned the new industrial structure" (see W.W. Rostow (ed.), *The Economics of Take-off into Sustained Growth*, Macmillan, London, 1963, pp. 6–7).

[23] See, in this respect, Fishlow, *American Railroads*, which is a rigorous and imaginative attempt to measure the economy-wide impact of a single innovation.

[24] The economic impact of Schumpeterian "epochal" innovations would presumably be dependent upon their spatial implications, with sizable population shifts triggered by such innovations being accompanied by large-scale construction and other subsidiary activities.

characteristic of technological innovation that it leads to wholly new patterns of specialization both by firm and by industry, with the result that it is impossible to compartmentalize the consequences within conventional Marshallian industry boundaries, or to read their impact directly off an input-output table.[25]

The ways in which technological changes coming from one industry constitute sources of technological progress and productivity growth in other industries defy easy summary or categorization. In some cases relatively stable relationships have emerged between an industry and its supplier of capital goods, and that becomes of decisive importance for the rate and direction of technical change in that industry, as evidenced by the postwar experience of the American aluminum producers. On many occasions the availability of new and superior metals, or new alloys, has played a major role in bringing performance and productivity improvements to a wide range of industries, such as railroads, machine tools, electric-power generation, and jet engines, among others.

Often an innovation from outside will not merely reduce the price of the product in the receiving industry, but make possible wholly new or drastically improved products or processes. In such circumstances it becomes extremely difficult even to suggest reasonable measures of the impact of the triggering innovation, because such innovations, in effect, open the door for entirely new economic opportunities and become the basis for extensive industrial expansion elsewhere. In the twentieth century the chemical industry exercised a massive effect upon textiles, at the time a very "mature" industry, through the introduction of an entirely new class of materials – synthetic fibres. Technological change in the chemical industry has exercised a similar triggering function in industries other than textiles. In the case of the electrical industry, the chemical industry played a critical role through the provision of refractory materials, insulators, lubricants, and coatings, and provided metals of a high degree of purity for use in conductors. And yet the profound effects of chemical innovations have had a relatively limited visibility because of the intermediate good nature of most chemical products.

In sum, the interindustry flow of new materials, components, and equipment may generate widespread product improvement and cost reduction throughout the economy. This has clearly been the case in the past among a small group of producer-goods industries – machine tools,

It would still need to be demonstrated, of course, why such a process added up to cycles of the periodicity postulated by Kondratiev, rather than, for example, the much shorter ones postulated by Kuznets for the pre First World War period.

[25] Input–output analysis, however, may be extremely useful in estimating some of the relevant magnitudes. The following discussion draws in part on Rosenberg (*Inside the Black Box*, chapter 3).

chemicals, electrical and electronic equipment. Industrial purchasers of such producer goods experienced considerable product and process improvement without necessarily undertaking any research expenditure of their own. Such interindustry flow of technology is one of the most distinctive characteristics of advanced capitalist societies, where innovations flowing from a few industries may be responsible for generating a vastly disproportionate amount of technological change, productivity improvement, and output growth in the economy. It is certainly conceivable that technological change generates long cycles through such interindustry flows and their consequent macroeconomic effects. Yet, given the difficulties of knowing what is the nature of the benefits flowing from each innovation, and where exactly within the structure of the economy these benefits eventually accrue, this can at best be regarded as no more than an untested hypothesis until systematic attempts at quantification have been undertaken.

Recurrence

The final requirement for a theory of long waves based upon technological innovations involves demonstrating their cyclical or recurrent character. In fact, it is not sufficient to show that causality runs from innovation to investment; that the economic and technological factors which determine the adoption of new technologies do so in a manner compatible with the stringent timing requirements of a Kondratiev; and that patterns of diffusion and inter-industry linkage of new technologies involve sufficient amplitude for long cycles to be perceived in the form of sizable variance in aggregative growth rates. It still has to be shown, if the argument is going to be logically complete, that the waves repeat themselves over time, either because the wave-generating factors in the form of innovation clusters are themselves cyclical (or at least recur with a certain regularity), or because there is an endogenous mechanism in the economic system which necessarily and regularly brings a succession of turning points.

What are the conditions under which long cycles become a historical necessity, in the sense that there are structural reasons for one long wave to follow another?

a. The availability of an elastic supply of inventions, at a time when risk-return combinations appear propitious for innovations;

b. the formation of a cluster of innovations at the base of the upswing, that is a technologically dense set which undergoes a rapid process of diffusion under favorable macroeconomic conditions;

c. the reaching of an upper turning point of the technologically driven cycle due to increasing macroeconomic instability, as well as forces that deter the introduction of substitute technologies;

d. the arrival of the economy at a technologically fertile ground, after an appropriately extended period of time. At this point, old innovation paths have been largely exhausted, but previously postponed ones have not yet been taken up.

This schema brings numerous problems. One would be hard pressed to show that Kondratievs are regulated on a purely internal basis, and that, in the past, exogenous factors have had only a marginal effect upon such long-term movements. It can in fact be plausibly argued that the recurrence of innovation clusters has been more in the nature of *an historical accident* than endogenously generated fluctuations in the rate of innovation.[26] Moreover, our earlier discussion of timing provides no compelling reason to expect recurrence at 45- to 60-year intervals, even if innovations cluster and such clusters appear regularly.[27]

Furthermore, in view of the widely varying lengths of individual innovation cycles, one cannot be certain, in observing a Kondratiev upswing, that the upswing is a consequence of a recent innovation or innovation bunch, rather than the protracted acting out of the longer-term impact of

[26] O. Lange, in his review of Schumpeter's *Business Cycles* in *Review of Economics and Statistics*, 23 (November 1941), although readily agreeing that recurrence was a theoretical possibility, argued that "there is serious doubt whether the Kondratievs can properly be called cycles. Professeur Schumpeter's explanation in terms of the three great waves of innovation in the history of capitalism seems quite correct. But these three waves of innovation appear to be more of the nature of historical 'accidents' due to discoveries in technology than regular fluctuations in the risk of failure ... Schumpeter has extended the theory of business cycles, worked out originally with references to Juglars, rather mechanically to Kondratievs and Kitchins" (p. 192). See also S. Kuznets, "Schumpeter's Business Cycles," *The American Economic Review*, 30 (June 1940), for a comprehensive critique of Schumpeter's 3-cycle model as presented in *Business Cycles*, and his skeptical comments on recurrent 50-year cycles.

[27] Let us make this point more precise. If we represented the structure of our model economy, and its movement through time, by a system of linear difference (or differential) equations, then a persistent cyclical behaviour would be obtained if one of the following is true: (a) the solution of the system, the complex conjugate roots, has unitary modulus, and the structural parameters are of the right magnitudes to generate cycles of appropriate periodicity and amplitude; (b) the modulus of the complex roots are less than unity (the motion of the system being strongly damped), yet random disturbances (not necessarily serially correlated) generate, or are smoothed into, a cyclical pattern; (c) the modulus of the complex is greater than unity (in which case we observe an increasing amplitude over time) or the value of the dominant positive real root is greater than unity, yet the existence of floors and ceilings constrains the movement of the economy in a cyclical fashion. Insofar as the characteristic roots depend on all structural parameters of the system, it would therefore take its *complete specification* to ascertain what sort of periodic motion it is able to generate, if any. We have not fully specified the model in this manner, not only because of the complexity of the undertaking, but because of the difficulties of ruling out the possibility of a Kondratiev through this sort of formal exercise. Moreover, further examination of the data might not be conclusive, even if long and reliable production time series existed. In particular, as Sidney Winter has reminded us, if our model economy is represented by a set of non-linear dynamic equations, even simple deterministic systems can mimic a periodic motion for many periods and then shift to other motions without any change of parameters or shocks to the system. Thus, historical evidence that would appear to suggest a particular cycle in the data needs to be interpreted with extreme caution.

earlier innovations. We suspect that this is a much more serious problem than is generally recognized in recent attempts to associate specific cyclical upswings with specific antecedent innovations. At any time, the investment opportunities generated by specifically recent innovations are likely to be small compared with the aggregate of opportunities made available by ongoing improvements and modifications in older technologies. Moreover, much empirical evidence suggests that many innovations (such as the car) play a major role in more than one Kondratiev. As a result, we suspect that the saturation notion cannot be made to support the heavy burden placed upon it by long-wave exponents.

In our view a critical gap in establishing the recurrence of a long cycle is the absence of a clear economic mechanism that causes the system to move upward from its lower turning point.[28] The most forceful attempt to fill this lacuna is Gerhard Mensch's book, *Stalemate in Technology*. Mensch asserts that innovations tend to be bunched during depressions, even though they build upon knowledge that was generated at an earlier stage and could have been embodied in innovations at an earlier date.[29]

There are two sources of difficulty with Mensch's case for the bunching of innovations during periods of stagnation and depression: the questionable nature of the data base that he employs for his purpose and the inconclusiveness of his economic argument for the pattern of bunching that he purports to find. On the identification and dating of inventions and innovations, there are still no satisfactory criteria whose application would command widespread consensus.[30] The issue is, unfortunately, fundamental because, some would argue, it is only certain peculiarities of Mensch's categorization that allow him to say that "up to now Western industries

[28] N.D. Kondratiev, "On the Problem of Major Economic Cycles," *Planovoe Koziaistvo*, 8 (August 1928), did have such a mechanism, however primitive. As we recall (see note 4, p. 63), the depreciation and ensuing replacement of the most durable and costly forms of fixed capital were at the basis of Kondratiev's explanation of long waves. The capital goods Kondratiev was referring to were "big plants, important railways, canals, large land improvement projects, etc." and their investment spurts were connected to the large sums of free loanable capital available at the bottom of the cycle. Thus the lower turning point would come as interest-rate levels were driven down by the accumulation of funds by those on fixed incomes, as the general price level declined. The upper turning point occurred with the depletion of these loanable funds and the ensuing rise in interest rates, which would lead to a curtailment of investment.

[29] Mensch, *Stalemate in Technology*, pp. 156–157, 193–194. Mensch argues, for example, that "most of the essential basic inventions later to be applied in the innovative surge of the 1930s were already well known by 1925. Thus we see that the paradox of unused technologies existed even in the 1920s" (p. 156).

[30] For most purposes, Mensch, in his twentieth-century sample, makes use of a subset of the inventions listed by J. Jewkes, D. Sawers, and R. Stillerman in their book, *The Sources of Invention* 2nd edn., W.W. Norton, New York, 1968. For a careful criticism of Mensch's sources and uses of data, see Freeman, Clark, and Soete, *Unemployment and Technical Innovation*, chapter 3.

have largely dwelled on the swell of basic innovations that came in the 1930s, and in the 1950s and 1960s very little basic innovation push developed on which we could expand in the 1970s and 1980s" (pp. 30–31). In fact it would not be difficult to compile a most impressive list of major innovations that occurred in the 1950s and 1960s, drawing from such burgeoning fields as pharmaceuticals, electronics, computers, instrumentation, communications, nuclear power, materials (synthetic and otherwise), etc. Regrettably, lists of inventions and innovations, and their appropriate dating, remain notoriously subjective and arbitrary, and cannot yet support the burdensome structure of argument placed upon them. To invoke Mensch's own plaintive note: *tot homines, quot sententiae*.

The economic argument for the bunching of innovations is also far from convincing. Mensch's view is that innovative activity is finally undertaken in the depths of an economic downturn because, in their inability to generate profits from older and better-established products whose markets have been saturated, businessmen eventually turn in desperation to new products. Thus, the adverse economic circumstances of the depression are perceived as providing a push into new product lines that were rejected under earlier, more favorable economic circumstances.[31]

It is not, however, easy to see how economic adversity itself would accelerate such substantial long-term financial commitments *before* a lower turning point had yet been reached. On the contrary, there is much in the economic logic and in the environmental conditions of a depression, as it confronts the individual members of the business community, that would seem to militate against it. Although perceptions of risk may be expected to become more favorable once it is clear that the recovery phase has already begun, it is difficult to see how depression conditions could provide such an improvement either in perception or opportunity. In fact, depressions tend to make entrepreneurs and managers (as well as sources of financial capital) overly cautious, committing resources to purposes that generate, in the short run, only marginal improvements in the existing technology. This practice, *a fortiori*, excludes major projects directed toward an immediate restructuring of the firm's technical base of production of a kind that requires long planning horizons and favorable assessment of risk. It does *not* exclude committing resources to the basic design of new products that, in spite of providing the eventual development basis upon which whole new technological trajectories can be built, do not in themselves produce

---

[31] "In the preceding chapter for the 220 years surveyed, the empirical findings showed that surges of technological basic innovations emerged after economies had fallen into a serious crisis and then passed through years of depression. A graphic representation of the fluctuations in innovative implementation shows that there is a damming up of innovative activity until the onset of economic crises, and then innovations break through the floodgates" (Mensch, *Stalemate in Technology*, p. 138).

significant macroeconomic effects. Research and development expenditures during phases of retardation (or depression) provide, at most, the technological basis for sustained growth during expansion. This is so to the extent that such commitments do not necessarily lead to large-scale investments of a kind associated with major innovations. Research and development expenditures should therefore appropriately be viewed as a necessary but *not* a sufficient condition for bringing about the commercialization of new products and the actual application of new techniques of production.[32] Other conditions have to be present, in the form of acceptable perceptions of future risk and returns, before firms will commit large amounts of resources to the construction of new plant capacity.

Of course, the commercialization of some new products involves long gestation periods (e.g. commercial jets and telecommunications systems) and setting up a new facility for the production of even well-established products will often require a similar long gestation period (e.g. a conventional hydroelectric-power generating plant). The decision to proceed on such projects, in anticipation of some future demand, may well necessitate commencement during the depression phase of business cycles. This is, however, very different from the assertion that it is the depression that is *responsible* for initiating the new undertaking.

In addition, whatever economic cogency Mensch's timing argument might conceivably retain with respect to product innovations, such arguments are of no obvious relevance with respect to process innovations. They can hardly suffer from the "crowding out" phenomenon that might afflict new products during prosperity phases of the cycle. Indeed, the one phase when the construction of the new plant and equipment embodying process innovations might be *least* welcome and feasible would be during a depression when, presumably, firms are already suffering from excess productive capacity and facing additional financial constraints. Here again it is difficult to understand the economic logic that would present such innovations as providing the momentum that would generate the lower turning point.

Thus, we reject as economically implausible and unsubstantiated

---

[32] The Charpie Report has been widely quoted for its suggestion that research and development expenditures constitute only a small fraction of the total costs of successful innovations. According to that report a "typical distribution" might be that research and development activity accounted for 5–10% of the total cost of introducing an innovation, while engineering design accounted for 10–20%, tooling for 40–60%, and manufacturing start-up costs for 10–15%. See Panel on Invention and Innovation, *Technological Innovation: Its Environment and Management*, Dept. of Commerce (Washington DC), 1967, p. 9. Although there is no empirical basis for these numbers, and although the actual numbers doubtless vary enormously among firms and among industries, it is sufficient for our purposes to assert that research and development expenditures may be, and often are, only a small proportion of total innovation costs.

Mensch's view that depression conditions themselves are responsible for the innovations that, in turn, bring the depression to an end. In the specific instance of the 1930s, we would argue that there were numerous other stimuli. The ominous prospects of large-scale warfare in Europe (and eventually war itself) concentrated minds wonderfully upon innovations of great military significance, as in the growing commitment of government funds to the development of the jet engine, radar, and substitutes for especially scarce strategic materials. The ongoing thrust of scientific research in the biological and chemical sciences opened up numerous specific innovative possibilities in fields such as synthetic fibres and pharmaceuticals. The continuing diffusion of an "old" innovation, the automobile, operated as an increasingly powerful stimulus not only in automobiles directly but in a number of ancillary industries such as glass, rubber, metallurgy, and petroleum refining. This brings us, in a sense, full circle to the issue of causality, which we regard as far more complex and multifaceted than it was made out to be in Mensch's account.

Conclusions

What we have attempted to show are the far-from-trivial requirements that are necessary in order to demonstrate that technological change, in conjunction with macroeconomic factors, can indeed be the preponderant force behind long waves. Having made these conditions explicit, we have also argued, first, that none of the present-day authors who work within a neo-Schumpeterian paradigm has clearly specified the causal links connecting innovation, investment, and aggregate rates of growth. Second, that the complexities entailed in the timing of the diffusion process, with its technological and macroeconomic determinants, are such that the requirements they impose upon a technologically induced long-wave theory are very stringent, to say the least. Third, that the essential exercise of measuring the impact of a set of major innovations upon the economy as a whole has yet to be undertaken by any long-wave proponent. In spite of its difficulties, such an exercise is an important necessary step to add credibility to the notion of long cycles. Finally, it has yet to be shown why the factors responsible for a Kondratiev and its turning points should be expected to have a recurrent character.

We feel we are now entitled to conclude that the conceptual framework of a model of long waves in economic growth, which has at its core the process of technological innovation, has still not been adequately formulated. If long waves are to become a credible notion and serve as a useful analytic framework for understanding changes in capitalism over time, there is a clear need to specify their conceptual underpinnings in a more cogent and precise way, in particular the theoretical adequacy of the idea that large or widely diffusable innovations (together with the related investment flows) are responsible for the generation of Kondratievs. Until such a model is developed, the assessment of its historical validity remains unresolved.

We close, therefore, on a skeptical note or, at the very least, on a verdict of "unproven." At the same time, we trust that the route that we have travelled in arriving at our present position has been one that has enlarged the awareness of the extreme complexity of the connections that link technological innovation, structural change, and the long-term dynamics of advanced capitalist economies.

Part II

Technology in context

Technology in context

5　Economic experiments

This chapter will offer an historical examination of a certain kind of freedom and the economic consequences that have flowed from it. It will focus upon the freedom to perform economic experiments, understanding the expression in the broadest sense to include experimentation with new forms of economic organization as well as the better-known historical experiments that have been responsible for new products and new manufacturing technologies. It will be argued that the freedom to undertake such experiments has been the essential element accounting for the fact that industrialization has been, uniquely, an historical product of capitalist societies.

The perspective suggested here is not, of course, entirely novel. Marx understood very well that the new technology that was transforming Great Britain in the century before the publication of *The Communist Manifesto*[1] was inseparably linked to capitalist institutions. Marx grasped a part of this story so firmly that his treatment must, necessarily, be the starting point for this chapter, but, as we will see, Marx missed some fundamental parts of the story. Moreover, we now have the distinct advantage over Marx of more than a century of further capitalist performance and more than seventy years of history of a large socialist economy that adopted a distinctly different posture toward the freedom to conduct organizational experiments. Thus, we start with Marx and the big issues connected with the economic growth experience of the west.

This chapter appeared in *Industrial and Corporate Change*, vol. 1, no. 1, 1992. A substantially different earlier version was presented at a conference, "What is Political Economy?: Some Issues at the Foundation," held at Claremont McKenna College in November, 1987. The chapter draws heavily, in parts, upon N. Rosenberg and L.E. Birdzell, Jr., *How the West Grew Rich*, Basic Books, New York, 1986. I would like to acknowledge my intellectual debt to L.E. Birdzell, Jr., from whom I have learned a great deal. I have also benefitted from the suggestions of several anonymous referees of *Industrial and Corporate Change*.
[1]　K. Marx and F. Engels, *The Communist Manifesto*, 1848

The argument will be advanced through a consideration of some of the salient features of western institutional history and more recent developments in the eastern European socialist world. There is, of course, a considerable body of theoretical literature examining the weaknesses of market capitalism and the strengths of central planning. Market economies underinvest in research generally and private incentives may drive the pool of potential inventors into commitments of their resources that are socially suboptimal. Decentralized exploration of the technological frontier may lead to a "lock-in" to an inferior path of technological development that is not subject to correction by market forces. On the other hand, one can postulate a central planning authority of a socialist society that appropriately addresses society's long-term interests, that can internalize positive economies external to the innovating unit, and that can avoid the many pitfalls generated by profit-maximizing firms that consider only private and not social returns. Nevertheless, it now seems plausible, especially in view of the recent economic collapse of eastern European socialism, to render certain judgments on why the two systems have in fact performed so differently with respect to technological change.

The central argument of this chapter is a simple one. The freedom to conduct experiments is essential to any society that has a serious commitment to technological innovation or to improved productive efficiency. The starting point is that there are many things that cannot be known in advance or deduced from some set of first principles. Only the opportunity to try out alternatives, with respect both to technology and to form and size of organization, can produce socially useful answers to a bewildering array of questions that are continually occurring in industrial (and in industrializing) societies.

Marx on the history of capitalism

How does Marx (and Engels) account for the intimate historical association of capitalism and industrialism? How are these connected with the decline of feudalism? Is the independent variable technological or economic? Although Marx is sometimes portrayed as a technological determinist, he surely did not believe that it was technological change that initiated social change. Rather, as the economic determinist that he surely was, he visualized economic forces as shaping the forces of technology.

In the case of the rise of capitalism itself, its emergence was not directly associated with any major changes in the methods of production. Indeed, in Marx's view, capitalism arose in the sixteenth century, but the dramatic changes in technology that are associated with the industrial revolution only came more than 200 years later, in the second half of the eighteenth century.[2]

In the opening pages of *The Communist Manifesto*, Marx and Engels emphasize that it was the economic opportunities associated with the expansion of trade and overseas markets that provided the initiating impulses to the growth of capitalism and the unique technologies that capitalism brought with it.

From the serf of the Middle Ages sprang the chartered burghers of the earliest towns. From these burgesses the first elements of the bourgeoisie were developed.

The discovery of America, the rounding of the Cape, opened up fresh ground for the rising bourgeoisie. The East-Indian and Chinese market, the colonization of America, trade with the colonies, the increase in the means of exchange and in commodities generally, gave to commerce, to navigation, to industry, an impulse never before known, and thereby, to the revolutionary element in the tottering feudal society, a rapid development. The feudal system of industry, under which industrial production was monopolised by closed guilds, now no longer sufficed for the growing wants of the new markets. The manufacturing system took its place. The guild-masters were pushed on one side by the manufacturing middle class; division of labour between the different corporate guilds vanished in the face of division of labour in each single workshop.

Meantime, the markets kept ever growing, the demand ever rising. Even manufacture no longer sufficed. Thereupon, steam and machinery revolutionized industrial production. The place of manufacture was taken by the giant, Modern Industry, the place of the industrial middle class, by industrial millionaires, the leaders of whole industrial armies, the modern bourgeois. Modern industry has established the world-market, for which the discovery of America paved the way. This market has given an immense development to commerce, to navigation, to communication by land. This development has, in turn, reacted on the extension of industry; and in proportion as industry, commerce, navigation, railways extended, in the same proportion the bourgeoisie developed, increased its capital, and pushed into the background every class handed down from the Middle ages.[3]

Marx's account, therefore, emphasizes the growth in profit opportunities that were associated with the growth of overseas markets – it is, in fact, quite noteworthy that Marx and Engels pay no attention to the internal growth taking place in European markets. The feudal economy lacked the capability to respond to these market opportunities. The organization of its industry was fundamentally restrictive and conservative. The craft guilds that controlled handicraft industry severely restricted entry into specific trades, dictated the quality of the product, and controlled the relationship

[2] F. Engels, *Socialism: Utopian and Scientific*, Clark H. Kerr and Co., Chicago, 1910, pp. 12–13.   [3] Marx and Engels, *The Communist Manifesto*.

between buyer and seller, including the price at which a product could be sold. The feudal system is therefore overthrown by an emerging class of capitalists who sweep away feudal institutions and replace them with institutions of their own making. Above all, these institutions accord a more prominent role to market forces than would have been possible in the Middle Ages.

Perhaps the most striking aspects of *The Communist Manifesto* are the passages calling attention to the unique role of capitalism in bringing about an historic growth in human productivity.

The bourgeoisie has ... been the first to show what man's activity can bring about. It has accomplished wonders far surpassing Egyptian pyramids, Roman aqueducts, and Gothic cathedrals ...

The bourgeoisie cannot exist without constantly revolutionising the instruments of production, and thereby the relations of production, and with them the whole relations of society. Conservation of the old modes of production in unaltered form, was, on the contrary, the first condition of existence for all earlier industrial classes ...

The bourgeoisie, by the rapid improvement of all instruments of production, by the immensely facilitated means of communication, draws all, even the most barbarian, nations into civilisation ...

The bourgeoisie, during its rule of scarce one hundred years, has created more massive and more colossal productive forces than have all preceding generations together. Subjection of Nature's forces to man, machinery, application of chemistry to industry and agriculture, steam-navigation, railways, electric telegraphs, clearing of whole continents for cultivation, canalisation of rivers, whole populations conjured out of the ground – what earlier century had even a presentiment that such productive forces slumbered in the lap of social labour?[4]

Why, according to Marx, is capitalism such an immensely productive system? (Note that, in the paean of praise in the last paragraph quoted, the great accomplishments cited are specifically creations of the bourgeoisie, not the Protestant Ethic or some other force exogenous to a particular form of economic organization.)

Marx's answer is that the bourgeoisie is a unique ruling class on the stage of world history. It is the first ruling class whose economic interests are inseparably tied to change and not the maintenance of the status quo.[5] The bourgeoisie "cannot exist without constantly revolutionising the instruments of production." In essence, capitalism has created a very powerful set of incentives that drives the system in the direction of continuous technical change and capital accumulation. The market pressures of competitive capitalism force the capitalist to maximize the output from his labor force. These pressures compel the capitalist to plow back the profits that he has

---

[4] *Ibid.*   [5] For Schumpeter's discussion of this insight, see chapter 3.

earned by adopting new, economically superior, labor-saving technologies as rapidly as possible.

It is not Marx's view that capitalism was, *ab initio*, a highly productive system, although some passages in his writings often sound that way. Such an interpretation overlooks the intermediate steps in Marx's historical analysis of capitalism because, in its earliest stages, it still made use of an essentially handicraft technology. This system – of manufacturing – was more productive than the handicraft system that it displaced, but not enormously so. While it involved a much more extensive division of labor, it did not yet utilize any drastically new technology. Capitalism did provide the necessary incentives to raise productivity. However, that great improvement in productivity was only realized when capitalism's more powerful incentive structure led to the emergence of Modern Industry. And that took a couple of hundred years, in Marx's view.

Marx's argument here has an important component that was foreshadowed in the last quotation from *The Communist Manifesto*. The great increases in productivity are attained only when capitalism leads to a mode of production to which science can be directly applied. This is perhaps the most distinctive feature of what he refers to as Modern Industry. For Marx, then, the application of science to industry is the essential step to the rapid productivity growth of modern industrial societies, but it was uniquely capitalism that made that application possible. In fact, Marx's view is that modern science itself developed primarily in response to the problems that first expressed themselves historically in the sphere of production. Far from being some exogenous force, science arose out of the incentive structure and culture of capitalism.[6]

Thus, the Marxian view is that capitalism has served as a remarkable vehicle for the increase of human productivity because:

a. It provided powerful incentives to generate new technologies.
b. It generated high rates of investment that led to the rapid diffusion and exploitation of new technologies.
c. It generated incentives for the development of science as well as for the application of science to the problems of industry.

Of course it was also central to Marx's thinking that advanced capitalism would finally give way to socialism after it became caught up in its own internal contradictions, but also after it had brought about the vast increases in human productivity that it was, uniquely, qualified to bring

---

[6] For an extended discussion of this point, see N. Rosenberg, "Karl Marx on the Economic Role of Science," *Journal of Political Economy* (July–August 1974); reprinted in N. Rosenberg, *Perspectives on Technology*, Cambridge University Press, New York, 1976. See also J.A. Schumpeter, "The Civilization of Capitalism," *Capitalism, Socialism and Democracy*, Allen and Unwin, London, 1943, chapter 11.

about. It is perfectly obvious, from the present vantage point, that this was wrong. The fact of the matter is that socialism was never introduced into a country that had attained an advanced stage of capitalism – at least not without the assistance of the Soviet army. On the contrary, twentieth-century socialist revolutions occurred only in societies that had not yet passed through the advanced stage of capitalism, with all of its attendant expansion of productive capacity.

One of the ironies of the twentieth century is that socialism was embraced not only as an anti-capitalist ideology; in addition, many socialists looked to Marx and his writings for guidance on how to organize a socialist society in order to generate rapid economic growth in poor countries. The irony, of course, is that Marx himself did not believe that this bypassing of the capitalist stage on the road to socialism was possible. Marx believed that a socialist revolution had to be preceded by a capitalist stage because only capitalism could bring about the improvements in productivity that would make it possible for socialist societies to be indifferent to *further* productivity growth. Socialist societies would not have to be concerned with raising productivity to high levels, because it was the historic mission of capitalism to accomplish precisely that. Marx was wrong in believing in the inevitability of that sequence. But at the same time, recent events in the socialist world suggest that Marx was at least right in believing that societies with socialist objectives could not so casually bypass the capitalist stage. As a joke in the former Soviet Union used to go: question: "What is communism?" Answer: "The most painful of all possible roads from capitalism to capitalism."

Features of technological innovation

Marx's account of the reasons why industrialization first occurred within a framework of capitalist institutions is incomplete, or at least incompletely specified. He is much more explicit about the importance of the special incentive mechanisms of capitalism – the large financial rewards – than he is about the specific forms that economic organizations have taken and why they have taken those particular forms. Capitalism's historic success in generating new technologies depended heavily upon its ability to fulfill certain other conditions. What were the additional features of capitalism that have rendered it such a powerful instrument for technological innovation? The general answer that has already been advanced is that capitalism has offered the freedom to engage in experiments of all sorts. But to see why that freedom has been so critical, it is first necessary to examine with greater care certain aspects of technological innovation.

The essential feature of technological innovation is that it is an activity that is fraught with many uncertainties. This uncertainty, by which we mean an inability to predict the outcome of the search process, or to predetermine the most efficient path to some particular goal, has a very important implication: the activity cannot be planned. No person, or group of persons, is clever enough to plan the outcome of the search process, in the sense of identifying a particular innovation target and moving in a predetermined way to its realization – as one might read a road map and plan the most efficient route to a historical monument.

If we wanted to draw an analogy, we might say that achieving an attractive technological innovation is much more like a military engagement. Its execution cannot be completely planned in minute detail because the commanding officer does not know how the enemy will respond, or what the outcome to that initial response will be.

Without pushing the analogy too far (because, after all, a battle has a simple, unambiguous goal, whereas the search for a technological improvement typically has a number of possible tradeoffs), what innovation and military combat have in common is that decisions need to be made in a sequential way. That is to say, vital information will become available at some future point which cannot, in the nature of the case, be made available now. It would be folly to lock oneself into a predetermined pattern of behavior, because this amounts to depriving oneself of the benefit of additional information, of a kind that may be decisive to success or failure, that can only become available in the future.[7]

It is inherent in the research process that information accumulates, even if it is only the information that certain alternatives are unproductive and should be discarded – for example, dry wells. There is no way of knowing, in advance of the research (experiments), which alternatives are worth pursuing further and which are not. This is one reason why taking out a patent discloses valuable information to a firm's competitors, even though the award of the patent provides the owner with certain legal protections, and even though the contents of the patent document may not disclose sufficiently detailed information to permit imitation. The mere knowledge that something is possible (say, in pharmaceuticals) or that a particular procedure can achieve a particular end result, is likely to be extremely valuable. It is important evidence that research in certain specific directions, or employing certain specific methods, is likely to prove fruitful. The appropriate analogy here is to the information provided when someone has struck oil. A competitor may want to locate her drilling equipment as close as possible to the successful well.

Thus it is in the nature of the research process that it is more likely to

---

[7] R. Nelson, "Uncertainty, Learning and the Economics of Parallel Research and Development Efforts," *Review of Economics and Statistics*, 43 (1961), pp 351–364.

prove successful, and far more likely to proceed efficiently, if decision-making is sequential in nature. However, it is also very important to realize that failed experiments often generate valuable information of a kind that is not exhausted by the analogy with the information produced by the drilling of a dry well. Those engaged in both search and research of an unsuccessful nature may accumulate a great deal of understanding along the way that may enhance their prospects for success in the future. The design of a new product does not proceed directly from scientific principles. Rather, product designers necessarily deal with multiple tradeoffs with respect to product characteristics, as well as tradeoffs between performance and cost. It is in the nature of the research process that it is more likely to be successful, and far more likely to proceed efficiently, if decision-making is sequential in nature. It is also likely to be the case that experience with poorly designed products (or failed experiments) may contribute to the ability to produce superior designs in the future.

Moreover, quite independently of the improvement of skills, there is an additional tradeoff between time and cost. Proceeding more rapidly, and on a large scale, is costly. The reason is that, when one is allowed to proceed slowly and sequentially, one can keep numerous options alive. As new information becomes available from the ongoing research enterprise, and as uncertainties are reduced, options can be re-evaluated and more informed allocative decisions can be made. Unpromising avenues can be dropped. By committing larger amounts of money only at a later and better-informed stage, research resources are utilized more efficiently.[8]

The trouble with a War on Cancer, as with Supersonic transport, is that large amounts of money are committed to a particular project, or to a particular design, long before sufficient information is available to permit an intelligent evaluation of the research options. Where government funds are involved the problem is likely to be compounded by the failure to terminate a project, or a design, even after compelling evidence has accumulated that the thrust of R&D expenditures is in a direction that is unlikely to yield acceptable results. The post-war American experience is littered with such instances in nuclear energy, synthetic fuels, and the procurement of new military hardware of all sorts.[9] Although there may on occasion be a compelling case for rapid development, as in the Manhattan Project of the Second World War, the evidence is overwhelming that there is an inherent pathology of wastefulness in such an approach, as compared with a slower pace of development that permits frequent revision and redirection as new information becomes available.

---

[8] For example, chemical engineers are trained to reduce the cost and uncertainty associated with building large-scale plants. For a further discussion, see chapter 10 below.

[9] Richard Nelson, *The Moon and the Ghetto*, W.W. Norton and Co., New York, 1977, provides a valuable discussion of some of these issues.

There is an additional advantage to a system that encourages, or at least tolerates, multiple sources or decision-making. Not only do human agents differ considerably in their attitudes toward risk; they differ also in their skills, capabilities, and orientations, however those differences may have been acquired. This heterogeneity of the human input, insufficiently stressed in microeconomics, constitutes a valuable resource that is much more readily enlisted into the realm of potentially useful experimentation by an organizationally decentralized environment. An economy that includes small firms and easy entry conditions is likely to benefit from this pool of human talent far more than one dominated by centralized decision-making.

Distinctive features of capitalism

The relevance of this discussion for the historical efficiency of capitalist institutions in encouraging innovation is clear. Capitalism has provided multiple sources of decision-making and initiative, strong incentives for proceeding one step at a time, and the possibility for drawing upon a wide range of human potential – all valuable features of activities that are carried out in an environment of high uncertainty. The notion that planning and centralization of decision-making are likely to be more efficient appears to be the opposite of the truth when there is a high degree of uncertainty and when goals and objectives cannot be clearly defined in advance.

One of the less-heralded but considerable virtues of competitive capitalism has been the speed with which firms have unsentimentally cut their losses as it became apparent that a particular direction of research was likely to prove unfruitful. Where funds come from the public sector, by contrast, monies are likely to be spent on unpromising projects for rather longer. Inertia and the reluctance to admit failure publicly play important roles here, but so does the fact that the decision-makers in government are not personally concerned over the financial losses involved.

The historical creativity of capitalism as an institutional mechanism for encouraging technological and organizational innovation has to be examined against this background of the centrality and pervasiveness of uncertainty. The uncertainties that are inherent in the search for new technologies have meant that the risks associated with this search could best be approached in certain specific ways. Capitalism historically has developed a cluster of novel organizational forms that have had the result of reducing certain intolerable risks to more tolerable levels. These were the risks that were unavoidably associated with the decision to commit financial resources to the search for technological improvements. These high levels of risk were inseparable from technological innovation because, as we have seen, the outcome of the search for new technologies was uncertain in the extreme. Moreover, even if one did succeed in developing a new technology that was a clear improvement over anything that already existed, the prospect of making any money out of it was still highly uncertain.

It is of particular interest to note that Marx himself recognized this uncertainty, although the recognition only made its public appearance in the third volume of *Capital*, published after his death and many years after the publication of the immensely influential first volume of that book. In the third volume Marx called attention to "the far greater cost of operating an establishment based on a new invention as compared to later establishments arising *ex suis ossibus*. This is so very true that the trail-blazers generally go bankrupt, and only those who later buy the buildings, machinery, etc., at a cheaper price make money out of it."[10] This is an extremely interesting passage, since it constitutes explicit recognition on Marx's part of the extreme vulnerability of the capitalist in his social role as a carrier of technological innovation. Had Marx given more attention to this vulnerability in volume I of *Capital*, it would have been necessary to portray the capitalist in a distinctly different light. It would also have been necessary to face up more candidly to the painful tradeoffs that all societies must confront between greater equity and greater efficiency.[11] But such an examination would have highlighted the weakness of capitalists whereas Marx was intent on portraying their social power and their consequent capacity for exploiting others.

The history of capitalism involved the progressive introduction of a number of institutional devices that facilitated the commitment of resources to the innovation process by reducing or placing limitations upon risk while, at the same time, holding out the prospect of large financial rewards to the successful innovator. Among the most critical were new institutions, laws, and legislation that (1) limited the liability of an investor in any particular enterprise, (2) provided for the easy marketability of ownership shares, (3) established stock markets which were essential to the achievement of ready marketability, (4) reduced risk by the fundamental technique of insurance, and (5) defined the obligations between principals and their agents.[12]

The emergence of business firms with limited liability for their owners, and ownership shares that were easily marketable, was central from the point of view of facilitating investment in risky undertakings. From the

---

[10] K. Marx, *Das Capital*, vol. III, Foreign Languages Publishing House, Moscow, 1959. See also chapter 2, pp. 36–37.

[11] Insofar as Marx may be said to have dealt with the tradeoff between equity and efficiency, he did so by assigning to capitalism the historical role of providing efficiency and to a later socialism the role of delivering equity.

[12] These matters are discussed in detail in N. Rosenberg and L.E. Birdzell, Jr., *How the West Grew Rich*, Basic Books, New York, 1986, especially in chapters 4–8.

point of view of the individual investor, a limited-liability corporation made it possible to convert a long-term risk involving large amounts of capital into a short-term risk that was limited to small amounts of capital. Marketability of assets and the existence of efficient markets for the sale of these assets meant that owners were not undertaking commitments equal in duration to the life of long-lived capital assets. On the contrary, they could realize their financial gains or cut their financial losses whenever doing so appeared to be expedient. In this way a capitalist proprietor's long-term risk was converted into an investor's short-term risk. At the same time, the ownership of the firm's assets was effectively divided into two levels: first, those of the corporation as an ongoing entity; and second, those of the shareholders who supplied the firm with its capital. The first-level risks remained as great as they always had been, but the second-level risks were of a different order and were much more readily acceptable. This division of risk obviously bears a close analogy to the redistribution of risk that takes place between a property owner and his insurance company.

Looking back on Marx, it is apparent that, although he had a profound appreciation for the technical dynamism of capitalism, he did not appreciate the extent to which this was due to such institutional measures that reduced risk and, by reducing risk, encouraged the experimentation that made innovation so commonplace under capitalism.[13] There has obviously been a close connection between reducing risk and encouraging experimentation. The willingness to undertake experiments in both the social and technological spheres depends upon some sort of limitation upon the negative consequences for the individual if the risky enterprise should fail, as it frequently did. The great technological dynamism of capitalism has been inseparable from the system's success in reducing risk to more tolerable levels while, at the same time, offering the prospect of huge financial rewards if the risky enterprise should succeed.

These technological achievements were thus based upon capitalist legal institutions, especially with respect to contracts and property rights, which legitimized the right to experiment with new organizational forms as well as with new technologies. The final arbiter of whether something new was socially desirable was not a government authority, or the religious clergy, or the guild members, or the merchants whose personal interests might be adversely affected by some innovation. Rather, the final arbiter was the marketplace. Capitalism did legitimize innovation, but only if it could pass the market test. It was indeed, as Marx recognized, the first form of social organization in which economic life was dominated by groups whose economic interests caused them to threaten the status quo.

---

[13] Of course, it is also true that some of the risk-reducing innovations achieved their full development after Marx's main writings had been completed.

Autonomy of the economic sphere

The freedom to conduct experiments, in turn, required that yet other conditions be fulfilled. One of these conditions was that the economic sphere had to attain a higher degree of autonomy from external forces, especially freedom from arbitrary and unpredictable interventions by government authorities.

A critical aspect of this increasing autonomy was that new political institutions emerged that reduced the risk of arbitrary exactions and appropriations (or even expropriations) by a powerful ruler. The rise in western Europe of parliaments in control of government financial purse strings was an essential part of this story. So was the emergence of new legal concepts, precedents, and institutions for the enforcement of contracts and property rights generally. In this respect, the bourgeois political revolutions of the seventeenth and eighteenth centuries were central to the economic achievements of capitalism.

The swiftness and the extent to which business organizations were rendered free of government control in the early years of capitalism should not be exaggerated. Government approval, in the form of a charter or franchise, long remained the normal practice, at least for specific forms of organization – for example, with limited liability; or for companies that wished to trade in certain regions – the Hudson's Bay Company, East India Company, Muscovy Company, etc.; or for organizations providing certain kinds of services, such as canal building, road building, etc.[14] It was only in the course of the nineteenth century that business firms attained a reasonable degree of freedom in selecting new activities or new product lines. Nevertheless, the trend in western Europe and North America in the eighteenth and nineteenth centuries was in the direction of an expansion of the freedom of action of the enterprise.

The freedom to conduct experiments required not only a high degree of autonomy; it also required, as already discussed, a large number of decision-makers, as opposed to a high degree of centralization and/or hierarchy. In effect this meant not only decentralization but also the inability of the experimenters to influence the outcome of the market evaluation of the new product. In fact, some of the most decisive failures of twentieth-century socialism flow from the failure to allow experimentation, and from the consequent failure to benefit from the opportunity to observe the *outcome* of such experiments.

---

[14] Of the regulated companies, which controlled so much of foreign trade even in the late eighteenth century, Adam Smith made the sardonic observation: "To be merely useless, indeed, is perhaps the highest eulogy which can ever justly be bestowed upon a regulated company." A. Smith, *Wealth of Nations*, Modern Library edition, Random House, Inc., New York, 1937, p. 693.

The need to expose investment decisions to the risk of being proven wrong implies the decentralization of decision-making authority, since any central authority will have a strong motivation for withholding financial support from those who are bent on proving that the central authority made a mistake, or on imposing on the central authority the cost of scrapping splendid-looking facilities whose only fault is that some interloper has devised more productive facilities or discovered that the work done in the facilities can be accomplished more cheaply in some other country – or perhaps need not be done at all. The social costs and risks associated with such moves might be well worth financing, but the costs and risks *to centralized decision-makers* might well be prohibitive.

Historically, one of the most distinctive features of capitalist economies has been the practice of decentralizing authority over investments to substantial numbers of individuals who stand to make large personal gains if their decisions are right, who stand to lose heavily if their decisions are wrong, and *who lack the economic or political power to prevent at least some others from proving them wrong*. Indeed, this particular cluster of features constitutes an excellent candidate for *the* definition of capitalism. Its importance for western economic growth turns on the point that the choice of capital investments includes the selection of the proposals for innovation that are to be funded. The diffusion of authority to select programs for capital expenditure and the diffusion of authority to select projects for innovation thus cover much the same ground.[15]

Organizational diversity of capitalism

The historical outcome of this long-term freedom to conduct experiments which, as I have argued, has been the central feature of western capitalism, has been an economy characterized by a truly extraordinary pattern of organizational diversity. This diversity may usefully be thought of as the end result of a process of social evolution in which a wide range of organizational forms has been introduced, and in which firms have been allowed to grow to sizes that were influenced by underlying conditions of technology, location, market size, range of products, etc. The particular outcomes achieved with respect to firm size, pattern of ownership, product mix, etc., have been essentially determined by a market process in which the underlying conditions of different industries have generated patterns of survival reflecting their own special circumstances, not some a priori notion of a single best model to which they were expected to adhere.

It is very common to stress the importance, indeed the dominance, of

---

[15] The last two paragraphs are drawn, with only slight modification, from Rosenberg and Birdzell, *How the West Grew Rich*, pp. 234–235.

large firms in western capitalist economies. This perspective has been particularly common among Marxists (although of course not confined to them), who have seen the trend toward bigness and greater industrial concentration as part of the "inner logic" of capitalism. According to the Marxist version, the emergence of monopoly capitalism not only reflects the pervasive advantages of bigness; it also conveniently facilitates the transition to socialism through the mechanism of nationalization of giant firms. Unfortunately, the commitment to this view has absolved several generations of critics from the much more serious task of examining, and accounting for, the remarkable institutional complexity of contemporary capitalist societies. Had they done so, it would have been apparent that, for example, although large firms are the predominant users of capital, smaller firms are the predominant employers of labor. Further, organizational structures not only differ immensely among the agricultural, manufacturing, public utilities, and services sectors, but immense differences also exist *within* each of these sectors. Giant corporations do indeed play a most important role, but so do millions of self-employed individuals. Any perspective that sees only giant corporations misses a most impressive feature of western economies: the great subtlety with which organizational modes have been adapted to, and modified by, the particularities of products and markets. Thus, even in those manufacturing industries that contain the largest firms, as measured by assets, size, and sales – petroleum, automobiles, aircraft, chemicals, computers, photographic equipment – dozens, or even hundreds, of smaller firms also persist.

Problems of twentieth-century socialism

The discussion of organizational diversity as the outcome of a process of prolonged experimentation forms an appropriate bridge on which to cross over to a consideration of some of the economic problems of twentieth-century socialism. The failure of socialist societies to permit experimentation was compounded by an undiscriminating ideological commitment to the economic advantages of bigness – a commitment that had its origins in the writings of Marx. The reluctance to allow organizational size and structure to be tailored to the specific needs of different economic activities was combined with an incentive system that is pervasively hostile to risk-taking. This combination goes a long way toward explaining one of the most fundamental, and perhaps surprising, difficulties of socialist societies: their failure to take full advantage of superior technologies.

It is, on first consideration, not so obvious why hostility toward experimentation and risk-taking should have created such serious obstacles toward the exploitation of better technologies. After all, in a world where technologically advanced capitalist economies already exist, a socialist economy has the invaluable option of acquiring such technologies from abroad. There are no compelling reasons why foreign capitalist economies cannot serve as sources for the more sophisticated technologies that socialist economies are unable to develop internally.

Of course, to a considerable extent, that is precisely what happened. The Soviet Union, beginning in the 1920s, was a large-scale importer of western technologies. Her inability to generate the incentives, or to provide the social space and opportunity for experimentation, was at least partially offset by the ability to import technologies developed by the technologically dynamic capitalist west. Thus, although Marx was wrong in arguing that socialism would arrive only in societies that had already passed through the state of mature capitalism, one might argue that this did not carry as severe a penalty as one might expect because advanced capitalism in the west has made its technologies universally available. This is, indeed, an important truth, and it should be further acknowledged that *all* industrializing countries have managed to grow more rapidly by borrowing foreign technologies. This was, as is widely acknowledged, true of Japan in the twentieth century, but it was also a central element of America's rapid industrialization in the nineteenth century, an industrialization that built upon the already existing technologies of metallurgy, power generation, railroads, and textiles in Great Britain.

But even though twentieth-century socialist societies did not have to develop their own technologies, the mode of organization of their economies imposed sharp limits on the economic benefits they could derive from the availability of foreign technologies. First of all, technology transfer is not simply a matter of shipping hardware from one location on the earth's surface to another. Rather, such borrowing presupposes a sizable cadre of engineers, technicians, and managers to modify, adopt, maintain, and repair such technology. This implies a competent infrastructure of skills, organization, and facilities. Unless these very considerable preconditions are reasonably fulfilled, the prospects for successful exploitation of foreign technologies are poor.

But there are other systemic considerations at issue here. Central planning, and the negligible freedom of action accorded to plant managers under the Soviet system, has been deeply hostile to the introduction of new technologies. New technologies are, by their nature, disruptive of established routines. Although they hold out the considerable promise of long-term improvements in productivity, they also exact a high short-term cost in terms of installation of new equipment, teaching of different skills, establishment of new work routines, working out of inevitable bugs with respect to product design and process technologies, developing new arrangements with suppliers of doubtful reliability, etc. However, the entire central planning apparatus has been geared to short-term goals. The success of a plant manager has been based relentlessly upon his ability to fulfill the annual output quota given to his firm by the central planners. Although there have been innumerable attempts to introduce greater flexibility into this system, those attempts have consistently failed. The system inflicted severe penalties upon the manager who failed to fulfill his annual output goal while, at the same time, the managerial reward for fulfillment or overfulfillment has been small – such as a modest, once-and-for-all bonus. Thus, risk aversion with respect to new technology has been endemic to the structure of incentives. The system not only lacked the capitalist incentive of large financial rewards, which Marx understood well; it also lacked the threat of competition, and the large risks of *failing* to innovate in an environment containing competitors who were likely to do so.

Indeed, the situation was typically even worse than this. Since the setting of annual targets was based upon the estimate made by the central planners of a plant's productive capabilities, it has been distinctly dangerous to the plant manger to reveal a capability considerably in excess of the most recent annual target. The plant manager has had a strong incentive to underrepresent his capabilities in order to keep his future targets low and therefore easily attainable.

This managerial risk aversion and dissimulation was, of course, powerfully reinforced by a huge and well-entrenched Soviet bureaucracy. Drastic reforms in the direction of greater managerial discretion and autonomy would threaten both the power and the perquisites of that bureaucracy. Decentralization would carry with it a devolution of power to the regions and to the plant managers. For these reasons, a greater reliance upon the associated apparatus of markets and market-determined prices remained anathema to planners and bureaucrats.

In addition, the systematic neglect of the consumer or, at best, the attachment of a low priority to consumer needs, weakened even further the incentive at the plant level to introduce improved products.[16] It is notorious that, within the perpetual seller's market which the Soviet system created, selling the product was never a problem. As a result, the effort involved in improving a product, or the disruption involved in changing the

---

[16] It has been a deliberate policy in the Soviet Union in the past to limit the number of models of a given product and the frequency of model changes. For a discussion of the impact of this policy, see J. Berliner *The Innovative Decision in Soviet Industry*, MIT Press, Cambridge (MA), 1976, pp. 195–198.

productive apparatus in order to introduce an entirely new product that would be more attractive or useful to consumers, offered a zero payoff to the plant manager. His continual preoccupation has always been not with the marketing of his product, but with the unreliability of his suppliers in providing him with the inputs essential to annual goal fulfillment.[17] Here again the system provided no incentive to innovation.

The problem is the lack of institutions and organizations which despite all obstacles can effect the introduction of revolutionary new technical innovations, accepting all the risk concomitant with this work, including that of failure, the struggle against conservatism and deep-rooted habit. Why should an enterprise director accept this risk and take up a struggle when . . . he is able without such effort to sell the products of his firm easily? With the buyers lining up for the firm's old product, why take upon oneself all the trouble involved in the introduction of a new product?[18]

The failure of socialist societies to learn from the conduct of experiments has been most conspicuous, of course, with respect to the uncritical acceptance of the desirability of large size, or what is sometimes referred to as "giantism" in Soviet central planning. Giantism may be defined as an uncritical commitment to a belief in the existence of indefinitely continuing economies of large-scale production.[19] Its intellectual antecedents undoubtedly lie in Marx's admiration for the large-scale technologies of the British industrial revolution and his forceful articulation of the view that, in the competitive process, the larger-scale capitalist always beats the smaller one. In Marx's words: "The battle of competition is fought by cheapening of commodities. The cheapness of commodities depends, *ceteris paribus*, on the productiveness of labour, and this again on the scale of production. Therefore, the large capitals beat the smaller."

---

[17] One important by-product of supplier unreliability is an incentive to vertical integration in order to achieve greater control over the supply of inputs and thereby to reduce dependence upon others. This translates, of course, into another incentive to increase the size of the firm.

[18] J. Kornai, *Anti-Equilibrium*, North Holland Press, Amsterdam, 1971, pp. 288–289.

[19] See L. Smolinski, "The Scale of the Soviet Industrial Establishment," *American Economic Review Papers and Proceedings*, 52 (1962), pp. 138–148. Smolinski asserts that giantism began with the first of the Five Year Plans in 1928. Giantism "started in 1929 when the original draft of the First Five Year Plan was scrapped as being too conservative, and both the output goals and the size of the new projects, from which the bulk of the additional output was to come, underwent a series of drastic upward revisions. The sky was soon the limit. Coal mines of 10 million tons annual capacity were being designed (some 4 times larger than the world's largest mine and some 150 times larger than an average Soviet mine in operation), the world's largest cement works of 930,000 tons, steam condensing power stations of 1 million kw . . . etc. At the same time, hundreds of smaller projects included in the original draft were being dropped, even when they were complementary to the 'giants' themselves. Giantism reached its peak around 1932, was condemned in 1938, and revived, in a modified form, in 1950" (pp. 139–40).

Marx was certainly one of the first economists (together with John Stuart Mill) to call attention to the economic significance of large-scale production.[20] He appreciated the importance of indivisibilities and pointed to numerous cases (especially in the capital goods sector) where economic advantages were derived from doing certain things on what he called a "cyclopean scale." Marx also pointed to the possibilities in certain industries, when the scale of production was sufficiently large, of utilizing wastes, or by-product materials.[21]

As a very careful and perceptive observer of the industrial scene, it is far from clear that Marx would have advocated indiscriminate giantism in the way that goal was to be pursued in the Soviet Union. There is evidence, moreover, that the thrust toward giantism was fed, during the Stalinist years, by a determination to emulate certain of the largest American establishments that were believed to be highly efficient – for example in the steel industry.[22] (It is tempting to say that, in their determined pursuit of the economies of large-scale production, the Soviet Union has provided the world with much additional evidence on the diseconomies of large-scale production). Finally, as a matter of administrative convenience, central planners undoubtedly found it much simpler to deal with a small number of large plants rather than a large number of small ones. Bigness clearly served the interests of the central bureaucracy. This was most apparent in the disastrous experience in agriculture, the sector where bigness was least appropriate. However inefficient the large collective farm may have been in terms of the productivity of agricultural inputs, it served as a powerful organizational device for *collecting* an agricultural surplus that could then be made to serve the interest of rapid industrialization.[23]

An ironic historical outcome is that, whereas Marx predicted that bigness would emerge out of the competitive process under mature capitalism, the size distribution of industrial firms shows a far greater concentration of employment in large firms in the Soviet Union than in the United States or

---

[20] Both of these authors were preceded and guided by Charles Babbage. See chapter 2 above pp. 41–45.

[21] The general requirements for the reemployment of these "excretions" are: "large quantities of such waste, such as are available only in large-scale production, improved machinery whereby materials, formerly useless in their prevailing form are put into a state fit for new production: scientific progress, particularly chemistry, which reveals the useful properties of such waste" (Marx, *Das Capital*, p. 100).

[22] Smolinski, "The Scale of the Soviet Industrial Establishment," p. 141. For an account of some of the early Soviet difficulties in the establishment of large-scale industrial complexes, see T.P. Hughes, *American Genesis*, Viking Penguin, 1989, chapter 6. Hughes documents the important role of American ideas, as well as the direct participation of American industrialists and engineers, in the early years of Soviet industrialization.

[23] China's dramatic improvement in food production after 1979 provides strong evidence of the earlier costs of collectivized agriculture.

Japan. Data for the 1960s indicate that 24 percent of Soviet enterprises had more than 500 employees. The corresponding figure for the United States was only 1.4 percent and for Japan a mere 0.3 percent. At the other extreme, only 15 percent of Soviet enterprises had fewer than fifty employees, whereas 85 percent of American firms and 95 percent of Japanese firms had fewer than fifty workers.[24] Obviously, the larger size of Soviet firms has been imposed by deliberate government policy and was not the outcome of historical experience of an earlier, mature capitalism or socialist experimentation.

The purpose of experimentation, of course, is to provide useful information for answering certain kinds of questions. But Marxism, in at least some of its most influential twentieth-century forms, has been unwilling to admit that the answers to some questions were subject to doubt. This has often taken the form of simply asserting the priority of ideological purity over technical expertise. In China, both the Great Leap Forward and the later, disastrous Cultural Revolution involved a denial of the role of technical expertise in the attainment of an efficient industrial society. Chairman Mao further claimed that a new socialist man would pursue economic efficiency and embrace an ideal of hard work merely out of a sense of commitment to socialism, and without any strong material rewards. His followers made important technical and economic decisions with no reference to technical specialists. The only litmus test for occupying important managerial and technical positions was an ideological one. It is fair to say that these episodes set back the industrialization of China by at least a generation. (Curiously, the Great Leap Forward may be said to have involved experimentation of a very perverse sort: the attempt to set up

---

[24] Berliner *Innovation Decision*, pp. 33–34. Some more recent World Bank data show a much greater concentration of industrial enterprises at the high end of the spectrum, with respect to the number of employees in Yugoslavia and Hungary as compared to South Korea and Japan. Mainland China occupies an intermediate position, reflecting the large number of small rural enterprises.

	Size distribution of industrial enterprises (%)				
	China (1982)	S. Korea (1981)	Japan (1972)	Yugoslavia (1981)	Hungary (1981)
5–33 employees	59.2	70.6	80.2	6.6	2.2
33–75 employees	19.5	14.4	10.7	15.8	4.8
75–189 employees	12.2	9.2	6.1	32.1	18.7
189–243 employees	8.5	1.5	0.8	12.0	9.2
More than 243 employees	0.6	4.3	2.2	33.5	65.1

Source: World Bank, as reported in *The Economist*, 1 August 1987, China's Economy Survey, p. 10.

backyard blast furnaces and chemical plants involved a "test" of the non-existence of economies of large-scale production in precisely those sectors of the economy where they are of critical importance!)

The socialist preoccupation with bigness in industry has been hostile to technological innovation in another very fundamental way. Some of the disadvantages of bigness are minimal in an environment characterized by a high degree of stability and routine. But where the technology is changing rapidly or might be *made* to change more rapidly, bigness is much more likely to be a serious handicap. Many experiments are easier and less costly to conduct on a small scale. It is inherently difficult to experiment and to introduce numerous small changes, and to do so frequently, in a large hierarchical organizational structure where permissions and approvals are required from a remote central authority.

The history of industries that have recently been undergoing rapid technological change – such as electronics and biotechnology – suggests that the flexibility offered by small firms may be highly advantageous to experimentation and exploration, especially in the early stages of the development of a new technology. Large firms, operating through layers of management with rigid rules, are not well-suited to environments undergoing rapid changes and requiring frequent, on-the-spot decisions. Where technological uncertainties are high, it is often far more efficient to be able to conduct experiments on a small scale in small firms.[25]

However, as Alfred Chandler has so extensively documented, as new technologies have gradually matured and entered commercialization on a national and eventually global scale, large firms have come to play a far more prominent role.[26] But what it is essential to realize is that the large western firms, which perform most of the R&D activity, bear little resemblance to large firms in socialist economies, although some parallels in the decision-making process of large hierarchical organizations, with elaborate rules, are easy to find. In the Soviet economy the largest firms have commonly been single-function plants or retailing organizations.

---

[25] Of course, firms of different sizes are likely to differ with respect to the *kinds* of innovative activity in which they are most competent to engage. Given the varying requirements of different classes of innovation, it would be natural to expect patterns of specialization based upon size. Moreover, many innovations actually carried out by large firms, such as du Pont, have been based upon inventions originally made in small firms. For a suggestive analysis of the role of firm size in innovation, see K. Arrow, "Innovation in Large and Small Firms," in J. Ronen (ed.), *Entrepreneurship*, D.C. Heath and Co., Lexington (MA), 1983, chapter 1. Arrow's conclusion is "that there is likely to be a tendency toward specialization – less costly and more original innovations will come from small firms, and those involving higher development costs but less radical departures in principle will come from larger firms" (p. 16).

[26] See A.D. Chandler, Jr., *Scale and Scope: The Dynamics of Industrial Capitalism*, the Belknap Press of Harvard University, Cambridge (MA), 1990.

Planning and coordination of the flow of goods have been the responsibility of government agencies such as Gosplan and Gosban. By contrast, in western capitalist economies over the past century the large firm has been responsible for integrating production with distribution and has coordinated the flow of goods to the market. Equally important, the firm's current financial performance and future earnings' expectations have powerfully influenced the commitment of resources to new product and new process development. Retained profits have played a major role in the financing of investment for expanding the firm's future capacity to produce new products and to deliver them to the appropriate markets. Large firms in socialist economies conspicuously lack these essential functions.

The Soviet thrust toward larger scale and centralization has even pervaded the organization of R&D activities within each of the ministries that has had planning responsibilities for major sectors of the economy. Among other consequences, this has resulted in the isolation of R&D from managerial decisions relating to production planning, and has thus intensified the difficulties, discussed earlier, of introducing new technologies.[27] It has also further isolated the findings of Soviet science from possible industrial applications. This is a consideration of great significance. Improving the links among the separate components of the R&D process is crucial to success in innovation in all industrial economies.[28] In the case of the Soviet Union the costs of poor linkages have undoubtedly been very great, since much Soviet research at the basic end of the R&D spectrum is at the highest international standards.

This last point is in fact of more general significance than the specific context in which it has been raised. Institutional innovation can foster technical change, not just by the risk reduction that has received primary emphasis in this chapter, but also by fostering improved communication among specialists with the necessary knowledge. Such reductions in the cost

---

[27] Within each ministry, there is a separation between R&D and production. "The decision was taken early in the development of Soviet economic institutions to pursue the presumed advantages of scale and specialization, and to concentrate R&D within branch institutions rather than to have individual R&D departments at each enterprise. This separation of R&D units from production units extends to the separate subordination of each to different channels of planning, finance, and supply. This has proved a considerable barrier to the transfer of new technology from the laboratory to production. Similar Western experience clearly demonstrates how important it is to maintain a close linkage between the management of production and that of R&D, to coordinate the two activities, and to ensure that the new technology is compatible with the technical production procedures and organizational characteristics and needs of the adopting enterprise" H. Levine, "On the Nature and Location of Entrepreneurial Activity in Centrally Planned Economies. The Soviet Case," in Ronen (ed.), *Entrepreneurship*, pp. 249–250.

[28] See M. Aoki and N. Rosenberg, "The Japanese Firm as an Innovating Institution," in T. Shiraishi and S. Tsuru (eds.), *Economic Institutions in a Dynamic Society*, Macmillan and the International Economic Association, London, 1989.

of technological change in market economies have been achieved in various ways. The emergence of capital good sectors has, in some instances, brought about a concentration of technological communication that has proven to be highly efficient; and a great strength of many integrated firms has been their ability to integrate the R&D function with marketing as well as manufacturing and other functions. Thus, in technologically sophisticated economies, success in the innovation process is likely to depend strongly upon improved communication among a number of specialized agents, especially agents in different organizations. Carrying through an innovation may depend upon effective relations with a variety of organizations, such as universities and input suppliers, and especially upon feedbacks from marketing specialists. Put somewhat differently, the existence of incentives to facilitate the learning process underlying innovation can be found only in a highly attenuated form in socialist societies. The upstream diffusion of incentives that originate in perceived possibilities for larger profits in the marketplace has been a powerful source of incentives to improve communication and to reduce its costs in capitalist economies. This incentive has essentially been aborted in centralized socialist economies.

Conclusion

The purpose of this chapter has been to assert the strategic role played by the freedom to experiment in the long-term process of economic growth and industrialization. It has been argued that a peculiar strength of capitalism, historically, has been the manner in which it has accommodated the special needs of the innovation process. It has also been argued that the failure to provide for such accommodation, in terms of organization and incentives, has been responsible for the persistent failure of socialism to generate new technologies or even to adopt technologies that already exist. It should be obvious that this discussion does not exhaust all the significant things that one might say about capitalism and socialism as alternative ways of organizing economic activity. However, it should also be obvious, as recent developments in eastern Europe and China have emphasized, that it is extremely difficult to make socialist societies more amenable to technological change without, at the same time, making them more capitalistic.

6   Why in America?

Let me try to clarify just what question it is I am trying to answer. I am not going to discuss the high overall rate of economic growth in the United States after 1800, that is, the rate of increase of per capita income. In fact, the rate of growth was not particularly high by comparison with later experience, although many scholars believe that it accelerated during the 1830s. If we extend our time horizon well back into the colonial period, we find that the rate of growth of per capita income between 1710 and 1840 did not exceed one-half of 1 percent per year.[1] Nor are we considering the overall rate of technological innovativeness which characterized the American economy, although that rate was doubtless very high. In spite of continued obeisance to the idea of Yankee ingenuity, it cannot be over-stressed that America in the first half of the nineteenth century was still primarily a borrower of European technology. Although the rate of technical change was indeed high, most of the new technologies were not American inventions. Americans were rapid adopters of foreign technologies when it suited their economic needs, and they were also skillful in modifying someone else's technology to make it more suitable to their needs. They made abundant albeit selective use of European innovations in power generation, transportation, and metallurgy.[2] It is worth noting, moreover, that high rates of technological improvement were not always a part of the American experience. Such improvements seem to have played an insignificant role in the American economy in the eighteenth century.

Originally published in Otto Mayr and Robert C. Post (eds.), *Yankee Enterprise, the Rise of the American System of Manufactures*, Smithsonian Institution Press, Washington (DC), 1981. The focus here on demand- and supply- side factors to explain the particular direction of American technological development complements the discussion of technological change in the energy and forest products sectors in chapters 9 and 12, respectively.

[1] Robert Gallman, "The Record of American Economic Growth," in Lance Davis, Richard A. Easterlin, and William N. Parker (eds.), *American Economic Growth*, Harper & Row, New York, 1972, p. 22.

[2] Nathan Rosenberg, *Technology and American Economic Growth*, Harper & Row, New York, 1972, chapter 3.

The latest scholarship on the colonial period suggests that the rate of inventive activity was very low, and that the slow but steady growth in productivity was dependent upon a cumulatively powerful combination of forces centering upon improvements in the organization of industries and the more effective functioning of markets and ancillary institutions.[3]

The question I propose to address, then, is not the high rate of technological change in America when that rate indeed became high in the nineteenth century. Rather, the question is one of direction and character. By the time of the Crystal Palace Exhibition in London in 1851, there was something so distinctive about many American goods that the British coined the phrase "the American system of manufactures." The expression was used to describe goods which were (1) produced by specialized machines, (2) highly standardized, and (3) made up of interchangeable component parts.[4] I propose to address myself to the question of causality. Why did this system emerge first in America? By midcentury it was apparent that there was an important class of goods which was being produced in a distinctive way in America.[5] It is important, however, that the distinctiveness should not be overstated, nor should it be thought that America had also assumed a role of broad technological leadership across the whole manufacturing sector. That was far from the case. Indeed, even in gunmaking, commonly regarded as the main triumph of the American system of manufactures, American barrelmaking may still have lagged well behind Britain at midcentury.[6]

Now, if you call upon an economist to try to explain a particular phenomenon, such as why the technology which we have come to call the

[3] See James Shepherd and Gary Walton, *Shipping, Maritime Trade and the Economic Development of Colonial North America*, Cambridge University Press, Cambridge, 1972.

[4] The degree or ease of interchangeability varied between products and over time. The degree of precision required for interchangeability varied considerably from one product to another. As one nineteenth-century commentator observed: "The more prevalent modern idea of the interchangeable in mechanism supposes a super-refinement of accuracy of outline and general proportions that is not always necessary or even desirable. It would be a criminal waste of time and substance to fit a harrow tooth with mathematical accuracy, but yet any harrow tooth should have a practical interchangeable relation to all harrows for which it is designed. The instructive rewards of folly would certainly overtake him who should attempt to make ploughshares and coulters with radical exactness; nevertheless, these essential parts of ploughs should be interchangeable among all ploughs to which they are adapted." W. F. Durfee, "The History of Interchangeable Construction," *American Society of Mechanical Engineers Transactions*, 14 (1893), p. 1228.

[5] The role of the manufacturing sector had increased very sharply during the decade of the 1840s. According to Gallman's estimates the contribution of manufacturing to national commodity output grew from 17 percent to 30 percent during the decade 1839–1849. Robert Gallman, "Commodity Output, 1839–1899," in the Conference on Income and Wealth's *Trends in the American Economy in the 19th Century*, Princeton University Press, 1960, p. 26.

[6] Paul Uselding, "Henry Burden and the Question of Anglo-American Technological Transfer in the Nineteenth Century," *Journal of Economic History*, 30 (1970), pp. 312–337.

American system of manufactures first arose in the United States and not elsewhere, you are not entitled to express surprise over an explanation couched in terms of supply-and-demand analysis. That is what I propose to give, and I do so without apology. Presenting an historical explanation in terms of supply-and-demand forces does not *necessarily* mean that I am committed to some form of economic determinism. Supply and demand are nothing more than convenient conceptual categories which enable us to think about an event or process in a more systematic way and to organize our analysis in a way which lends itself more readily to an understanding of cause–effect relationships. The forces *underlying* these economic categories may be social, geographic, technological, or ideological, but such forces have economic content and effects, and I am particularly interested in focusing upon the economic implications or consequences of these forces. There is a difference, which I trust that I need not belabor, between *translating* certain phenomena into their economic consequences and insisting that economic variables are all powerful.

I have already suggested a distinction between the rate and direction of technological progress. However, these two factors are not as easily separable as may be thought at first glance. The point is that differences in the resource endowment and demand conditions of an economy go a long way toward determining what kinds of inventions – with what kinds of product characteristics and factor-saving biases – it will be profitable to develop and exploit. To the extent that technological progress is responsive to economic forces – and I would agree that it is highly responsive and needs to be understood in these terms – the inventions actually brought forth in a particular country will tend to be compatible with those special needs. We need to distinguish here between invention and adoption. It is obvious that only those inventions which are compatible with a country's needs will be widely adopted. I am making here the stronger assertion that a high proportion of the *inventions made* will also reflect the peculiar needs of the economic environment in which they are developed.

If, at any given time and state of technical knowledge, certain *kinds* of inventions are easier to create, for whatever reason, economies where such inventions are also economically appropriate would be expected (*ceteris paribus*, as economists are fond of saying) to find it easier to generate new and improved technologies. If economic forces tend to push economies with different factor endowments in different directions in the attainment of technological progress, and if the technical problems which have to be overcome are more difficult in some directions than others, then the rate of technological progress may not be independent of the direction in which the economy is being pushed.

I have developed this argument because I believe it has merit. The

American experience in the nineteenth century involved an economy with resource endowment and demand conditions that pushed it in a direction somewhat different from the one that prevailed at the time for the economies of western Europe. This turned out to be a direction in which the inventive payoff was rather high. You may, if you wish, take this as a confirmation of the belief that a benevolent Providence watched over the affairs of America in the nineteenth century. Or you may simply regard it as luck or as the consequence of a particular resource endowment.

Whatever the label, I want to argue that what we call the American system of manufactures was a part of a larger process of economic adaptation, or even, if you prefer, economic evolution. American economic and social conditions in the nineteenth century pushed the search for new technologies in a specific direction. It was a direction which, both for social and economic reasons, was less appropriate in Europe. And, as it turned out, it was a direction in which there happened to exist a rich layer of inventive possibilities. In this sense, I will argue, the American system of manufactures was a species of a larger genus and, in this sense also, the high *rate* of technical progress was not entirely independent of the *direction* which that progress took.

The notion that the American system of manufactures requires explanation is reinforced by the facts that (1) the United States was, in the first half of the nineteenth century, still largely a technical borrower rather than a pioneer, and (2) technical innovations incorporating some of the elements of the system had been introduced earlier in Britain, mainly in the Portsmouth naval dockyards, but were not widely adopted elsewhere in that country.

Demand

What were the factors on the demand side that were so conducive in early-nineteenth-century America to the emergence of the American system of manufactures? There was a very rapid rate of growth in the aggregate demand for certain classes of commodities, which encouraged entrepreneurs to devise or adopt new production processes whose profitability required very long production runs. Adam Smith long ago taught that "the division of labor is limited by the extent of the market." The proposition applies to the use of specialized machinery as well as to specialized men. The fixed costs embodied in special-purpose machinery are warranted only if they can be distributed over a large volume of output. Therefore the confident expectation of rapidly growing markets is an extremely powerful inducement. Furthermore, the use of highly specialized machinery, as opposed to machinery which has a greater general-purpose capability, is contingent upon expectations concerning the *composition* of demand – specifically, that there will be strict and well-defined limits to permissible variations. Both of these conditions – rapid growth in demand and circumstances conducive to a high degree of product standardization – were amply fulfilled in early-nineteenth-century America.

What forces were responsible for these conditions? Probably the most pervasive force of all was the extremely rapid rate of population growth, primarily from natural increase but with immigration assuming a role of some significance in the 1840s. Between 1790 and 1860, the American population grew at a rate of nearly 3 percent per year (immigration included), a rate more than twice as high as that achieved by any European country even for much shorter periods. American fertility levels at the beginning of the nineteenth century were close to fifty per thousand – again, a rate far higher than European levels – and crude death rates were somewhere around twenty per thousand. The factors underlying this rapid expansion in population are many, but most important was probably the abundant supply of high-quality land in a society which was still predominantly agricultural. The abundance of good land, and the concomitant optimism about the future, were conducive to high fertility levels as well as an inducement to immigration.[7]

Although scholars differ concerning the long-term trend in the rate of growth of per capita income during the nineteenth century, there can be no doubt that the strong rate of population growth resulted in an exceedingly rapid rate of market growth. As early as 1840 the net national product of the United States was two-thirds or more of the size of Great Britain's.[8] In subsequent years America's net national product grew far more rapidly than Britain's.

Rapid population growth resulted in a very high rate of new household formation and therefore a rapid rate of growth in the demand for a wide range of manufactured commodities. This growth in market size was reinforced by other developments. Improvements in transportation, especially after the beginning of the canal-building period in 1815 and the beginning of railroad construction in the 1830s, served to link industrial centers with remote potential markets that previously had been largely self-sufficient. Thus, in many cases industrial producers and consumers were in a position to establish economically feasible market relationships with one another for the first time.

Many of the distinctive characteristics of the American market can be

[7] For an excellent, concise treatment of long-term demographic trends in America, see Richard A. Easterlin, "The American Population," chapter 5 in Davis, Easterlin, and Parker (eds.), *American Economic Growth.*
[8] Gallman, "Commodity Output, 1839–1899," p. 33.

properly appreciated only in the context of its predominantly rural and agricultural character. Over 80 percent of the American labor force was in agriculture in 1810 and this remained true for well over 60 percent in 1840.[9] The predominance of the agricultural sector in the nineteenth century, and the abundant endowment of natural resources more generally, served to shape the American environment in numerous ways which made it more receptive to the American system of manufactures. First of all, we have already noted how the rich and abundant supply of agricultural land contributed to high fertility levels and therefore to a rapid growth in the market. In addition, the abundance of land conferred another advantage upon the American economy, for it meant that food prices were relatively low. As a result, for any given income level or family size, there was a larger margin left over for the purchase of nonfood products, including those produced under the American system of manufactures. Thus the structure of relative prices in the United States, as a result of its resource endowment, was distinctly more favorable than in Europe for the emergence of manufactured goods. Both American farmers and urban industrial workers spent less of their income on food than did their European counterparts. Empirical evidence in support of this hypothesis has been carefully marshalled and analyzed by Albert Fishlow, relying upon data collected for the period 1888–91.[10] Since American food prices were, relatively, lower earlier in the nineteenth century, the case for the more favorable American conditions is even stronger.[11]

Yet another advantage conferred by America's natural-resource abundance was the easy accessibility to land ownership and the relatively egalitarian social structure which consequently emerged – with the major exception, of course, of the southern plantation system. Outside of the south there had emerged in colonial times and later a rural society which

---

[9] Lebergott's estimates of the percentage of the labor force in agriculture are as follows: 1810 – 80.9%; 1820 – 78.8%; 1830 – 68.8%; 1840 – 63.1%; 1850 – 54.8%; 1860 – 52.9%; 1870 – 52.5%; 1880 – 51.3%. Stanley Lebergott, "Labor Force and Employment, 1800–1960," in *Output, Employment and Productivity in the U.S. after 1800*, ed. Dorothy Brady, Studies in Income and Wealth, vol. XXX, National Bureau of Economic Research, New York, 1966, p. 119.

[10] Albert Fishlow, "Comparative Consumption Patterns, the Extent of the Market, and Alternative Development Strategies," in *Micro-Aspects of Development*, ed. Eliezer Ayal, Praeger Publishers, New York, 1973.

[11] "The very fact that food prices should have been relatively lower earlier would have given them more leverage at precisely the right moment – when per capita incomes were smaller and the percentages allocated to food higher. What is significant is that they did not rise rapidly thereafter and impede the extension of the market. American food prices in the 1830s and 1840s were not only lower relative to those of a nonfood composite, but also compared to British foodstuffs. That is, British food prices fell more rapidly from 1831–50 to 1866–90 than did American, and we have already seen that American foods were absolutely cheaper at that later date. Hence, the comparative advantage the United States enjoyed was greater in the earlier period." *Ibid.*, pp. 77–78.

was far less hierarchical, and with property ownership far less concentrated, than in Europe. American society included a large component of middle-class farmers and craftsmen. This was in sharp contrast with European societies in which poor peasants and farm laborers, with very little income beyond subsistence needs, constituted a large fraction of the total population, while at the top of the social pyramid was a small group of large landowners whose expenditure patterns made little contribution to the emergence of a sector producing standardized manufactured goods.

In America, to a degree which is now largely lost from the collective memory of a highly urbanized population, markets in the first half of the nineteenth century were dominated by the tastes and requirements of middle-class rural households.[12] In such households, often living under frontier or at least isolated conditions, there was little concern – indeed there was little opportunity – for ostentation or conspicuous consumption. Out of these social conditions emerged a relative simplicity of taste and a stress upon functionalism in design and structure. Rural isolation also strongly favored reliability of performance and ease of repair in case of breakdown. Such characteristics were particularly important for agricultural machinery and firearms. Simplicity of design and uniformity of components meant that a farmer could repair a broken plough in the field himself without having to depend upon a skilled repairman or distant repair shop. Thus, out of the social and geographic conditions of land-abundant America emerged a set of tastes and preferences highly congenial to a technology capable of producing large quantities of standardized, low-priced goods. These circumstances even left their indelible imprint on the American automobile in the early years of the twentieth century. The Ford Model T was designed in a manner which strongly resembled the horse and buggy, and the primary buyers were farmers for whom a cheap car offered a unique opportunity for overcoming rural isolation.

Supply

The point has already been made that in the early nineteenth century America was a large-scale borrower of European technology. But the point

---

[12] "The share in aggregate expenditures of different groups in the population in the nineteenth century and earlier can be estimated only roughly, for want of statistical information representative of all sections of the country. Even a crude statistical picture, however, can indicate how important rural households were in the market for manufactured goods and services. In the 1830s, about 66 percent of all households were on farms, 23 percent in villages, and 11 percent in cities. On the supposition that farm families on the average were able to spend $100, village families $200, and city families $300 over and above their outlays for housing and fuel, rural families (farm and village) would have accounted for 76 percent of all such expenditures." D. Brady in Davis, Easterlin, and Parker (eds.), *American Economic Growth*, p. 62.

also has been made that America's factor proportions, especially its rich abundance of natural resources, differed substantially from Europe's. These two propositions have an interesting implication that provides a useful way of entering into an examination of supply-side influences upon the emergence of the American system of manufactures. For, if factor proportions between the two continents were sufficiently disparate, it would follow that the technology devised to accommodate European needs did not always constitute, in present-day terminology, an "appropriate technology" in America. We now need to consider, therefore, how differences in the supply of available resources pushed Americans in a direction that helps to account for the country's unique technological contributions.

An abundance of natural resources means, in economic terms, that it is rational to employ methods of production which are resource intensive. Much of American inventive activity in the first half of the nineteenth century aimed at substituting abundant natural resources for scarcer labor and capital – although this aim is often not apparent from a present-day examination of the hardware devised for the purpose. America's early world leadership in the development of specialized woodworking machinery – machines for sawing, planing, mortising, tenoning, shaping, and boring – was a consequence of an immense abundance of forest products. Although these machines were wasteful of wood, that was of little consequence in a country where wood was very cheap. The substitution of abundant wood for scarce labor was, in fact, highly rational.[13]

Similarly, the immense available supply of potential farmland was not conducive to inventive activity that would maximize output per acre (as would be sensible in a land-scarce economy like Japan's), but rather to activity that would maximize the amount of land that could be cultivated by a single worker. This is precisely the thrust of nineteenth-century American mechanical innovation in agriculture, based upon animal power which supplied the traction for the steel plough (as well as Jethro Wood's earlier plough which already had replaceable cast-iron parts); the cultivator which replaced the hand-operated hoe in the corn and cotton fields; and the awesome reaper which swept away what once had been a basic constraint upon grain cultivation – fluctuations in labor requirements that reached a sharp peak during the brief harvesting season. Later, output per worker was further increased by binders and threshing machines and, eventually, by combine harvesters. In corn cultivation, the corn sheller and the corn picker were particularly valuable for their laborsaving characteristics.

In the gunmaking trade, usually regarded as the *locus classicus* of the distinctly American mass-production technology, some of the most origi-

---

[13] For a more detailed treatment, see Nathan Rosenberg, *Perspectives on Technology*, Cambridge, 1976, chapter 2, "America's Rise to Woodworking Leadership."

nal contributions were in the development and elaboration of a set of lathes for shaping the gunstock with a minimum amount of labor. The fact that these laborsaving machines were initially highly wasteful of wood – as compared to the shaping of a gunstock by a Birmingham craftsman – was a trivial consideration in a wood-abundant economy. Blanchard lathes were widely adopted in America.

What is the relevance of these woodworking and agricultural machines to the emergence, by midcentury, of the American system of manufactures? The essential point is that resource abundance provided an incentive in America to explore the possibilities of certain new machine technologies earlier and more deeply than in Europe.[14] The fact that these machines, particularly in their early stages of development, were not only laborsaving but also resource intensive, was not the economic deterrent that it was in Britain or France. Thus, in a wide range of manufacturing activities, Americans had a strong incentive to develop and adopt new technologies which, in effect, traded off abundant natural-resource inputs for labor, as well as machines which were wasteful of natural resources yet could be constructed more cheaply. But the pressures generated by America's unique resource endowment led to exploratory activities and to eventual learning experiences the outcome of which cannot be adequately summarized merely in terms of factor-saving of factor-using biases. For they also led to new patterns of specialization and division of labor between firms – especially between the producers and users of capital goods – as a result of which the American economy developed a degree of technological dynamism and creativity greater than existed in other industrial economies in the second half of the nineteenth century.

I believe that this technological dynamism was due in large measure to the unique role played by the capital-goods industries in the American industrialization process and the especially favorable conditions under which they operated. For these capital-goods industries – I refer here primarily to those involved in the forming and shaping of metals – became learning centers where metalworking skills were acquired and developed, and from which such skills were eventually transferred to the production of a sequence of new standardized products – interchangeable firearms, clocks and watches, agricultural machinery, hardware, sewing machines, type-writers, office machinery, bicycles, automobiles. A key feature of the story of American industrialization is that it involved the application of certain basically similar production techniques to a growing range of manufac-tures. Moreover, the technological knowledge and competence that gradu-ally accumulated in this sector were directly applicable to generating cost

---

[14] The rest of this paragraph draws upon Nathan Rosenberg, "American Technology: Imported or Indigenous?" *American Economic Review Papers and Proceedings*, Feb. 1977.

reduction in the production of capital goods themselves. A newly designed turret lathe or universal milling machine, or a new steel alloy permitting a lathe to remove metal at higher speeds – each of these innovations not only resulted in better machines but also reduced the cost of producing the machines in the first place.

Thus, although the initial shift to the capital-using end of the spectrum was generated by the unique pattern of American resource scarcities, it is by no means obvious that the final outcome of this process was in terms of factor biases. For the capital-using path was also a path which, *eventually*, generated a much-increased capacity for capital-saving innovations. The attempt to deal with labor scarcity in a regime of natural-resource abundance pushed us quickly in a direction in which there turned out to be rich inventive possibilities. In turn, the skills acquired in a more capital-abundant society with an effectively organized capital-goods sector provided the basis – in terms of knowledge and engineering skills and expertise – for innovations which were capital saving as well as labor saving. Indeed, most new products, after their technical characteristics became sufficiently stabilized, have passed through such a cost-reducing stage during which capital-goods producers accommodated themselves more efficiently to the large-quantity production of the new product. American industry seems to have particularly excelled at these activities.

Aside from the highly visible major inventions, capital-intensive technologies have routinely offered extensive opportunities for improvements in productivity which seem to have had no equivalent at the labor-intensive end of the spectrum. Knowledge of mechanical engineering, metallurgy, and, perhaps most important of all, the kind of knowledge which comes from day-to-day contact with machine technology, provide innumerable opportunities for small improvements – minor modifications, adaptation to some special-purpose use, design alterations, substitution of a superior or cheaper material – the cumulative effects of which have, historically, been very great.

It is important that these developments be seen in their actual historical sequence. America began the growth of her capital-goods sector not only with a strong preoccupation with standardization and interchangeability, but also with some early experience with techniques as well as a market which readily accepted standardized products. This shaped the eventual outcome of the industrialization process in some decisive ways. The acceptance of standardization and interchangeability vastly simplified the production problems confronting the makers of machinery and provided the technical basis for cost reductions in machinemaking. At the same time it provided the conditions which encouraged the emergence of highly specialized machine producers as well as the transfer of specialized technical skills from one industrial application to another. Indeed, America's most significant contributions to machine-tool design and operation and related processes – profile lathes, turret lathes, milling machines, die-forging techniques, drilling and filing jigs, taps and gauges – were associated with specialized, high-speed machinery devoted to the production of standardized components of complex products.

Thus, as a result of certain initial conditions, America's industrialization in the early nineteenth century proceeded along one out of a variety of possible paths. It was a path dictated by peculiar resource conditions and also a path rich in inventive possibilities. Movement along this path generated a dynamic interaction of forces, a dialectical process in which cause and effect become exceedingly difficult to disentangle. While greater homogeneity of tastes was originally conducive to the introduction of goods produced according to the American system of manufactures, it is also true that, once this technology began to spread, it in turn shaped and influenced tastes in the direction of simplicity and functionality.[15] Further-more, although American factor endowment pushed in the direction of mechanization, the experience with mechanization *in itself* brought about an improvement in inventive ability and its more rapid diffusion. This was an interactive process, whereby the successful application of mechanical skills in one sector improved the likelihood of their successful application in other sectors.

What, finally, can we add by way of explaining why Britain – which was far more advanced industrially than the United States in the early nine-teenth century – did not go further than it did in developing the distinctive features of the American system of manufactures? Much of the answer is already implicit in the preceding discussion of Anglo-American differences in conditions of demand-and-resource endowment. There is, however, an additional factor which deserves mention, namely, the persistence and continuing powerful influence of certain traditional values and attitudes which had their roots in a preindustrial craft society. Such values and attitudes had, of course, played a much more significant role in shaping the outlook of workers and engineers in Britain than in the United States. Strong craft traditions, with their emphasis upon pride in workmanship, individuality, and high standards of product quality, were often inimical to standardization and the alterations in final product design which were essential to low-cost, high-volume production. To some extent the persist-ence of traditional craft attitudes in Britain reflected the demand-side phenomena to which we have already referred, as well as other market

[15] Dorothy Brady, "Relative Prices in the Nineteenth Century," *Journal of Economic History*, 24 (1964), pp. 147–148.

peculiarities. But beyond that there is evidence from many industries – firearms, automobiles, locomotives, a wide range of production machinery, clocks and watches – suggesting a preoccupation with technical perfection beyond what could be justified by narrowly utilitarian considerations.[16] And perhaps this observation suggests what should be an appropriate final comment upon why this particular system first emerged in America. For the American system of manufactures was, above all, a totally unsentimental approach to the productive process in industry, one in which purely commercial considerations prevailed. The British long consoled themselves with the belief that standardization and mass-production techniques inevitably resulted in an inferior product. Unhappily, from their point of view, they persisted in this belief long after it ceased to contain even an element of truth.

[16] S.B. Saul, "The Market and the Development of the Mechanical Engineering Industries in Britain, 1860–1914," *Economic History Review*, 41 (1967); S.B. Saul, "The Engineering Industry," chapter 7 in *The Development of British Industry and Foreign Competition, 1875–1914*, ed. D. Aldcroft, University of Toronto Press, Toronto, 1968; S.B. Saul, "The Motor Industry in Britain to 1914," *Business History*, 5 (1962); R.A. Church, "Nineteenth Century Clock Technology in Britain, the U.S., and Switzerland," *Economic History Review*, 49 (1975); and Nathan Rosenberg, introduction to *The American System of Manufactures*, Edinburgh University Press, Edinburgh, 1969.

7 Can Americans learn to become better imitators?

NATHAN ROSENBERG AND W. EDWARD STEINMUELLER

Despite American success in previous historical eras at imitating the technology and organizational structure of industrial rivals in other nations, there is mounting evidence that its capacity to absorb and adapt rivals' advantages to its own purposes has diminished in recent years. While these concerns are voiced with regard to a number of nations, the recent success of Japanese firms has been noteworthy and deserves special attention.

One reason Americans have been such poor imitators is that, until very recently, they were not even aware that there was much in Japanese industry that was worth imitating. Japanese economic competitiveness was, for a long time, dismissed as simply reflecting lower labor costs, which were regarded as decisive in certain industries. Later, Japanese success was dismissed as ephemeral, reflecting the ease of rapid growth on the part of a "mere imitator" following the innovative leads of other nations, particularly those of the United States.

More recently, as competition has become more heated and as certain American industries suffered heavily from Japanese imports, the successes of Japanese firms have been attributed to policies of "industrial targeting" orchestrated by the Ministry of International Trade and Industry (MITI), usually said to involve extensive government subsidies and coordination of import policies that unfairly tilted what should have been a "level playing field."

We do not wish to deny that there may have been some truth in each of these beliefs at one point in time. However, an unfortunate consequence of such beliefs has been that they have delayed efforts to monitor and study the performance of the Japanese manufacturing sector with any care.

Certainly an earlier complacency has now unravelled. It is abundantly clear that there is much to admire, and, perhaps to emulate, in some parts of

A shorter, earlier version of this paper was published in *American Economic Review Papers and Proceedings*, May 1988, under the title "Why Are Americans Such Poor Imitators?"

the Japanese manufacturing system. In retrospect it is obvious that Americans, even when they have become aware of this, have been poor imitators.

The essence of these concerns was summarized by Harvey Brooks in congressional hearings:

Although Japanese success in recent years has been based on adaptation of Western, mainly American, technology, and on the capacity to commercialize it more rapidly than its competitors, it would be wrong to conclude from this that the Japanese are mere imitators who, once they have attained to the world state-of-the-art in a field, will not continue to move forward the frontiers of technology. On the contrary, history suggests that imitation, followed by more and more innovative adaptation, leading eventually to pioneering, creative innovation forms the natural sequence of economic and industrial development.

Successful imitation, far from being symptomatic of lack of originality as used to be thought, is the first step of learning to be creative. This is probably true of nations, as it seems to be of individuals, something which Americans may have forgotten in our almost obsessive belief in originality and individual creativity. It may be only those who try continually to reinvent the wheel that will lose out in the innovative race. In my opinion, the United States, so long accustomed to leading the world, may have lost the art of creative imitation, and is deficient in scanning the world's science and technology for potential commercial opportunities relative to what is done by its competitors, particularly Japan.[1]

Why should this have been so? Why have the Japanese been so much better at imitation than the American? What has made the Japanese such "creative imitators?"

I

During the past twenty-five years, the composition of Japanese exports to the United States has shifted dramatically away from industries where labor intensity provided comparative advantage, to industries where sophisticated manufacturing skills and technology are of central importance. This shift has been so marked that, in 1986, over 80 percent of Japanese exports to the United States were in electrical, electronic, transportation equipment, and machinery sectors. In short, Japanese "imitation" has been concentrated in a few specific sectors where American industry had previously been dominant for many years following the

---

[1] House Subcommittee on Investigations and Oversight and the Subcommittee on Science, Research, and Technology of the Committee on Science and Technology, *Japanese Technological Advances and Possible United States Responses Using Research Joint Ventures*, 98th Congress, 1st Session, June 29–30, 1983.

Second World War. The imitative processes that were used by Japanese industry in catching up to United States firms in these sectors should now be recognized as having major implications for how Japanese firms are prepared to succeed at the more difficult task of forging ahead.[2]

Table 7.1 provides a guide to the main categories of Japanese success in recent years. These data show the composition of Japanese exports, by industry, to the United States for the year 1986. The expansion of Japanese exports to the United States over the previous decade was very rapid. In 1976, the nominal value of exports was $15.7 billion compared with the 1986 nominal value of $81.9 billion. Deflating these numbers by the consumer price index still reveals a remarkable 10 percent annual rate of growth in Japanese exports to the United States.[3] In comparing the 1986 percentage distribution of imports with 1976, the main difference is the replacement of steel imports by growth in the categories reported in the lower half of table 7.1, particularly transport equipment and consumer audio and video equipment.[4] It is readily apparent that Japan's great successes have been highly selective in nature. Japanese "creative imitation" has been concentrated in a few sectors where American industry had traditionally been very strong: machinery, automobiles, and electronic equipment. Indeed, these and related categories account for 86.5 percent of 1986 United States imports from Japan. Compared to twenty years earlier, both the scale and composition of Japan's exports have changed dramatically.[5]

The composition of Japanese exports reflects the very rapid progress that Japanese firms have made toward competitive dominance in markets where high degrees of "systemic complexity" are significant. Goods with high levels of systemic complexity include plain-paper copiers, automobiles,

[2] See Moses Abramovitz, "Catching Up, Forging Ahead, and Falling Behind," *Journal of Economic History*, 46 (2) (June 1986), pp. 385–406, for criticism of the proposition that "catch up" is a self-limiting tendency, and speculation about the role of social capabilities as a foundation for forging ahead.
[3] While comprehensive measures of import prices are not tabulated by the United States, inflation in some important categories has been much lower than the consumer price index. For example, the index for telecommunications equipment rose at a 1.2 percent annual rate during the 1976–1986 period. See US Department of Commerce, Bureau of the Census, *Statistical Abstract of the United States: 1987*, Washington (DC), 1986, p. 461, and US Department of Commerce, Bureau of the Census, *Statistical Abstract of the United States: 1980*, Washington (DC), 1980, p. 485.
[4] In 1976, iron and steel constituted about 15 percent of imports compared to the 3 percent for 1986 reported in table 7.1.
[5] On the rise of Japanese industrial exports see Lawrence B. Krause and Sueo Sekiguchi, "Japan and the World Economy," in Hugh Patrick and Henry Rosovsky (eds.), *Asia's New Giant: How the Japanese Economy Works*, The Brookings Institution, Washington (DC), 1976.

Table 7.1. *Composition of United States Imports from Japan – 1986*

Category	· Value	% of total
Food and live animals	$445,684,104	0.54
Beverages, tobacco, and crude materials	143,168,011	0.17
Mineral fuels, oils, and fats	78,375,254	0.10
Organic chemicals	732,204,409	0.89
Crude chemicals, dyeing, and coloring materials	396,582,084	0.48
Medicines and pharmaceuticals	124,231,381	0.15
Essential oils, perfumes, and soaps	45,334,089	0.06
Other chemicals including synthetic resins and plastics	493,269,872	0.60
Non-metallic manufacturing (including rubber manufacturing and textiles)	2,551,655,918	3.12
Iron and steel	2,240,493,428	2.74
Nonferrous metals	504,577,058	0.62
Metal goods (not elsewhere specified)	1,535,892,624	1.88
House fittings, furniture, luggage, and handbags	252,185,725	0.31
Wearing apparel and footwear	477,098,130	0.58
Other (including special transactions and low valued items)	836,174,412	1.02
Subtotal	10,856,926,499	13.25
Non-electrical machinery	8,303,752,016	10.14
Electrical machinery and electronics	18,963,888,060	23.15
Transport equipment	31,049,263,222	37.91
Scientific and photographic equipment	3,471,678,461	4.24
Miscellaneous manufactured items (including audio/video equipment)	9,265,626,609	11.31
Subtotal	71,054,208,368	86.75
Grand total	$81,911,134,867	100.00

Notes:
(1) Machinery related to electric power generation (codes 716.6, 716.9, and 718.8) was made part of the Electrical machinery and electronics total rather than a more general power-generating machinery category in the original table.
(2) Audio and video equipment are included with miscellaneous manufactured equipment and constitute $6.38 billion of that category. This separates them from electrical machinery and electronics, where they appear in the original table.
(3) Parts for audio and video equipment remain in the electrical machinery and electronics category.

Source: US Department of Commerce, "US General Imports: World Area and Country of Origin by Schedule A Commodity Groupings," FT155/1986, Washington, DC, Bureau of the Census, Foreign Trade Division, pp. 760–777.

some machine tools, and consumer electronics. Producing such goods, which have many interacting parts or "sub-systems," requires a high degree of effort in manufacturing design and development.[6] To be competitively successful, Japanese firms have not only had to achieve high levels of reliability and performance in such products, they have also had to foreclose opportunities for competitors to improve inexpensively upon their efforts.

The first part of our answer to the question of why Americans have been such poor imitators compared to the Japanese is that there has been a distinct asymmetry in the strengths developed by each of these industrial economies. This asymmetry partly accounts for why it has taken so long to appreciate fully the sources of Japanese industrial capabilities. The Japanese have been very successful in borrowing and developing technologies initially created by American firms. These technologies have been largely of a hardware nature, in particular a stream of highly visible product innovations.

By contrast, what may be most worth imitating on the Japanese side is much more subtle and much less visible. It includes ways in which certain *activities* are carried out, rather than readily identifiable pieces of hardware. These differences lie at the levels of organization and incentives for improvement of manufacturing operations, and they have been mobilized to address two key goals in manufacturing improvement. The first is the efficient coordination of product design and manufacturing functions.[7] The second is effective solutions to the myriad small problems that are key to efficient mass-production techniques.[8] An important part of the reason why it has been so difficult to appreciate the nature of Japanese achievements is that they are heavily concentrated in a collection of activities – Development – that economists have, so far, failed to unpack and subject to detailed and critical analysis.

This is surprising for a number of reasons, not the least of which is that

---

[6] As Abegglen and Stalk note, "The Japanese labor productivity advantage is enormous in high volume assembly processes where hundreds, even thousands, of interdependent steps must be coordinated. In simpler processes, such as a foundry, where perhaps thrifty operational steps are required, the Japanese advantage is slight, and sometimes non-existent." James C. Abegglen and George Stalk, *Kaisha, The Japanese Corporation*, Basic Books, New York, 1985, p. 61.

[7] See Masahiko Aoki, "Horizontal vs. Vertical Information Structure of the Firm," *American Economic Review*, 76, (5) (December 1986), pp. 971–83, and Ken-ichi Imai, Ikujiro Nonaka, and Hirotaka Takeuchi, "Managing the New Product Development Process: How Japanese Companies Learn and Unlearn," chapter 8 in Kim B. Clark, Robert H. Hayes, and Christopher Lorenz (eds.), *The Uneasy Alliance: Managing the Productivity-Technology Dilemma*, Harvard Business School Press, Boston (MA), 1985, pp. 337–375.

[8] See Abegglen and Stalk, *Kaisha*, 1985 and Masaaki Imai, *Kaizen: The Key to Japan's Competitive Success*, Random House, New York, 1986.

R&D is, in fact, overwhelmingly D. Yet, we know more about the 12 percent of R&D that constitutes basic research than about the 68 percent that constitutes development. While this may be understandable on the part of natural scientists, it is less so on the part of economists. Nevertheless, American thinking about the innovation process has focused excessively upon the earliest stages – the kinds of new products or technologies that occasionally emerge out of basic research, the creative leaps that sometimes establish entirely new product lines, the activities of the "upstream" inventor or scientist rather than the "downstream" engineer. American discussions of technical change are more likely to be presented in terms of major innovations and pioneering firms rather than in terms of the success of particular sectors or firms at catching up and overtaking other organizations through sustained effort and small improvements. In this respect, the dominant view of the innovative process is still overly Schumpeterian, in its preoccupation with discontinuities and creative destruction, and its neglect of the cumulative power of numerous small, incremental changes. We suggest that the Japanese have had a much deeper appreciation of the economic significance of these vital development activities than their American counterparts.

II

Development, of course, covers a range of activities whose content differs widely from one industry to another. It generally includes the designing of new products, testing and evaluating their performance (which, in some industries may involve the building and testing of prototypes, or experimentation with pilot plants), and inventing and designing new and appropriate manufacturing processes. In each of these activities, the roles of minor modifications and small improvements that better integrate design and production, establish closer feedbacks from users to suppliers, and more effectively "tune" existing production methods, are critically important. Individually, each of these modifications and improvements will bring about some slight reduction in cost or improvement in performance. Their cumulative effects may, however, be immense, as when the semiconductor industry moves, through a multitude of small steps, from a handful of transistors on a chip to a million such transistors, or when the channel capacity of a 3/8-inch coaxial cable expands, through a succession of small improvements, by more than an order of magnitude, or when the speed of computers increases by several orders of magnitude.

It is the essence of these development activities that they have no well-defined terminus. They do not end when a new or improved product is brought to market. Quite the contrary. A continual stream of small improvements is often the essence of success in the competitive process. In industries such as those that currently account for the bulk of Japanese exports to the United States, development is a never-ending activity. They are not, from some points of view, very exciting activities. They are activities that do not win Nobel Prizes; nor, for the most part, do they even win recognition at the Patent Office. This low visibility partly accounts for the very limited awareness of their economic importance. Nevertheless, poor performance in the development process can easily be commercially fatal to firms that are highly successful at research. Such poor performance can readily translate into final products of inferior design, lower quality, and poor reliability. It can also translate into higher cost and, therefore, inability to sustain a market position originally achieved through the innovation process. These shortfalls can convert a technological head start, resulting from successful innovation, into a scramble to retain what turns out to be a shrinking market share against the cost and performance advantages of competitors, including those who may have had no role in the initial innovation or in the antecedent research that made it possible.[9]

These possibilities are, of course, not offered as mere idle rumination. There is an accumulation of evidence that many Japanese successes in recent years are a consequence of greater effectiveness in organizing and providing strong incentives for these "downstream" development activities. In the internal organization of their firms, the Japanese commonly provide for much closer interaction between product designers and production engineers, they devote far more attention to the refinement of the appropriate process technologies, and they also assign a more prominent role to the engineering department.[10] In considerable measure, then, their skill in imitation has been an accompaniment of their skill in, and concern with, development activities. Sustained efforts to master the development process carry with them a further connection with imitation. Success in development often involves imitating and improving upon one's own prior performance, rather than starting from scratch. If American industry were to improve its development skills it would also, simultaneously, improve its capacity to imitate. The two capabilities overlap heavily.

[9] As Abegglen and Stalk note in commenting on United States problems in competing in the domestic Japanese market, "As [Japanese company production] volumes increase and their costs fall, they will increasingly be able to fund an upgrading of their technology and products." Abegglen and Stalk, *Kaisha*.

[10] In a recent comparison of innovation in Japan and the United States, Mansfield has observed a striking difference with respect to the allocation of R&D budgets between product and process technology. According to Mansfield, the American firms in his sample devoted two-thirds of their R&D budgets to improved product technologies and only one-third to improved process technologies, whereas among the Japanese firms only one-third of their R&D budgets were devoted to improved product technologies and two-thirds to improved process technologies. Edwin Mansfield, "Industrial Innovation in Japan and the United States," *Science* (30 September 1988), pp. 1769–1974.

This statement applies with particular force to the cultivation of a strong interface between product design and engineering. Japanese strength at this interface has facilitated her technology-imitation activities by the ease with which it enables foreign products to be quickly adapted, modified to suit domestic requirements and achieve low production costs. In a study of innovation among Japanese and American firms, Mansfield notes a major difference in the time it took firms to commercialize technologies originating outside the firm. Japanese firms were able to do this much more rapidly than American firms.[11] Furthermore, a strong interface between design and engineering makes it possible for Japanese firms to move to positions of leadership when new technologies call for simultaneous optimization on both the process and product sides.

The more rapid exploitation of robotics in Japan appears to be due, in important measure, to greater producer expenditures in adapting robotics to the needs of customers and to the alacrity with which Japanese user firms have modified and simplified product design in order to accommodate the new robotics technology.[12] With regard to product-design adaptation, it has probably been more sensible to simplify the design of products so that robots could readily assemble them – reducing the number of component parts, simplifying the method by which parts are attached to one another – than to design robots of more general, and therefore more sophisticated, assembling capabilities.[13]

A central theme in the study of the development process has been its integrated, interactive, and iterative nature. In sharp contrast, American firms have often compartmentalized research and manufacturing functions.[14] Often, this has led to breakdowns in the development process characterized by "finger pointing," in which functionally specialized groups within the firm assign blame to each other or to external suppliers.

---

[11] Mansfield, *ibid.* Significantly, Mansfield found that the amount of time that it took United States and Japanese firms to reduce internally developed technologies to practice was essentially the same.

[12] In a study of robotics adoptions in Japan, Mansfield found that Japanese robotics producers spent five times as much on tooling and manufacturing equipment as American companies. Edwin Mansfield, "Technological Change in Robotics: Japan and the United States," *Managerial and Decision Economics: Special Issue* (1989), pp. 19–25.

[13] The possibility that users would prefer simpler systems was suggested by a report by the Office of Technology Assessment, *Computerized Manufacturing Automation: Employment, Education, and the Workplace*, US Congress, OTA-CIT-235, Washington (DC), April 1984. That report cites Frank Cogan, "Some Robots Being Simplified to Attract Users," *American Metal Market/Metalworking News* (September 13, 1982).

[14] As the Office of Technology Assessment noted in describing design-manufacturing connections, "A common description of the relationship is, 'The design engineer throws the set of drawings over the wall to manufacturing,'" *ibid.*, p. 77. See Stephen Kline and Nathan Rosenberg, "An Overview of Innovation," *The Positive Sum Strategy: Harnessing Technology for Economic Growth*, ed. Ralph Landau and Nathan Rosenberg, National Academy Press, Washington (DC), 1986, pp. 275–305.

In spite of this, United States firms are often very good at innovation since individual ingenuity and sharply focused specialization can overcome many obstacles. But these same firms often find it difficult to make the small steps that are crucial to the ongoing development process. This leaves competitors with a host of opportunities for imitation and modification for improving performance or reducing costs, thereby truncating the appropriation of returns from innovation.

The Japanese have, on numerous occasions, been the leaders in the commercialization of new products, in spite of the fact that the new product, or some essential component, was invented elsewhere. Although the United States pioneered both the scientific and technological frontiers in the invention of the transistor, Japanese firms were the first to succeed in large-scale application of this technology for radios and later obliterated America's earlier dominance of the market for color-television receivers. Japanese success at quality and design improvements for mass-produced goods such as compact automobiles and consumer electronics are highly visible. Products requiring smooth coordination of different technologies (e.g. electrical, electronic, and mechanical) for such things as plain-paper copiers, facsimile machines, floppy disk drives, and personal computer printers, are strongholds of Japanese commercial and export success. None of these technologies rests on a single critical innovation. Instead, Japanese success in each of these areas can be traced to the cumulative impact of her great development capabilities.

Japanese success in development has often been able to overcome America's much-heralded innovative capabilities. The more specialized an activity becomes, the greater the importance of efficient information exchanges if inappropriate tradeoffs or inappropriate optimization criteria are to be avoided.

For specialists to work well in a large organization, there must be an intimate familiarity with one another's goals and priorities. There must be a set of shared understandings and concerns. The development efforts of Japanese firms strongly emphasize rotation of personnel among departments in teams, whose stability augments the retention of information and the formation of common goals. In many cases, close communication among functionally separate specialists is strengthened by the awareness of a commonality of interests flowing from stable, long-term employment (and supplier) relationships.[15] Japanese firms appear to make more

---

[15] For comparisons of United States and Japanese job-tenure patterns see Masanori Hashimoto and John Raisian, "Employment Tenure and Earnings Profiles in Japan and the United States," *American Economic Review*, 75 (4) (September 1985), pp. 721–735. Stable supplier relationships in the Japanese automobile industry are discussed later in this paper.

systematic use of engineering skills and production-worker experience throughout the entire sequence of development activities associated with the introduction of new products, including the most minute aspects of the eventual manufacturing process.

These activities are not well appreciated when, as is commonly the case, development is thought of as the *application* of scientific knowledge.[16] Development in fact incorporates knowledge from many sources. Even in those instances in which new scientific knowledge *does* provide the initial stimulus for a new product, the subsequent development process will draw upon a wide variety of sources, the most common of which is likely to be the existing "in-house" engineering knowledge. Organizational structures and incentive systems that can exploit these sources effectively will create economic advantages over competitors who cannot do so, even if these competitors have superior research capability.[17] If these development capabilities are sufficiently strong, the stage of commercialization may be reached sooner, and will certainly be reached by firms in a better position subsequently to reduce cost and improve performance.[18]

In short, the economic value of "first-mover" advantages in capturing the economic returns from innovation is overrated, because innovations are commonly very poorly designed in their earliest stages and in numerous ways ill-adapted to their ultimate applications.[19] To put it another way, first-mover advantages accrue to the firm that develops the first *economically* feasible product, which may be very different from the first *technologically* feasible product. The incremental improvements underlying development thus play a critical role in the eventual capture of returns from innovations.

Thus, there are two reasons for the primacy of development in capturing the returns from innovations in markets such as those in which the Japanese have demonstrated success. The first is that efficiency gains in mass production are often easier to achieve through large numbers of small

[16] The NSF defines Development as "the systematic use of knowledge or understanding *gained from research*, directed toward the production of materials, devices, systems, or methods, including design and development of prototypes or processes." National Science Board, *Science Indicators*, National Science Foundation, Washington (DC), 1985, p. 221. Our italics.

[17] Major productivity advances in the Japanese automotive industry were attained prior to advanced manufacturing methods primarily through improvements in organizational technique. See Richard M. Cyert and David C. Mowery (eds.), *Technology and Employment: Innovation and Growth in the US Economy*, National Academy Press, Washington (DC), 1987, p. 28.

[18] Masahiko Aoki and Nathan Rosenberg, "The Japanese Firm as an Innovating Institution," *Economic Institutions in a Dynamic Society*, ed. Takashi Shiraishi and Shigetu Tsuru, Macmillan Press Ltd., Hampshire, 1989, pp. 137–154.

[19] See Nathan Rosenberg, "Factors Affecting the Diffusion of Technology," chapter 11, *Perspectives on Technology*, Cambridge University Press, Cambridge, 1976.

improvements than through major revisions. The second is that cost reduction and performance improvements in a well-established technology are often capable of overtaking efforts to advance technology through discontinuous "leaps" or major innovative steps. The creative elements of imitation involve not only the adaptation of new or externally created technology but a continuing refinement of existing technologies and manufacturing methods.

III

The organizational and incentive structures that foster imitation of major technological advance as well as "in house" refinements of knowledge have proven particularly effective in the expansion of Japanese consumer-electronics industries. Japanese and American efforts to develop a mass-market video cassette recorder (VCR) provide an illuminating account of the effectiveness of incremental and continuous technical change versus a strategy of striving for huge innovative leaps.[20]

United States efforts to achieve a VCR suitable for the consumer market illustrate the weakness that can occur in seeking a dominant position solely through product innovation. As Abegglen and Stalk concluded in summarizing Japanese firm success,

At least two Western companies had prototypes in hand at an earlier date than their Japanese competitors. It was the Japanese competitors, however, who managed to extract the product from the clutches of engineering departments bent on further refinements, move the product into the marketplace, cascade improved versions into the market and conclude with over 90 percent of the world output of VCR's, which are now the largest-selling single consumer electronic products in the world.[21]

Japanese firms sought, at an early stage of the development effort, a collection of product designs that both solved technical feasibility problems and provided opportunities for manufacturing improvements. To solve these problems, Japanese firms simultaneously developed several technologies in their efforts to discover where further manufacturing development efforts might succeed. For example, at Sony, the project leader, Nobotoshi Kihara, felt there were at least ten different ways to implement VCRs with desirable characteristics, and he assembled teams working in parallel to develop prototypes of all ten methods.[22] By focusing on close coordination

[20] See Richard S. Rosenbloom and Michael A. Cusumano, "Technological Pioneering and Competitive Advantage: The Birth of the VCR Industry," *California Management Review*, 29 (4) (Summer, 1987), pp. 51–76.   [21] Abegglen and Stalk, *Kaisha*, 1985, p. 135.
[22] Rosenbloom and Cusumano, "Technological Pioneering and Competitive Advantage," 1987, p. 63.

of the design and manufacturing technologies, the resulting system was well-positioned for mass production.

Development efforts for consumer VCRs and the related "scale up" of these designs to mass production at Sony, Matsushita, and Victor Company of Japan, Ltd. were aided by the transfer of personnel from development to manufacturing. By comparison, while United States firms had demonstrated prototypes of acceptable systems based on genuinely innovative solutions to some of the design problems of essential components such as the recording sub-system, moving these designs into large-scale manufacture faltered. In short, Japanese firms were able to begin delivery of complete systems while United States firms were still trying to develop or contract for mass manufacturing of their innovations.

Successive small improvements and close coordination between design and manufacturing have also been characteristic of Japanese success in electronic businesses located "upstream" from consumer electronics, such as semiconductors. The origins of the Japanese semiconductor industry during the 1950s were based on efforts of electronics system companies, such as Sony, to establish a domestic semiconductor supply for their principal business.[23] Japanese success at consumer electronics export during those years required high levels of reliability to compensate for their underdeveloped dealer and service networks in foreign countries. Reliability and cost, rather than performance, provided a focus for Japanese semiconductor development efforts from the outset. As a consequence, Japanese semiconductor firms achieved small improvements that would have immediate cost reduction and reliability payoffs in consumer products.[24]

Consumer electronics companies demanded that component suppliers (internal and external) achieve a very low failure rate, not only to assure final product reliability, but also to minimize manufacturing costs where component testing was viewed as involving an unacceptable cost. To achieve their development targets, consumer-electronics companies analyzed failures in great detail, tracing problems back to their source, whether it was in components or assembly, and pursued refinement in both components and assembly techniques that we have noted as key to success in development. As a result, a high standard of component reliability was

[23] Sony licensed Western Electric's transistor patents in 1954 and subsequently created the first commercially successful transistor radio. Japanese firms, however, had only modest success at creating state-of-the-art product and process technology until the late 1970s.

[24] The market for the highest performance consumer electronics systems (with the exception of VCRs) is still internationally diversified, with United States and European companies playing important roles. The size of this market is, however, very small compared to that of the mass-market consumer-electronics products.

achieved, albeit at a more modest performance level than was being achieved by United States computer and industrial electronic producers.

In the case of consumer electronics, Japanese company's focus on price and reliability, combined with a high level of features and performance for that market, created major long-term growth opportunities. During the past twenty years the income elasticity of demand for consumer electronics has proven to be quite high, reflecting both a very broad consumer acceptance of consumer electronics items as household items in advanced economies and the consumer's increasingly sophisticated demands for performance and features in such items. In addition, product innovations in consumer electronics, such as calculators and digital watches, provided renewed opportunities for Japanese firms to "tune" the production of complex but inexpensive systems as well as coordinate the design of semiconductors to the particular needs of system products. In many cases, this has involved development of effective vertical and horizontal relationships among Japanese electronic companies. The rapid growth of these markets provided excellent opportunities for extending and refining manufacturing methods. What may originally have been a rational specialization to lower Japanese wage levels in electronic assembly operations has matured into a production system employing high levels of engineering skill and sophisticated components. These capabilities were most effective in mass-produced products where incremental advance rather than major innovative advance determined competitive dominance. In products characterized by smaller production runs, both in the relatively small markets for "high-end" consumer electronics and in the larger markets for computer and industrial electronics, the innovative capabilities of United States firms were effective through the mid 1970s.[25]

By the 1970s, it had become apparent to Japanese companies that incremental improvement in consumer electronics, alone, would be insufficient to carry semiconductor technology to a state-of-the-art position in other electronic system markets such as computers and telecommunications. To match United States technological capabilities in these industries, Japanese integrated circuit (IC) firms would require an infusion of basic and applied research. This conclusion was reached after Japanese firms reflected on United States success in computer markets and noted that the

---

[25] For example, Japanese firms have yet to be successful in international competition for hard-disk-drive markets. These markets have been characterized by rapid innovative advances by United States firms over a prolonged period. In the market for large-capacity drives used by mainframe computers, IBM and other United States firms have sustained a technological and manufacturing lead over Japanese firms for twenty years. For almost a decade, small United States firms have led the Japanese in producing medium-capacity drives for the personal computer market.

most successful firms were not only active IC buyers, but were also active in their own IC development or production activities.[26] This conclusion led Japanese firms and the Japanese government to organize several cooperative government–industry projects during the 1970s. These projects were nominally oriented toward specific end-use markets. The first, organized in 1975, involving telecommunications applications, initially focused on photolithography technology, the fundamental process technology that "draws" the pattern of the IC. The second, organized in 1976, focused on the development of a large number of processing and design technologies for the computer industry.[27] These projects were funded at relatively modest levels as government loans to be repaid from future industry profits. The largest was $100 million for four years, or about 1 percent of the value of Japanese semiconductor production in a four-year period at that time.

Here again, the issue is one of imitation since the centralized effort sought to imitate United States leads as well as making independent advances. Individuals were transferred into the projects by companies to absorb the new technology and returned to their companies to find substantial complementary development efforts under way. These programs successfully divided applied research from development, leaving companies to develop technologies in-house where each company could employ its own strategies for making small modifications and improvements. Both personnel transfer and specialization in applied research contributed to the incentive compatibility of the effort, since the returns from the project could be and were sought through the development efforts of individual companies.

The development efforts at each of the major IC companies were harnessed to the task of performance improvement and cost reduction as well as to sustaining the previous levels of components reliability. The principal IC market that Japanese companies chose to focus on was commodity production of random access memories (RAM). RAM ICs provided several important advantages that parallel Japanese experience in consumer electronics. They are standard commodities that do not require

---

[26] The largest United States IC firm is IBM, a fact that was influential in reaching this conclusion. Some United States computer firms have attained major market positions without an in-house manufacturing capability, but all have considerable expertise in the design of ICs.

[27] Daniel I. Okimoto, Takuo Sugano, and Franklin B. Weinstein (eds.), *Competitive Edge: The Semiconductor Industry in the US and Japan*, Stanford University Press, Stanford (CA), 1984, pp. 18–24. See W. Edward Steinmueller, "Industry Structure and Government Policies in the US and Japanese Integrated Circuit Industries," *Government Policy Towards Industry in the United States and Japan*, Cambridge University Press, Cambridge, 1987, on other government programs in both the United States and Japan.

the high level of engineering services support of products such as micropro-
cessors. They are mass-market products – the largest single class of IC
products. The reliability of these ICs is both very important and easily
monitored by users. And product price is the major factor affecting user
adoption of a particular product. With regard to cost reductions that could
support low prices, the economics of IC production have a central focus,
that is yield, or the proportion of workable devices emerging from
manufacturing.[28] High yields, achieved through conservative design
standards, but combined with attention to manufacturing process and
incremental refinement or tuning of technology, were key elements in
Japanese success in memory-market competition.[29] Japanese strength in
international competition for mass-produced RAM IC sales is now well
known.[30]

What is less well recognized is that process improvements associated with
mass-produced RAM have opened major new opportunities for Japanese
IC firms and their capital equipment suppliers to extend their previous
success in consumer electronics to other electronic products. Past American
success in ICs has been based on a rapid pace of innovation in both
manufacturing processes and products. In recent years, however, process
innovation has been replaced by incremental improvement of existing
process methods and technological advance in many of the major IC
markets has tilted toward product innovation. The key manufacturing
technologies underlying IC production, including lithography, which sets
the pattern of connections on the IC and device fabrication, which
determines transistor size and characteristics, are now relatively mature.
While major new innovations are expected to materialize from a wealth of
technological possibilities, the last decade of technological improvement in
IC manufacturing methods has been achieved primarily through the

---

[28] See W. Edward Steinmueller, "Microeconomics and Microelectronics: Economic Studies
of Integrated Circuit Technology," unpublished dissertation, Department of Economics,
Stanford University, Stanford (CA), 1987. Improvements in yield easily dominate any
conceivable cost reduction in other areas.

[29] American firms initially responded to this success by claiming that Japanese firms were
pricing below cost, and prevailed in dumping claims before the US International Trade
Commission. At the same time, most United States firms withdrew from the production of
RAM ICs. Currently, Japanese companies produce three-quarters of the world output of
the largest class of memory devices (dynamic RAMs) while the United States consumes one
half of world production. William J. McClean (ed.), *Status 1987: A Report on the Integrated
Circuit Industry*, Integrated Circuit Engineering Inc., Scottsdale (AZ), pp. 7–8.

[30] Higher Japanese manufacturing yields for memory ICs may be the major source of this
competitive advantage. See William F. Finan and Annette M. LaMond, "Sustaining U.S.
Competitiveness in Microelectronics: The Challenge to U.S. Policy," in Bruce R. Scott and
George C. Lodge (eds.), *U.S. Competitiveness in the World Economy*, Harvard Business
School Press, Boston (MA), 1985, pp. 144–175.

extension of existing techniques, through the development process that, we argue, is a particular strength of Japanese companies.[31]

According to the United States Commerce Department:

Since 1979, there has been a general change in the nature of technological innovation in the semiconductor manufacturing industry. All the important front-end processes presently in use (e.g., ion implantation, dry etching, step and repeat microlithography, E-beam mask generation) were developed by 1978. It was expected that new generations of microlithographic equipment (such as X-ray, direct write E-beam, focused ion beam) would become necessary as the level of chip integration increased and line widths shrank. However, refinements of the existing visible and ultraviolet lithography have extended the capabilities of this type of equipment to the point that it will continue to be used for production into the foreseeable future. The same is true even for contact and proximity photoaligners. More advanced lithographic techniques are, and will continue to be, used primarily for research and development and, in a limited way, for customized production of ICs. This shift in the nature of technological change from generational to incremental has had the effect of slowing down the pace of technological advancement allowing the Japanese to close the gap. US equipment-makers now find themselves in a situation where the rate at which they can extend the technological frontier is drastically reduced, greatly simplifying the efforts by the Japanese to overtake the technological leaders.[32]

Technological leadership in the IC industry once required innovative leadership in both product and process technology. If the Commerce Department is correct in its conclusion that both the United States and Japan will have comparable abilities at process innovation, technological leadership will, in the future, be based solely upon product innovation. Moreover, continued American leadership in IC technology that depends exclusively on product innovation without a corresponding rapid rate of innovation in process technology is untested. Therefore, there is a significant basis for concern over future United States IC industry prospects and the United States electronics industry as a whole, to the extent that the IC industry contributes to the general health of United States electronics production through close ties between IC and equipment producers.[33]

Japanese efforts at incremental improvements of consumer electronics

---

[31] For an overview of these new technologies and the significant leads that Japanese companies have in many of them, see National Research Council, *Advanced Processing of Electronic Material in the United States and Japan*, National Academy Press, Washington (DC), 1986.

[32] US Department of Commerce, International Trade Administration, *A Competitive Assessment of the US Semiconductor Manufacturing Industry*, US Department of Commerce, Washington (DC), March 1985, p. 60.

[33] There are significant prospects for revitalization of United States IC manufacturing technology through cooperative industry initiatives and restructuring of the industry. See W. Edward Steinmueller, *Government Policy Towards Industry*.

products have provided unexpected benefits to Japanese IC firms in a completely different fashion than the "catch up" effort. Among the many process technologies developed at one time or another in the United States, complementary metal oxide semiconductor (CMOS) technology has had a particularly close relationship to consumer electronics. Among other advantages, the low power requirements of CMOS are essential for battery-operated systems. While United States firms were pursuing product innovations based on other processes, Japanese firms continued the incremental improvement and "tuning" of production methods for CMOS technology. As it has turned out, CMOS is the most promising technology at present for attaining higher IC component densities and greater complexity. CMOS currently accounts for a dominant share of the total worldwide sales of ICs, and is a major source of United States-Japanese joint ventures. The prior experience of Japanese firms in this area, stemming from the sustained development of the technology for consumer applications, has proven to be advantageous. Here the success in consumer electronics developments, sometimes dismissed by United States firms as "second-tier" technology, has turned out to be an important source of competitive advantage. The knowledge necessary for subsequent developments is never gained once and for all; rather, incremental improvement can overtake discontinuous product innovation.[34]

Japanese electronics firms have also exploited the organizational features we previously identified as important.[35] A close relationship between component and final product design has made it possible for Japanese electronics firms to sustain their competitive advantage in electronic-system products in the face of growing competition from other Pacific Rim countries where lower wages and increasing skill levels might provide an opportunity for replicating the early history of Japanese electronics industry growth. The main vehicles for sustaining this advantage are recent major innovations including compact disks, video disks, digital audio recording, and digital television.[36] Building markets in each of these technologies requires inexpensive components and a tight coordination between component and product design, often involving coordination between IC suppliers and users. These same links have been important in

---

[34] W. Edward Steinmueller, "International Joint Ventures in the Integrated Circuit Industry," *International Collaborative Ventures in US Manufacturing*, ed. David Mowery, American Enterprise Institute, Ballinger Publishing, Cambrige (MA), 1988, pp. 111–146.

[35] In the case of the Japanese IC industry, these organizational features are further augmented by the higher degree of vertical integration of Japanese IC producers. See W. Edward Steinmueller, "Industry Structure.".

[36] For an account of how one American company failed to meet the development challenge for video disks see Margaret B.W. Graham, *RCA and the VideoDisc: The Business of Research*, Cambridge University Press, Cambridge, 1986.

the development of computer peripherals such as impact and laser printers. In the case of laser printers, Canon's adaptation of plain-paper-copier technology into a printer technology has been central to the growth of an entire new market segment of the personal computer industry, the desk-top publishing industry.

The electronics industry is not the only example of the efficacy of small improvements in establishing competitive dominance or the technological vitality of sustained efforts to extend well-established technologies. Close communication links between suppliers and users play a role at the inter-firm level that is analogous to our emphasis on effective communication links among functional specialists at the intra-firm level. Recent detailed studies of the organization of parts purchases in the Japanese automobile industry by Asanuma demonstrate the existence of long-term relationships with important institutional mechanisms for coordinating design and assuring timely supply.[37] Aoki cites an (unnamed) major auto manufac-turer as having 122 stable "first-tier" suppliers.[38] More importantly, Aoki characterizes these relationships as "quasi-permanent," noting that between 1973 and 1984 only three firms exited from this relationship while twenty-one firms entered. The consequences of such stable supplier rela-tionships are that development efforts can be jointly initiated and pressed forward, further extending the coordination of product design and manu-facturing beyond the level of the individual firms as well as improving the flow of information for making modifications and improvements in the manufacturing process.

We draw an ironic conclusion from our examination of American and Japanese technological skills. The Japanese have indeed been excellent imitators. But instead of flourishing a trump card stating that Americans are excellent *innovators*, Americans may need to fix their attention on the disconcerting prospect that innovative skills count for a great deal less than was once thought – unless they can learn to become better imitators themselves.

---

[37] Banri Asanuma, "The Organization of Parts Purchases in the Japanese Automotive Industry" and "The Contractual Framework for Parts Supply in the Japanese Automotive Industry," *Japanese Economic Studies*, 13 (4), Summer 1985, pp. 32–78.

[38] Masahiko Aoki, *Information, Incentives, and Bargaining in the Japanese Economy*, Cambridge University Press, Cambridge, 1988, p. 335.

8 Critical issues in science policy research

Everyone knows that the linear model of innovation is dead. That model represented the innovation process as one in which technological change was closely dependent upon, and generated by, prior scientific research. It was a model that, however flattering it may have been to the scientist and the academic, was economically naive and simplistic in the extreme. It has been accorded numerous decent burials, and I do not intend to resurrect it only to arrange for it to be interred once again.

However, in a world in which the economic role of science may reasonably be expected to grow over time, and in which policy-making will need to be based on a more sophisticated understanding of the ways in which science and technology interact and influence one another, a better road-map of the science/technology landscape is vitally necessary. I will therefore not be primarily examining the determinants of innovation. Rather, my main focus will be on some of the ways in which the two communities, of scientists and technologists, exercise influences on one another.

Obviously, while my central focus will not be on the determinants of innovation, what I say will, I hope, be highly relevant to that question. Indeed, I regard it as central to a more useful framework for analyzing the innovation process that it should be based on a more sharply delineated road-map of science/technology relationships. That road-map ought, at a minimum, to identify the most influential traffic flows between science and technology. Obviously, such a map cannot at present be drawn.

Consequently, this chapter offers no more than the preliminary findings of a reconnaissance expedition, identifying some of the most significant

This chapter first appeared in *Science and Public Policy*, 1991, volume 18, no. 6, pp. 335–346. It is reprinted with omissions. The paper was first presented at the celebration of the twenty-fifth anniversary of the Science Policy Research Unit, University of Sussex, in July 1991. The author has incurred substantial intellectual debts, in the preparation of this chapter, to Harvey Brooks, Ralph Landau, David Mowery, Richard Nelson, and Ed Steinmueller.

features of the landscape – including some rather intriguing features that have been surprisingly neglected – rather than providing a detailed map. But perhaps that will be sufficient to identify some of the major locations where research is most urgently called for. If it is successful in this, it will have achieved its major purpose of providing, in the time-honored academic locution, "a guide to further research."

It is, of course, a matter of definition that science/technology interactions are most significant in the so-called high-technology industries. But it must be recognized, to begin with, that there still remain crucial portions of high-technology industries where attempts to advance the technological frontier are painstakingly slow and expensive, because of the limited guidance that science is capable of providing.

The development of new alloys with specific combinations of properties proceeds very slowly because there is still no good theoretical basis for predicting the behavior of new combinations of materials, although materials science may now be getting closer to the point of developing models with predictive powers. Many problems connected with improved fuel efficiency are severely constrained by the limited scientific understanding of something as basic as the nature of the combustion process. The development of synthetic fuels has been seriously hampered in recent years by scientific ignorance of the relationship of the molecular structure of coal (which is known) to its physical and chemical properties.

The requirements of computer architecture remain badly in need of an improved scientific underpinning. The design of aircraft and steam turbines are both hampered by the lack of a good theory of turbulence. In the case of aircraft, wind-tunnel tests are still subject to substantial margins of error in terms of predicting the actual flight performance of a new prototype. Some of the functions of wind-tunnel testing in generating data for aircraft design have been taken over in recent years by computer simulation techniques, but by no means all of them.

It is noteworthy that the rapid growth in development costs in industrial economies shows no sign of subsiding. The extremely high development costs that prevail in most of the high-technology industries, and their rapid growth, are due to the inability to draw more heavily on a predictive model in determining the performance of specific new designs or materials.

More precisely, the true desideratum is a good predictive model that will lead to a reduction in the cost of determining optimal design. It needs to be a computationally simplifying model, which is not always the case. One can learn a great deal about reaction mechanism in the computational chemistry if one has unlimited access to a Cray computer, but Cray computers are extremely expensive.

If science provided a cheaper predictive basis for moving to optimal design configurations, development costs, which constitute about two-thirds of total R&D expenditures in the United States, wouldn't be nearly so high. They are as high as they are because engineers and product designers continue to need to engage in very extensive testing activities before they can be sufficiently confident in the performance characteristics of a new product.

On the other hand, although there continue to be sharp limits on the extent to which technology can draw on science, it is far less appreciated that scientific progress has become increasingly dependent on technology. Indeed, it is tempting to say that an alternative definition of a high-technology industry is one in which problems that arise at the technological frontier exercise a major role in shaping the research agenda of science. In these industries, it is not enough to say that scientific knowledge is *applied* to the productive process; rather, to a considerable extent, such knowledge is also being *generated* there.

An important source of scientific progress, in advanced industrial societies, has derived from the attempt to deal with difficulties, unexpected problems, or anomalous observations that first arose in connection with new product designs or novel productive processes. Additionally, the industrial context has identified highly specific areas of research in which some expansion of knowledge would make possible a significant improvement in quality or in the performance characteristics of a material.

In the course of the twentieth century, that additional knowledge has been produced to an increasing degree by scientists employed inside industrial research labs of high-tech firms. This has not been just some stroke of good fortune or act of a benign Providence. Scientists in industry are inevitably confronted with specific observations or difficulties that are extremely unlikely to present themselves in a university laboratory: premature corrosion of an underwater cable, unidentifiable sources of interference in electromagnetic communications systems, or extreme heat generated on the surface of an aircraft as it attains supersonic speeds.

The fact is that industrial activity, especially, but not only, in high-tech sectors, provides unique observational platforms from which to observe unusual classes of natural phenomena. In this respect, the industrial research laboratory may be said to have powerfully strengthened the feedback loop running from the world of economic activity back to the scientific community.[1]

It must be added that observations are sometimes made in an industrial

---

[1] See "How Exogenous is Science?", chapter 7 in Nathan Rosenberg, *Inside the Black Box*, Cambridge University Press, Cambridge 1982, and Stephen J. Kline and Nathan Rosenberg, "An Overview of Innovation," in Ralph Landau and Nathan Rosenberg (eds.), *The Positive Sum Strategy*, National Academy Press, Washington (DC), 1986.

context by people who are not capable of appreciating their potential significance, or who are simply uninterested in observations that have no immediate practical relevance. In 1883 Edison observed the flow of electricity across a gap, inside a vacuum, from a hot filament to a metal wire. Since he saw no practical application, he merely described the phenomenon in his notebook and went on to other matters of greater potential utility in his effort to enhance the performance of the electric light bulb.

Edison was of course observing a flow of electrons, and the observation has since come to be referred to as the Edison Effect. Had he been a patient scientist and less preoccupied with matters of short-run utility, he might later have shared a Nobel Prize with Owen Richardson who analyzed the behavior of electrons when heated in a vacuum, or conceivably even with J.J. Thomson for the initial discovery of the electron.

Edison's inventive contributions were so great that it would be rank ingratitude for later generations to chastise him for his "practical" orientation! But, ironically enough, the Edison Effect, together with other scientific discoveries, eventually had immensely important practical consequences through the development of the vacuum tube and the vast technology that was later associated with the emergence of modern electronics. However, perhaps it was not ironical after all. When one speaks of someone as being "practical," what is usually meant is that he or she is interested in matters of short-run utility only. Science is, surely, a very practical activity but, typically, only in the long run.

Impact of science on technology

These considerations suggest an important avenue through which the technological realm has shaped the research agenda, and therefore the eventual findings, of portions of the scientific community. In considering the flow of traffic in the opposite, and more "traditional" direction – the impact of science on technology – it is useful to make two separate observations.

First, where scientific findings have indeed profoundly influenced technological activities, these findings need not be derived from recent research at the scientific frontier. Indeed, many points of contention and dispute over the economic importance of science really derive from the fact that the science that was essential to some technological breakthrough was simply "old" science. Often this science was so old that it was no longer considered by some to be science.

The problem is compounded by the fact that many spokesmen for the economic importance of science are anxious to make a case for larger research budgets. In order to strengthen the case it helps considerably to emphasize the benefits that may be derived from what goes on at the research frontier, rather than the continuing contribution of, say, nineteenth-century analytical chemistry to the mining industry, or the economic contribution made by "old" science through the current education of engineers.[2]

The fact is that technology draws on scientific knowledge and methodology in highly unpredictable ways – and we are likely to cover up our ignorance by invoking such shameless tautologies as "When the time is ripe." The body of knowledge that is called "science" consists of an immense pool to which small annual increments are made at the "frontier." The true significance of science is diminished, rather than enhanced, by extreme emphasis on the importance of the most recent "increment" to that pool.

The lags may be very long indeed, often because much essential complementary technology needs to be developed before it can be said that "the time is ripe" for some major invention. Consequently, the perspective of the economist or the policy-maker needs to be distinctly different from that of the historian of science or, for that matter, of contemporary advocates of larger science budgets in the public sector.

Consider the laser. The first lasers were developed around 1960, since when they have expanded into a remarkably diverse range of uses, including the printer that produced the manuscript of this chapter. But, from the point of view of the historian of science, it could be argued that the basic science underlying the laser was formulated by Einstein as long ago as 1916.[3] A historian of science might say that everything of real interest had been completed by 1916, and the rest was "just" engineering and product development. At the same time, what is relatively uninteresting to her may be the most essential part of the story from the point of view of the technological innovation.

Amid this specialization of interests, it is essential to retain the point that there may be lags of many decades between a given increment to science and

[2] On the significance of old science, see Nathan Rosenberg, "The Commercialization of Science in American Industry," in Kim B. Clark, Robert H. Hayes, and Christopher Lorenz (eds.), *The Uneasy Alliance: Managing the Productivity-Technology Dilemma*, Harvard Business School Press, Boston (MA), 1985.

[3] "The underlying science involves an understanding of the energy levels of molecules and solids, and the specific principle was that described by Einstein in his 1916 work on stimulated emission. Much of the technology necessary for the laser emerged only during the Second World War from work on microwave radar – including magnetrons and klystron sources, semiconductor detectors, and wave-guiding networks." John R. Whinnery, "Interactions between the Science and Technology of Lasers," in Jesse H. Ausubel and J. Dale Langford (eds.), *Lasers: Invention to Application*, National Academy Press, Washington (DC), 1987, p. 124.

the useful application that may one day flow from it. This is one important reason (but only one) why the commercial benefits of basic research need not be captured by firms in the country where the basic research was performed. Perhaps equally important and equally neglected, the development of sophisticated, high-performance technologies, such as lasers and other complex electronics instrumentation, has generated much new basic research that was recognized as essential to the further improvement of the new technologies.[4]

The second major source of disjunction between an advance in science and its eventual influence on technology and the economy has received little attention. The problem is that, even when scientific research opens up an entirely new field of technological possibilities, it is usually a multi-stage process. The reason is that it is not ordinarily possible to proceed directly from new scientific knowledge into production, even when that new knowledge is actually of a specific final product, as opposed to the discovery of some new piece of information about the natural universe that may serve as an "input" into the eventual development of a new product.

In fact, the emergence of the two disciplines of electrical and chemical engineering, beginning in the late nineteenth-century, occurred for precisely this reason. It was not possible to move directly from the enlarged experimental and theoretical understanding of the electromagnetic and synthetic organic chemical realms into the production of goods that incorporated such new knowledge.

The reason was simple. The appropriate technologies could in no way be derived from or deduced from the scientific knowledge. On the contrary, distinctly different bodies of knowledge had to be drawn upon or generated before production could begin. Sometimes, this required the development of entirely new disciplines.

Consider the synthetic dye industry that was launched by Perkin's (accidental) synthesis of mauve, the first of the synthetic aniline dyes, in 1856. The subsequent growth of the synthetic organic chemicals industry did not occur immediately after this dramatic laboratory breakthrough. So long as dyestuffs could be produced only be enlarging the physical dimensions of the original laboratory apparatus, the industry was destined to remain a small-scale batch operation of little industrial consequence.[5]

Difficulties of transfer

The essential point is that the design and construction of plants devoted to large-scale chemical processing activities involves an entirely different set of

---

[4] See Harvey Brooks, "Physics and the Polity," *Science* (26 April 1968).
[5] See W.K. Lewis, "Chemical Engineering – A New Science." in Lenox R. Lohr (ed.), *Centennial of Engineering, 1852–1952*, Museum of Science and Industry, Chicago, 1953 p. 697.

activities and capabilities than those that generated the new chemical entities. To begin with, the problems of mixing, heating, and contaminant control, which can be carried out with great precision in the laboratory, are immensely more difficult to handle in large-scale operations, especially if high degrees of precision are required. Moreover, economic considerations play a much larger role in the design process, since cost considerations come to play a decisive role in an industrial context.

Thus, the discovery of a new chemical entity has commonly posed an entirely new question, one that is remote from the scientific context of the laboratory: how does one go about producing it? A chemical process plant is far from a scaled-up version of the original laboratory equipment. Experimental equipment may have been made of glass or porcelain. A manufacturing plant will almost certainly have to be constructed of different materials.

Moreover, efficient manufacturing is, inherently, something very different from a simple, multiple enlargement of small-scale experimental equipment. This is what accounts for the unique importance of the pilot plant, which may be thought of as a device for translating the findings of laboratory research into a technically feasible and economically efficient production process.[6] The translation, however, requires a kind of expertise that need not exist at the experimental research level: a knowledge of mechanical engineering and a careful attention to the underlying economics of the engineering alternatives.

Pilot plants have in the past been essential, and not only for the purpose of the reduction of uncertainties with respect to scale. Until a pilot plant was built, the precise characteristics of the output could not be determined. Test marketing could not proceed without the availability of reliable samples. Other essential features of the production process could not possibly be derived from scientific knowledge alone.

Consider the recycle problem. Very few chemical reactions are complete in the reaction stage. Therefore products of the reaction stage will not only

---

[6] "Often, in dealing with a complicated practical situation, the engineer arbitrarily reduces the number of variables in his theory by combining them into dimensionless groups, of which a well-known example is the Reynolds number characterizing the flow of fluid through a pipe. Such dimensionless groups are evaluated in the laboratory, and are used then for predicting the behavior in a large-scale chemical plant. But this procedure reduces somewhat our confidence in our predictions; though the group as a whole may have varied widely in the laboratory experiments, one or more of the variables within the group may have been virtually unchanged. Because of this reduced confidence in using dimensionless groups in scaling-up predictions, the chemical engineer usually builds a pilot plant, intermediate in size between the laboratory system and the proposed full-scale production plant, so that he can check whether the scaling-up predictions of his simplified theory are working sufficiently accurately." John T. Davies, "Chemical Engineering: How Did it Begin and Develop?" in William F. Furter (editor), *History of Chemical Engineering*, American Chemical Society, 1980, pp. 40–41.

include desired end products but also intermediates, unreacted feed, and trace impurities – some measurable and some unmeasurable.

Impurities, in particular, are identified by the operation of the pilot plant and methods of removing them devised to achieve a steady-state condition on a continuing basis.[7]

In the twentieth century, a gap of several years has separated the discovery under laboratory conditions of many of the most important new materials from the industrial capability to manufacture them on a commercial basis. For instance the first polymers that W.H. Carothers had produced with his glass equipment at the Du Pont Laboratories; and polyethylene and terephthalic acid, an essential material in the production of terylene, a major synthetic fibre.[8]

Eventually, to manage the transition from test tubes to manufacture, where output has to be measured in tons rather than ounces, an entirely new methodology, totally distinct from the science of chemistry, had to be devised. This new methodology involved exploiting the central concept of unit operations. This term, coined by Arthur D. Little at MIT in 1915, provided the essential basis for a rigorous, quantitative approach to large-scale chemical manufacturing, and thus may be taken to mark the emergence of chemical engineering as a unique discipline, not reducible to "applied chemistry."[9]

Moving from scientific breakthroughs to technologies ready for commercialization is a highly complex, inherently interdisciplinary subject that is far from well understood and far from adequately studied. Again in the realm of chemicals, the work of Staudinger and Mark in the 1920s on polymerization provided an excellent scientific basis for the development of polyester fibres. But the commercial introduction of such fibres required the use of a new raw material – paraxylene – which was not, at the time, an

---

[7] In recent years, computers have begun to displace the reliance on expensive and time-consuming pilot plants. In the hands of experienced designers, micropilot plant data, combined with good analytical equipment, may yield workable commercial designs.

[8] It is important to note that progress in the subdiscipline of polymer chemistry has been primarily an achievement of research in industrial laboratories.

[9] In Little's words: "Any chemical process, on whatever scale conducted, may be resolved into a coordinated series of what may be termed 'unit actions,' as pulverizing, mixing, heating, roasting, absorbing, condensing, lixivating, precipitating, crystallizing, filtering, dissolving, electrolyzing and so on. The number of these basic unit operations is not very large and relatively few of them are involved in any particular process ... Chemical engineering research ... is directed toward the improvement, control and better coordination of these unit operations and the selection or development of the equipment in which they are carried out. It is obviously concerned with the testing and the provision of materials of construction which shall function safely, resist corrosion, and withstand the indicated conditions of temperature and pressure. Its ultimate objective is so to provide and organize the means for conducting a chemical process that the plant shall operate safely, efficiently, and profitably." Arthur D. Little, *Twenty-five Years of Chemical Engineering Progress*, Silver Anniversary volume, American Institute of Chemical Engineers, D. Van Nostrand Company, New York, 1933, pp. 7–8.

article of commerce. It also required a new way of cheaply converting paraxylene to terephthalic acid, since the use of nitric acid was both too expensive and too messy – it produced an unacceptably impure product.

Eventual success in this major breakthrough not only took many years but owed little, if anything, to further scientific research. Here, as elsewhere, scientific breakthroughs are, at best, only the first step in a very long sequence of knowledge accumulation, if we think in terms of an economic perspective rather than that of the historian of science.

Consider the present-day world-wide search for products in which to embody the recently acquired knowledge of high-temperature superconductivity. The world may still be decades away from the large-scale commercial exploitation of this knowledge, just as the great breakthroughs in molecular biology of the 1950s are only now beginning to find an embodiment in the products of an emerging biotechnology industry.

Interdisciplinary research

The complexity of the science – technology interface, and especially the two-way movement of traffic across that interface, clearly calls for some new institutional responses. Decision-makers in both the public and private sectors will need to address the question of how to improve the organizational conditions and incentive structures at the science-technology interfaces. The ability to improve the functioning of various specialists at that interface will undoubtedly be an important determinant of future leadership in high-technology industries. This is so not only for the reasons that have already been suggested, but also because important changes appear to be occurring on the science side of the interface as well as on the technology side.

In particular, there is much evidence that scientific knowledge of a kind that is most likely to be useful in high-technology industries has to be pursued in an increasingly interdisciplinary fashion. Consider the realm of medicine, a truly high-technology industry, as can be readily verified by a quick walk through the intensive care unit of any major teaching hospital. In recent years, medical science has benefitted immensely, not only from such "nearby" disciplines as biology, genetics, and chemistry, but from nuclear physics (especially in diagnostic technologies such as magnetic resonance imaging, radioactive tracers, and radioimmunoassays), electronics, and materials science and engineering. Lasers are now a frequent instrument of choice in extremely delicate surgery, and the availability of fibre-optic technology has made possible the direct visualization of internal organs – as in the esophagoscope, the flexible sigmoidoscope, and the bronchoscope.

An interesting index of the growing importance of electronics in medicine is exhibited by Sony Medical Electronics, a recently established division of the giant consumer electronics company. This company is now promoting such new products as remote surgical consultation systems and cardiac recording systems. Other Japanese consumer-electronics companies are in earlier stages of a similar transition into medical applications.[10]

In pharmaceuticals, there have been remarkable advances drawing upon findings in such fields as biochemistry, molecular and cell biology, immunology, neurobiology, and scientific instrumentation. These advances are creating a situation in which new pharmaceutical compounds, with specific properties, can be targeted and perhaps eventually designed, in contrast with the randomized, exhaustive, and expensive screening methods that have characterized pharmaceutical research in the past.[11] The essential point is that the newly emerging pattern of innovation is, by its very nature, increasingly interdisciplinary. That is to say, success requires close cooperation among a growing number of specialists.

In other fields, some of the most fundamental innovations of the postwar world have been the product of interdisciplinary research. The transistor was the result of the combined efforts of physicists, chemists, and metallurgists. Optical-fibre light guides, now transforming the telecommunications industry, were essentially the product of these same three disciplines. Moreover, materials science has now emerged as an independent discipline, representing "a fusion of metallurgy, chemistry, and ceramics engineering with aspects of condensed-matter physics."[12]

The scientific breakthrough leading to the discovery of DNA was the work of chemists, physicists, biologists, biochemists and, far from the least, crystallographers. In agriculture, more productive seed varieties, such as the high-yielding rice varieties developed at the International Rice Research Institute in the Philippines, were the work of geneticists, botanists, biochemists, entomologists, and soil agronomists. These new varieties have totally transformed the food supply situation of Asia in the past twenty-five years.

In some cases, the continuing interdisciplinary nature of technological progress has been underlined by quite unexpected shifts in the bodies of scientific knowledge upon which progress has sometimes depended. The transition from the transistor to the integrated circuit brought with it a shift from essentially mechanical and metallurgical techniques of fabrication to chemical techniques. The increasing dependence of semiconductors on

---

[10] *Wall Street Journal*, 20 May 1991.
[11] See Alfonso Gambardella, "Science and Innovation in the U.S. Pharmaceutical Industry during the 1980s," Stanford University doctoral dissertation, 1991.
[12] *Scientific Interfaces and Technological Applications*, Physics Through the 1990s, National Academy Press, Washington (DC), 1986, page 6. See also chapter 4.

metallurgical inputs has played a major role in elevating metallurgy to what is now called "materials science."

More recently, the continued shrinkage in the size of electronic devices has led to a situation where further technological progress may eventually involve thinking in entirely different terms. Specifically, the unit of analysis for further progress in miniaturization may no longer be solid materials, but, perhaps, chains of molecules. If such a transition were to take place, the required knowledge base would no longer be the kind in which electronic engineers have been trained. It would become, rather, theoretical chemistry.

Institutional implications

Such a drastic shift in the underlying body of scientific knowledge, on which a technology is based, is not uncommon, and continued commercial viability may turn on the ease, or difficulty, that firms experience in making such a transition. Consider the shift in electronics from vacuum tubes to solid-state transistors to integrated circuits, or from propeller-driven aircraft engines to jet engines. The possibilities opened up by such shifts, and the potential difficulties of failing to make such transitions when a firm is suddenly "blindsided" by an unexpected shift, is an important reason for maintaining a substantial in-house scientific capability. Indeed, it may be a reason for maintaining a portfolio of research capabilities in a range of scientific disciplines. Unfortunately, only a relatively small number of firms have the resources for maintaining such a portfolio.

The increasing importance of interdisciplinary research has created serious organizational problems. Such research often runs counter to the traditional arrangements, training, priorities, and incentive structures of the scientific professions, particularly in the academic world where great emphasis is placed on working within well-recognized disciplinary, and therefore departmental, boundary lines.

The American university system in the past forty years or so has been very successful in combining the performance of basic research at the scientific frontiers with the training of future professionals. Nevertheless, the present organizational structure of American universities along disciplinary lines, as reflected in its departmental structures, poses some serious limitations as the solutions to research problems become increasingly interdisciplinary in nature.

Another major strength of the American university system has been the highly successful interface that it has developed with the industrial world. This relationship has not been without its problems and dangers. Industrial financing of university research runs the danger that universities will increasingly have their research agendas set by their external sources of finance. In so doing, there is the threat that they will compromise their autonomy, focus on short-term problems of immediate interest to industry, and thereby suffer a loss of effectiveness as leaders in fundamental research.

Perhaps even more serious is the possibility that the potentially great commercial value of scientific findings will lead to a loss of free and frank communication among university faculty members, and a reluctance to disclose research findings from which other faculty members or students might derive great benefit. Such developments could prove to be harmful to future progress in the realms of both science and technology, as well as to education itself.

Nevertheless, as is usually the case, there has been another side of the coin. Scientific autonomy is always subject to the potential pressures of its funding sources. Federal funding of research since the Second World War, which has been far greater than industrial funding, has given an immense prominence to the needs and the priorities of the military and to its notorious penchant for secrecy. But, at the same time, Department of Defense funding has played a highly creative role in the emergence of new specializations of great importance to high-technology industries, such as computer science and materials science.

Moreover, although I say this with some sense of trepidation to an academic audience, it is possible for the notion of autonomy to be carried to extreme lengths. The dominant role of the academic department in American universities has been, in some respects, excessive. It has, in particular, been very slow to provide professional career opportunities to those who have identified research problems at the edges, or interstices, of traditional academic disciplines. Indeed, it is highly significant that there is no research institution in the United States comparable to the Science Policy Research Unit in its commitment to interdisciplinary research at the intersection between science, technology, and economics.

Perhaps it should be added that there is nothing uniquely rigid about the department structure of American universities. Departmental rigidity is probably the inevitable price to be paid for the fact that, historically, scientific progress has required a high degree of disciplinary specialization. It is therefore, a widespread phenomenon. It is doubtful, for example, whether the department structures in German or Japanese universities are any less rigid. In fact, it may be suggested that the slow pace of German entry into the realm of biotechnology owed much to the inflexible role of German university departments.

The important role attached to the department as a unit of intellectual organization has not prevented the American higher educational system from being remarkably adaptive and responsive to changing social needs in general, and the changing requirements of business and industry in particular. Indeed, it has long been a recurrent criticism of European visitors, especially from Britain, that American colleges and universities have been excessively responsive to the changing dictates of the market-place and to vocational needs of all sorts.

Financial support

The determination to improve the links between the academic and indus-trial worlds has already led to a great deal of institutional innovation at many research universities. And, as is often the case, it has been the availability of new monies from external sources, and the associated possibilities for new hiring, that has generated a willingness to enlarge the traditional, single-discipline focus, and to contemplate new institutional arrangements. Earlier in the twentieth century the availability of funds from private philanthropies, such as the Carnegie and Rockefeller Founda-tions and the Guggenheim Fund, served as powerful and highly creative catalysts for intellectual and institutional innovation. It is fair to say that the financial stringency of recent years has rendered the American academic community more responsive to the introduction of new interdisciplinary arrangements.

The Center for Integrated Systems at Stanford is an interesting example of university-based research with industrial financing. The Center receives financial support from twenty corporations, and it is devoted primarily to developing methods for designing and manufacturing large-scale inte-grated microelectronic circuits. Its research activities draw heavily on computer science, integrated circuit engineering, solid-state physics, as well as other disciplines.

MIT has a Whitehead Institute, with a huge private endowment, which is devoted to biomedical research, as well as a ten-year contract with Exxon Research and Engineering Company to support research in the field of combustion. West Germany's huge chemical and pharmaceutical com-pany, Hoechst AG, has given the Massachusetts General Hospital, a teaching arm of the Harvard Medical School, $50 million for the support of basic research in the area of molecular biology.

At the federal level, the National Science Foundation has been instru-mental in establishing Engineering Research Centers at a number of major universities. These represent important institutional departures of a multi-disciplinary nature, typically involving a strong underlying emphasis on computers and specialized engineering skills working in close liaison with the rather more traditional scientific disciplines of physics, chemistry, and biology.

Columbia University has a center for telecommunications, Harvard University for the application of advanced computers to the design of communications systems, MIT for the improvement of manufacturing processes in the biotechnology industry, and Purdue University for research on highly automated manufacturing systems. The centers represent significant multi-disciplinary innovations. It is too early to appraise their overall effectiveness, although it may be noted that there have already been failures as well as successes.

Private industry

In some important respects, private industry in the United States has, in the past at least, had a substantial advantage over universities in the organization of multi-disciplinary research. It has not attached nearly the same significance to the rigid, disciplinary boundary lines that have loomed so large in the academic world.

It has proven easier to bring people from different disciplines together in an industrial environment where research is not organized by discipline but by problems, and where there has been a very different set of incentives and criteria by which the contributions of scientists are evaluated. In the best American industrial laboratories, unlike the universities, a high value and considerable recognition are likely to go to individuals who are useful in solving the problems encountered by colleagues in fields other than their own. The most successful American research laboratories in private industry have demonstrated that it is possible to perform research of both a fundamental and an inter-disciplinary nature in a commercial, "mission-oriented" context. The most successful appear to have been those that have managed to create close interactions, and exchanges of information, between those responsible for performing the research, on the one hand, and those responsible for the management of production and marketing, on the other. But it is far from clear exactly how this has been accomplished, and precisely what organizational, managerial, and incentive factors have differentiated successful from unsuccessful firms. The subject is one that deserves a high research priority.

One point worth emphasizing is that the firms with the most outstanding industrial laboratories – Bell Labs., IBM, General Electric, duPont, Eastman Kodak – have developed excellent interfaces with university-based research precisely because they are known to be involved in basic research of high quality. University scientists believe that they have much to learn from industrial scientists from such laboratories. Since the flow of knowledge, in these cases, is widely understood to move in both directions, industrial scientists from distinguished laboratories are likely to be enthusiastically received on university campuses, while university scientists welcome the opportunity to observe or even to become directly involved, as consultants, in industrial research.

A related comment about the Japanese scene may be appropriate at this juncture. It has been a common practice to point to the low level of commitment of Japanese universities to scientific research as a serious weakness, and as a potential threat to the prospects for continued expansion of Japanese technological capabilities. Certainly, Japanese universities represent a weak link within the Japanese science and technology systems.

Nevertheless, the concentration of scientific research in Japanese private industry has certain positive, or at least redeeming aspects. These include the problem orientation that comes so naturally in the industrial context, and the consequent weakness of the barriers to interdisciplinary research that can loom so large in the academic world. Equally important, perhaps, is the ease with which knowledge can be transmitted between the potential "producers" of new knowledge and those responsible for its eventual industrial application, and it cannot be emphasized too strongly that knowledge is readily transmitted in *both* directions.

This industrial context is not ideal for the pursuit of long-term basic research. But basic research is not always "the name of the game." The Japanese firm may be well-suited for producing and utilizing precisely the kind of new knowledge that is most directly relevant to providing improved industrial performance.[13]

Transfer between specialties

A further, significant category of science/technology interactions is closely related to the multi-disciplinary issues that have already been discussed, but nevertheless is sufficiently distinctive to warrant separate recognition. To put it in the most general terms, an important determinant of both the rate and direction of scientific progress in recent decades has involved the actual transfer of concepts, methodologies, or instrumentation from one scientific discipline, or specialty, to another.

In some cases the scale of these transfers has assumed almost the appearance of an invasion of one discipline by another (perhaps "migration" is a better term, since the transfer has often involved the permanent movement of scientists from one discipline to another). The field of chemistry has for a long time benefitted immensely from the work of physicists, whose interests in the fundamental nature of matter have

[13] See Masahiko Aoki and Nathan Rosenberg, "The Japanese Firm as an Innovating Institution," in T. Shiraishi and S. Tsuru (eds.), *Economic Institutions in a Dynamic Society: Search for a New Frontier*, Macmillan, London, 1989.

provided a natural intersection of common concerns between physics and chemistry. In the last couple of decades, the benefits to chemistry from such transfers from outside have increased considerably, in part as a result of the availability of new techniques of instrumentation. The primary instrument, of course, has been the computer.

In addition, both analytical and synthetic chemistry have experienced transformations in the very nature of their research as a result of new approaches based on the contributions of physicists, mathematicians, statisticians, laser experts, materials specialists, and a formidable arsenal of new computer-controlled instruments. One result, to which I have already referred, is the increasing capability for "designing" new pharmaceuticals instead of achieving them through crude empirical testing or experimentation.

The creative significance of these transfers to chemistry received broad recognition when the 1985 Nobel Prize in Chemistry was awarded to Herbert Hauptman (mathematician) and Jerome Karle (chemist). They were the developers of sophisticated mathematical techniques that made it possible to deduce the three-dimensional structure of natural substances from observations based on X-ray crystallography. The feasibility of their mathematical technique was, in turn, vastly improved by the availability of the computer:

They developed ways of actually calculating structure by analyzing the intensity of the points visible as dots in the X-ray pictures and calculating the "phase" of the atoms in the structures. In this context, phase is an angular measurement that can vary from zero to 360 degrees. The advent of powerful modern computers has made it possible to use the two scientists' mathematical formulations on intensity and phase to determine quickly the three-dimensional structure of a molecule under study.[14]

The 1986 Nobel Prize in Chemistry, awarded to Dudley Herschbach, Yuan Lee, and John Polanyi, for their work on "reaction dynamics," reflected some of these underlying trends:

They invented a set of tools in the 1950's and 1960's that helped bring both the theory and the technology of modern physics into chemistry. Among them is the technique of using beams of molecules, fired at supersonic speeds, to study chemical reactions molecule by molecule for the first time ... Like much of chemistry in the decades that followed, this work had a style that owed much to physics and depended on a broad understanding of theory.[15]

Although modern physics is probably the main "exporter" of concepts and methods to other scientific disciplines, it is by no means the only one.

---

[14] *New York Times*, 17 October 1985.   [15] *New York Times*, 16 October 1986, page 12.

The so-called "life sciences" of biology, genetics, and medicine have been heavily dependent on chemistry. The intellectual revolution that gave birth to molecular biology had diverse roots that certainly included the contributions of scientists trained in physics, such as Max Delbruck, Leo Szilard, Francis Crick, Maurice Wilkins, and George Gamow. But essential contributions also came from Mendelian genetics, X-ray crystallography, physical chemistry, and biochemistry.[16]

Within the realm of engineering disciplines, techniques developed in one area frequently turn out to be useful in others. Sometimes, they turn out to be of much broader significance and applicability. In aircraft design, a standard problem involves calculations of air flow over wings. In solving these problems in the very early years of the industry, Ludwig Prandtl devised what has come to be essentially a new branch of mathematics – known as asymptotic perturbation theory. Applications of that theory can be found in radar design and the study of the combustion process, but also in astronomy, meteorology, and even in biology. Recently, asymptotic perturbation theory has been used in designing pills so as to provide for optimal timing in the controlled release of medication.

One of the most powerful intellectual tools that has had extensive transfer experience in the past several decades has been information theory. Claude Shannon, who developed information theory at Bell Labs., actually provided a generalization for calculating the maximum capacity of a communication system for transmitting error-free information.[17] This generalization has been of great, and obvious, utility to the telephone industry, where a precise understanding of the determinants of channel capacity is central to engineering design.

However the theory, once it had received a rigorous formulation, turned out to be highly relevant in places very remote from the telephone system. For Shannon's central notion, that it is possible to give a quantitative expression to information content, had numerous ramifications. Information theory represented a distinctively new way of thinking about a range of problems that occur in many places, and it has powerfully influenced the design of both hardware and software. Eventually, information theory grew into a family of models of wide generality, with applications in the behavioral sciences as well as in the physical sciences and engineering.

[16] See Horace F. Judson, *The Eighth Day of Creation*, Simon and Schuster, New York, 1979, especially pages 605–613. For an account that emphasizes the contribution of physics, see Donald Fleming, "Emigré Physicists and the Biological Revolution," in Donald Fleming and Bernard Bailyn, *The Intellectual Migration: Europe and America, 1930–1960*, The Belknap Press of Harvard University Press, Cambridge (MA), 1969, pp. 152–189.

[17] Claude Shannon, "A Mathematical Theory of Communications," *Bell System Technical Journal* (July 1948).

It appears also that instrumentation requirements sometimes serve as a powerful device for bringing together research scientists from separate disciplines. X-ray crystallography played such a role in the development of molecular biology, precisely because it is, in effect, an instrument-embodied technique. In a very different way the increasing reliance on supercomputers is serving to bring members of different disciplines together. The impetus in this case is, to a considerable degree, the high cost of the technology and, consequently, the small number of locations where users need to convene.

Instrumentation as a production tool

Finally, there is another extremely important science/technology interaction that receives virtually no attention. It involves movement of new instrumentation technologies, not from one scientific discipline to another, but from the status of a tool of basic research, often in universities, to the status of a production tool, or capital good, in private industry. This is an "output" of basic research that has been of great significance in specific sectors of the economy. In fact, instrumentation originating in the world of academic research in the years since the Second World War has been responsible for critical contributions to certain industrial technologies. In the electronics industry, this would include instruments that are essential to the fabrication of semiconductors, such as ion-implantation technology and the scanning electron microscope.[18]

It is far from clear why this particular economic contribution of scientific research, including research of the most fundamental nature, has been so badly neglected. In the academic world, of course, high status is usually accorded on the basis of the "purity," or the abstractness, or the generality, of research findings. Conversely, matters involving "hardware," including techniques of instrumentation, are often dismissed as constituting an inferior form of knowledge, some of which may even (*mirabile dictu!*) turn out to be directly useful.

This sort of academic snobbery should surely have been discarded long ago, even by standards internal to this hierarchical manner of thinking, since a number of Nobel Prizes have been awarded to scientists for contributions that could be classed as hardware – the computer-aided tomography scanner, the electron microscope, and the particle accelerator. Moreover, a casual glance at the award of Nobel Prizes in science in recent years should make it apparent how crucial it has become in the realm of scientific research to have access to the most sophisticated instrumentation

---

[18] For further discussion, see chapter 13, pp. 255–257.

available. Much more to the present point, when the context of discussion is the economic impact of science, there is no obvious reason for failing to examine the hardware consequences of even the most fundamental scientific research.

Conclusion

The purpose of this chapter has been to raise questions about the science/technology interface by examining specific patterns of interaction at various points on that interface. No assertion is being made that these are the most important of the existing patterns. I merely call attention to them as being important as well as neglected. Their significance compared to other activities that have not been discussed here will obviously have to await the results of much further research.

Several policy issues already emerge clearly:

how can organizations and incentives be created that will be conducive to high quality interdisciplinary research?

To what extent is it reasonable to expect such research to be conducted inside individual firms, as contrasted with the resort to collaborative linkages with other firms, or with universities, in order to gain access to complementary skills and capabilities?[19]

How can fruitful interactions between scientists and technologists, as well as among scientists from different disciplines, be most effectively encouraged?

What measures can be taken to ensure that valuable findings or methodologies from any point on the science/technology interface will be transferred rapidly to other points?

It is essential that these issues are not approached in a piecemeal fashion. The realms of science and technology must be conceived of, not as disconnected bits and pieces of human activity, but as parts of large and complex, interrelated systems.

Equally important, it is apparent that these systems differ very significantly from one country to another. As a result, policies or institutional arrangements that work well in one country may not be readily transferable to other countries. Systemic differences need to be taken into account, which brings us back to the importance of mapping, with which this paper began.

Finally, far more attention needs to be devoted to what determines the profitability of private spending on science and technology. Although the

[19] For an analytical treatment of some of the underlying issues, see Ashish Arora and Alfonso Gambardella, "Complementarity and External Linkages: The Strategies of Large Firms in Biotechnology," *Journal of Industrial Economics* (June 1990).

linear model is no longer credible, the causal sequences that it emphasized still remain dominant in a subtle yet highly significant way, so that there is still a strong preoccupation with how research leads to economic consequences, and little attention is given to how economic factors influence the willingness to do research. In both the United States and the United Kingdom, for example, much attention is given to the argument that a weakening commitment to R&D may be responsible for the deterioration in the competitive position of these countries in international markets.

Much less noticed is the possibility that causality may also be the other way around. In the American case, at least, her overwhelming dominance in international markets in the twenty-five years or so after the Second World War surely provided a strong incentive to commit private money to R&D, since the prospects were excellent that American firms would receive the primary rents in international markets from the development of new technologies. Surely it is reasonable to believe that the private incentive to spend money on R&D in the United States weakened along with the growth of international competitors and the declining prospect of generating profits overseas, as well as at home, from larger R&D budgets.

In practice, far too much of the debate over R&D spending in the United States and the United Kingdom has been over the size of the public component of such spending and far too little on the determinants of private spending and on how private incentives can be strengthened. This has been particularly unfortunate, in my view, because it is the "downstream" development spending that plays a crucial role in determining who gets to capture the potential rents generated by scientific research.

This is a point that appears to be well understood in Japan, where approximately 80 percent of total R&D spending is financed by private industry – a far higher percentage than in either the United States or United Kingdom. This also suggests a conclusion which, coming from an economist, will occasion no great surprise: prospects for more rapid economic growth – surely a major though not exclusive goal of science and technology policy – will depend on success in providing a structure of economic incentives and rewards that are supportive of the rapid diffusion of new technologies, once they have been developed.

Decisions to adopt new technologies are, typically, investment decisions, involving the acquisition of new capital goods. Such decisions are therefore subject to the same sort of economic calculus that attends all investment decisions. Indeed, precisely the same is true of the decision to commit private resources to R&D in the first place. Science and technology policy, in this sense, is simply an aspect of economic policy-making and not an entirely separate subject. The wrong set of economic policies can guarantee the failure of any specific set of policies directed toward the realms of science and technology, no matter how ingeniously conceived.

Part III

Sectoral studies in technological change

9 Energy-efficient technologies: past and future perspectives

Energy efficiency: an introduction to the fundamental issues

A distinctive aspect of successful industrialization has been the increasingly intensive utilization of energy sources in ways that have raised the productivity of other inputs, most notably labor. The close relationship between high productivity and energy-intensity is a clear empirical regularity of long-run economic growth. However, for a host of reasons, industrialized nations since the early 1970s have become increasingly concerned with the adoption of energy-efficient technologies – technologies that minimize energy utilized per unit of output.

To understand the goal of energy efficiency, some analysis must necessarily be global in nature. For example, overall constraints upon energy supplies can only be explored at the international level. Energy sources are distributed in a highly uneven fashion among countries while, at the same time, the demand for energy inputs varies enormously among countries. It is important to note that per capita income and the extent of industrialization explain an unusually high fraction of the international variation in energy demand (see table 9.1).

On the other hand, there is a great deal that can be said about the prospects and benefits of energy efficiency by confining analysis merely to the American experience. Although there will be frequent reference to the experiences of other industrial countries, historical analysis of American energy use and technology adoption will, in general, highlight a number of important forces that influence the implementation of energy efficiency. Indeed, much of the underlying analysis, although drawing upon American experience, is equally relevant and valid elsewhere.

An earlier version of this chapter was presented at a conference, "How Far Can the World Get on Energy Efficiency Alone?", Oak Ridge National Laboratory, Oak Ridge (TN), August 1989. Thanks are due to Alison Peters for assistance in preparing this chapter. The historical discussion is complemented by the material in chapter 6 below.

Table 9.1. *Energy consumption in selected countries, 1982*

Country	Population (millions)	Commercial Energy Consumption[a] (exajoules)[c]	Per Capita Energy Consumption (gigajoules)[c]	Energy Imports As Share of Exports[b] (percent)
Argentina	28.4	1.7	61	11
Brazil	126.8	4.0	32	52
Canada	24.6	9.7	395	11
China	1,008.2	17.9	17	n.a.
East Germany	16.7	3.8	231	n.a.
France	54.4	8.5	156	33
India	717.0	4.9	7	81
Italy	56.3	6.2	110	41
Japan	118.4	15.8	134	48
Mexico	73.1	4.2	58	−76
Poland	36.2	5.0	138	20
Soviet Union	270.0	55.0	204	−77
United Kingdom	55.8	7.7	152	14
United States	231.5	75.1	324	36
West Germany	61.6	11.5	187	23
Total	2,880.0	232.0	80	—
World total	4,585.0	300.0	65	

Notes:
[a] Commercial energy consumption figures are Worldwatch estimates from 1981 data, assuming little change.   [b] A negative figure indicates the percentage of exports earned from energy sales.   [c] Giga- and exajoules equal a billion and a billion billion joules, respectively. The units are 0.95 million and 0.95 quadrillion (quad) BTU, respectively.
Source: World Bank, *World Development Report 1984*, Oxford University Press, New York 1984. Reproduced from William Chandler, *Productivity: Key to Environmental Protection and Economic Progress*, Worldwatch Paper 63, Washington, DC, 1985, p. 8.

Difficulties in implementing energy efficiency

From the outset, it is important to emphasize the peculiar content of the often-cited goal of energy efficiency. No policy-maker should be at all interested in pursuing energy efficiency alone, if that implies the blind minimization of the ratio of energy inputs to total output. There are innumerable possibilities for reducing that ratio. One can substitute capital, labor, and other inputs for energy in an unlimited number of ways; one can alter the quality and performance characteristics of final products; one can shift the composition of the economy's final output away from energy-intensive to less energy-intensive goods. Clearly, only some small subset of these approaches will be economically efficient.[1]

Although this point is obvious and unexceptionable, it has important implications that are not so obvious. Ever since the Arab oil embargo and the run-up in energy prices that began in 1973, the world has been awash with suggested ways of reducing the utilization of energy inputs, or substituting one source of energy for another. Frequently, these proposals suggest the substitution of renewable sources for nonrenewable ones.

Many of these proposals would succeed in reducing the requirements for certain fuels, but they do so by substituting certain other inputs for fuel in ways that raise total costs rather than reduce them. The rejection of such alternative technologies need not represent irrational decision-making procedures, insufficient willingness to undertake search activities, or a breakdown in the diffusion of information, to cite some common allegations. A much more plausible explanation is that firms and households remain overwhelmingly committed to decision rules that involve minimizing total private costs for a given volume of output rather than minimizing energy costs per unit of output.

Even when alternative technologies do indeed reduce total costs by reducing energy costs per unit of output, observers often protest that adoption is occurring at a rate that appears to be much slower than warranted. Once again, analysis need not rely on the intransigence or irrationality of consumers and firms to explain slow adoption rates. It is much more likely that these energy-efficient systems are embedded in expensive and long-lived assets. When this is the case, adoption of energy-efficient technologies might require the discarding of expensive assets in order to capture the (perhaps only temporary) reductions in energy costs. When viewed in this light, the observed adoption rate is no longer so baffling. It should be noted that when the asset has been more thoroughly depreciated and is approaching replacement, the replacement is likely to take place somewhat earlier and to incorporate newer technologies.

As it happens, a very large fraction of total energy use in industrial societies *is* embedded in long-lived capital equipment. New houses or factories built in any given year constitute only a small fraction of the total existing stock. Buildings that may have a life expectancy of fifty years or

---

[1] For a wide-ranging survey of the possibilities for further improvements in energy efficiency, see Christopher Flavin and Alan Durning, *Building on Success: The Age of Energy Efficiency*, Worldwatch Paper 82, Washington (DC), 1988.

more are not candidates for replacement (although they may be candidates for modification or retrofitting) when heating costs rise even very drastically. Similarly automobiles, with useful lives of a decade or so, are not immediately replaced even if fuel prices double. More than a decade was necessary before the sharp rise in gasoline prices during the 1970s was translated into the rapid replacement of the automobile stock by models that were significantly more energy-efficient. There is a general point here of immense significance to the formulation of energy policy, both public and private, and especially to decision-making with respect to R&D expenditures on energy projects: adjusting to changes in energy availability and price may take a very long time, frequently several years, as in the case of cars, and several decades in the case of houses, factories, and buildings generally. This long time horizon and the slow pace of adjustment is one of the most distinctive features of the energy problem and needs to be dealt with explicitly.

The emphasis on long-lived capital assets and long time horizons underlines one of the most basic considerations in the analysis of the prospects for improved energy efficiency. Energy efficiency is intrinsically tied to investment decisions, and these decisions need to be regarded and treated as such. The relevant calculation concerns some (usually large) expenditure that is made in the present in order to purchase a stream of distant benefits in the form of reduced spending on energy. Such decisions are therefore necessarily shrouded in uncertainties, including the prices at which various energy inputs will be available in the future and the possible availability of even more efficient energy technologies *after* the financial commitment has been made. Most basic of all, like all investment decisions, is the cost of capital, the financial terms on which it is possible to acquire the necessary funds. A society in which the cost of capital is low will have greater incentives to invest in long-lived technologies. Thus, when the cost of capital is low, individuals will find it more worthwhile to pursue improved energy efficiency than when the cost of capital is high. It is astonishing that this consideration does not receive far more explicit and prominent attention in discussions of prospects for greater energy efficiency. The world today is indeed full of ways of saving energy which, unfortunately, simply can not stand the financial test of comparing required present financial outlays with prospective energy-saving benefits. This suggests, however, that those macroeconomic policies that lower the cost and increase the availability of capital will also favorably affect the prospects for greater energy efficiency. The incentives to pursue energy efficiency are very much a function of the cost of capital.

Economic analysis thus highlights some of the principal difficulties in implementing energy efficiency. If decision-makers use rules that minimize total costs rather than energy use, many proposed energy-saving technologies will simply not be adopted. Even when adoption does make economic sense, the fact that energy technologies are overwhelmingly embedded in long-lived capital implies that adoption will take an extremely long time and will be tied to variables such as the interest rate and the availability of capital.

Possible payoffs from energy efficiency

Despite the difficulties that energy-efficient technologies might need to overcome in order to be widely utilized, the underlying concerns about energy utilization are not without basis. At the very least, consumption of nonrenewable resources generates two distinct externalities of serious social consequence:

a. There is obvious concern about limitations on the supply side. Existing stocks of resources, especially of fossil fuels, can not easily be increased, and apprehension has risen especially in the face of prospective increases in the demand for energy as a consequence of continued population growth and the expansion of demand from LDCs that are presently in the early stages of industrialization.

b. Improving energy efficiency has become more pressing as a result of growing awareness of the serious impact that burning fossil fuels has upon the environment. Increasing evidence in recent years indicates that acid rain is already having devastating ecological effects upon living things in lakes and forests. The evidence with respect to the greenhouse effect, although more tentative, suggests consequences that may be even more far-reaching in the long run. Thus, heightened awareness of the possible severity of ecological impacts now plays a major role in thinking about future energy supplies. At the very least, it is increasingly recognized that energy users' private costs of energy consumption are below the full long-term social cost of their energy consumption.

Consequences of energy efficiency

Historical considerations, however, raise fundamental questions about the relationship between energy efficiency and energy use: is it reasonable to expect that improved energy efficiency will necessarily reduce the utilization of limited fossil-fuel resources or offset negative environmental effects? That outcome, although commonly taken for granted, is far from self-evident. Historically, new technologies that improved energy efficiency have often led to a significant increase, and not to a reduction, in fuel consumption. This has been especially true in energy-intensive sectors where fuel costs have constituted a large proportion of total costs. In metallurgy, for example, innovations that drastically reduced fuel costs also significantly reduced the market price for important intermediate goods that faced elastic demand curves. Large increases in the quantities of goods bought due to the decrease in market price was, in fact, a manifestation of this elasticity.

For example, the Bessemer process, the fundamental innovation that made possible the refining of pig iron into steel, brought with it a dramatic reduction in the fuel cost of steelmaking. Indeed, it was this fuel-saving innovation that essentially transformed an iron industry into an iron-and-steel industry. Interestingly enough, Bessemer's 1856 paper to the British Association for the Advancement of Science bore the intriguing, if somewhat misleading title: "Manufacture of Malleable Iron and Steel without Fuel." The Bessemer process was one of the most fuel-saving innovations in the history of metallurgy. However, the innovation made it possible to employ steel in a wide variety of uses that were not feasible before Bessemer, bringing with it large increases in the demand for steel. As a result, although the Bessemer process sharply reduced fuel requirements per unit of output, its ultimate effect was to increase, and not to reduce, the demand for fuel.

Thus, when confronting the public policy debate over energy efficiency, the distinction between energy efficiency and other goals should be emphasized. Many paths are open to policy-makers; with enlightened policy-making, where the world ends up will depend very much on where it is that the world hopes to get. If the goal is reduced aggregate fuel utilization, then improved energy efficiency may, or may not, help to get it there. That will depend upon the elasticity of fuel utilization with respect to the price of fuel. While it is true that the demand for energy in many major-use categories in industrial countries appears to be reassuringly inelastic, improved energy efficiency may itself stimulate *new uses* of energy that are difficult to anticipate. Moreover, in poor countries where energy consumption is still low, demand curves for energy may well be far more elastic. Thus, when considering long-range policies in which the future price elasticity of energy is unknown, it will be important to recognize that the pursuit of energy efficiency alone may not be a sufficient condition for successful policymaking.

If reduced fuel utilization is the underlying goal of the policy-maker, high carbon-emission taxes provide one method for forcing energy users to pay the full social costs of their energy needs. This approach, long touted by economists but almost ignored in public debate, has recently become quite popular and has been incorporated in legislation throughout the industrialized world. Further, concerns about the world's energy future should lead to a focus upon possible alternative sources of energy. In particular, the benefits that will derive from R&D expenditures on alternative energy sources might become available only in the distant future. If this is so, private efforts might be lower than is socially optimal. Thus, support for research on alternative energy sources will need the continued and consis-

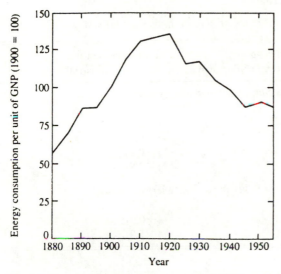

Fig. 9.1 Energy consumption per unit of GNP, excluding wood, United States, 1880–1950. Adapted from Sam Schurr and Bruce Netschert, *Energy in the American Economy*, The Johns Hopkins University Press, Baltimore, 1960, p. 159.

tent support of the public sector. High carbon taxes and directing inventive activity towards non-carbon-based fuels are two clear implications of economic analysis of the goal of reducing nonrenewable resource utilization. Public debate about the environment and natural resource utilization is unusually cloudy and often apocalyptic. Current environmental concerns would presumably appear in a very different light if the future of energy use seemed less clearly dominated by the burning of carbon-based fossil fuels.

The historical perspective

An historical perspective on energy use in industrial countries is dominated by several long-term trends. Industrial development over the past two centuries has involved an increase in the energy intensity of productive activity as measured by energy inputs per worker. One of the central features of industrialization over the long term has involved making larger amounts of energy available to each worker engaged in productive activity. Schurr has estimated that, between 1920 and 1969, energy inputs increased more than three times as rapidly as the number of man-hours employed.[2]

The amount of energy required per unit of output is, of course, a different question from that of energy per worker and has a more complex history (see Figure 9.1). Between 1880 and 1920 in the United States, energy

[2] Sam Schurr, "Energy Efficiency and Productive Efficiency: Some Thoughts Based on American Experience," *The Energy Journal*, 3, no. 3 (1982), p. 8.

Table 9.2. *Average annual rates of change in energy intensity, 1920–1969*

Period[b]	Total economy (Energy/GNP ratio)[c]	Industrial sector[a] (Energy/industrial output ratio)
Long period of persistent decline in national energy intensity		
1920–1953	−1.3	−1.7
1920–1929	(−2.2)	(−3.9)
1929–1937	(−0.5)	(−0.5)
1937–1948	(−0.4)	(−0.2)
1948–1953	(−3.2)	(−2.8)
Long period of comparative stability in national energy intensity		
1953–1969	+0.0	−0.3
1953–1960	(+0.2)	(+0.6)
1960–1969	(−0.1)	(−1.0)

Notes:
[a] Defined as manufacturing and mining.   [b] Business cycle peak years, but not each individual cycle is shown.   [c] Energy is measured in terms of primary energy inputs (excluding fuel wood). Output is measured in constant (1972) dollars of GNP (for the total economy), or of gross product originating in manufacturing and mining (for the industrial sector).
Source: Adapted from Sam Schurr, "Energy Efficiency and Economic Efficiency: An Historical Perspective," pp. 208–209, in Sam Schurr, Sidney Sonenblum, and David Wood (eds.), *Energy, Productivity, and Economic Growth*, Oelgeschlager, Gunn & Hain, Cambridge (MA), 1983.

intensity (energy consumption relative to GNP) grew at an annual rate of about 2.2 percent. Between 1920 and 1953, energy intensity for the total economy fell at an annual rate of 1.3 percent. During the 1950s and 1960s the ratio remained approximately constant (see Table 9.2. After 1973 there was a substantial decline, at an annual rate of 1.8 percent between 1973 and 1979 and at an annual rate of no less than 4.1% between 1979 and 1981. More recently, this ratio has again stabilized.[3]

A slight unpacking of these aggregate statistics reveals equally important dynamics with respect to the composition of the inputs that were drawn upon as energy sources (see Table 9.3). Given the very wide range of observed variation in input use, it is surprising that the energy debate so frequently centers around aggregate data. An examination of disaggregated data highlights a time-consuming process that gradually uncovered new sources of mineral deposits, and also the technological innovations

[3] Ibid., pp. 3, 7 and 9.

that vastly expanded the natural inputs that were usable as sources of energy. In fact, the diversity of energy inputs and the changing usage of those inputs over time is a central feature of the historical record that partially undermines any narrow focus on energy efficiency alone.

Long-term changes in technology have not only expanded the inputs that were usable as energy sources; they have also brought with them major changes in the *form* in which the energy had to be delivered. Technological innovations are often not neutral with respect to their energy requirements. Rather, their usefulness has commonly hinged upon the availability of energy in some particular form. For example, more efficient blast furnaces required the substitution of coke for charcoal before stack sizes could be increased. Charcoal crushes readily and can not support a heavy charge; coke is more resilient. Anthracite, usually considered a high-grade coal because of its chemical "purity," was a distinctly inferior fuel during the post-Civil War era, a period of rapid growth for the iron-and-steel industry. Using the original Bessemer technology, anthracite's physical structure rendered it incapable of achieving rapid combustion, an essential element of the productivity increases involving "hard driving" after 1870.[4] The original Bessemer technology – the acid Bessemer process – required ore with a low phosphorus content. It was the introduction, nearly twenty years later, of the "basic" process that allowed the Bessemer, as well as the later open-hearth process, to exploit a wide range of high-phosphorus ores.

Electricity might appear, at first sight, to contradict the importance suggested for the particular form of energy in the successful diffusion of new technologies. After all, technologies were invented that allowed for the production of electricity from a variety of fuel sources. However, although it could be generated from a variety of primary energy sources, a wide range of later technologies were specifically wedded to energy in the form of electricity. This dependence on electricity persists, even though electricity superficially seems to be an inefficient energy technology, as its generation involves large thermal losses. Once again, this non-neutrality of energy requirements is a critical feature of the history of energy. Examining energy prospects at the level of BTUs neglects the consideration that industrial economies have found it to be enormously valuable, in particular contexts, to deal with energy in the specific form of liquid fuel (petroleum and natural gas) or electricity. Of course, solid fuels can be converted into liquid forms, and electricity can be generated from a variety of primary energy sources. Nevertheless, it is often the case that energy needs can only be met by energy in a particular form. The form in which energy is required is essential and should not be suppressed by highly aggregated approaches to the problem.

[4] Peter Temin, *Iron and Steel in 19th Century America*, MIT Press, Cambridge (MA), 1964, p. 201.

Table 9.3. *Specific energy sources as percentages of aggregate energy consumption, five-year intervals, 1850–1955*

Year	Bituminous coal (1)	Anthracite (2)	Total coal (3)	Oil (4)	Natural gas (5)	Natural gas liquids (6)	Total liquids and gaseous fuels (7)	Total mineral fuels (8)	Hydro-power (9)	Mineral fuels and hydro-power (10)	Fuel wood (11)
											(measured in BTUs)
1850	4.7	4.6	9.3	—	—	—	—	9.3%	—	—	90.7%
1855	7.3	7.7	15.0	—	—	—	—	15.0	—	—	85.0
1860	7.7	8.7	16.4	0.1	n.a.	—	n.a.	16.5	—	—	83.5
1865	9.6	8.9	18.5	0.3	n.a.	—	n.a.	18.8	—	—	81.2
1870	13.8	12.7	26.5	0.3	n.a.	—	n.a.	26.8	—	—	73.2
1875	19.9	13.4	33.3	0.3	n.a.	—	n.a.	33.6	—	—	66.4
1880	26.7	14.3	41.1	1.9	n.a.	—	1.9	43.0	—	—	57.0
1885	33.4	16.9	50.3	0.7	1.5	—	2.2	52.5	—	—	47.5
1890	41.4	16.5	57.9	2.2	3.7	—	5.9	63.8	0.3	64.1	35.9
1895	45.8	18.8	64.6	2.2	1.9	—	4.1	68.7	1.2	69.9	30.1
1900	56.6	14.7	71.4	2.4	2.6	—	5.0	76.4	2.6	79.0	21.0
1905	61.2	14.5	75.7	4.6	2.8	—	7.4	83.1	2.9	86.1	13.9
1910	64.3	12.4	76.8	6.1	3.3	—	9.3	86.1	3.3	89.3	10.7
1915	62.7	12.2	74.8	7.9	3.8	—	11.8	86.6	3.9	90.5	9.5
1920	62.3	10.2	72.5	12.3	3.8	0.2	16.3	88.8	3.6	92.5	7.5
1925	58.4	7.3	65.6	18.5	5.3	0.6	24.4	90.0	3.1	93.2	6.8
1930	50.3	7.3	57.5	23.8	8.1	1.0	33.0	90.6	3.3	93.9	6.1

1935	45.6	6.3	52.0	26.9	9.4	0.9	37.1	89.1	4.1	93.2	6.8
1940	44.7	4.9	49.7	29.6	10.6	1.1	41.3	91.0	3.6	94.6	5.4
1945	44.8	4.0	48.8	29.4	11.8	1.5	42.8	91.6	4.5	96.1	3.9
1950	33.9	2.9	36.8	36.2	17.0	2.2	55.4	92.1	4.6	96.7	3.3
1955	27.2	1.5	28.7	40.0	22.1	2.9	65.0	93.7	3.7	97.4	2.6

Note:
n.a. Not available.
Source: Reproduced from Sam Schurr and Bruce Netschert, *Energy in the American Economy*, The Johns Hopkins University Press, Baltimore, 1960, p. 36.

In fact, a central – perhaps *the* central – feature of the history of improvements in energy efficiency is that it is not a subject that has really been separable from the search for energy in particular forms or for energy that satisfied certain specific performance characteristics. As a result, the search for improved energy efficiency has been part and parcel of the development of new technologies that opened up entirely new sources of energy. It is worth recalling that, when the American petroleum industry first emerged in Titusville, Pennsylvania, in 1859, the primary motivation for extracting petroleum from the ground was for kerosene, an illuminant. The most volatile fraction of the oil – gasoline – was regarded as little more than an awkward waste product. Petroleum in 1859 was not an energy source in the modern sense. Subsequent technological change in the form of the internal combustion and diesel engines obviously changed that, but only thirty or forty years later. Before those complementary inventions, petroleum was pumped out of the ground in large quantities, but little more than the kerosene fraction was utilized – an enormously wasteful practice.

Similarly, natural gas in the 1930s was still being treated as an unavoidable waste product.[5] After supplying local markets, natural gas was commonly flared in large quantities. Considering the fact that most natural gas deposits were found in relatively unpopulated areas, one of the most significant improvements in energy efficiency in American history was the development of techniques for producing high-pressure pipelines, which transformed this "waste product" of oil drilling into one of the largest and most attractive of all energy sources.

The possibility of flexibility in energy requirements

In spite of the long-term trend of growing energy utilization, there is much evidence that there is a great deal of flexibility in the relationship between output and energy requirements. In fact, there were very significant adjustments in energy utilization in response to the two sharp upward movements in energy prices in the 1970s. Between 1973 and 1985, all developed countries achieved significant reductions in energy intensity, the United States by no less than 23 percent (see table 9.4 and figure 9.2).

However, equally compelling evidence highlights the large variability of energy requirements per unit of output among countries. It is obvious that there is a great deal of slack in the energy system, in the specific sense that there is a considerable difference among industrial countries in the amount of energy required to generate a unit of GNP. Of course, the mere existence of such differences does not, *ipso facto*, demonstrate the possibility for

[5] Hans Landsberg and Sam Schurr, *Energy in the United States*, Random House, New York, 1968, p. 103.

Table 9.4. *Energy intensity of selected national economies, 1973–1985*

Country	1973	1979	1983	1985	Change, 1973–85
	(megajoules per 1980 dollar of GNP)				(percent)
Australia	21.6	23.0	22.1	20.3	− 6
Canada	38.3	38.8	36.5	36.0	− 6
Greece[a]	17.1	18.5	18.9	19.8	+ 16
Italy	18.5	17.1	15.3	14.9	− 19
Japan	18.9	16.7	13.5	13.1	− 31
Netherlands	19.8	18.9	15.8	16.2	− 18
Turkey	28.4	24.2	25.7	25.2	− 11
United Kingdom	19.8	18.0	15.8	15.8	− 20
United States	35.6	32.9	28.8	27.5	− 23
West Germany	17.1	16.2	14.0	14.0	− 18

Note:
[a] Energy intensity increased as a result of a move toward energy-intensive industries such as metal processing.
Source: International Energy Agency, *Energy Conservation in IEA Countries*: Organisation for Economic Co-operation and Development, Paris 1987. Reproduced from Christopher Flavin and Alan Durning, *Building on Success: The Age of Energy Efficiency*, Worldwatch Paper 82, Washington (DC), 1988, p. 8.

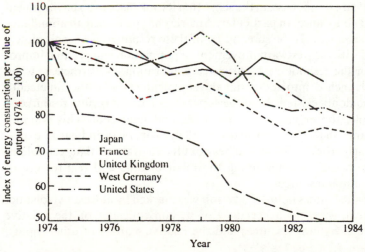

Fig. 9.2 Industrial energy intensity by country, all industries. Sources: United Nations, *Yearbook of Industrial Statistics. General Industrial Statistics*, vol. I, various years, and International Energy Agency (IEA), *Energy Balances of OECD Countries, 1970/1985 and Main Series from 1960*, OECD, Paris, 1987. Reproduced from *R&D Initiatives for Energy Competitiveness*, a report of the Energy Research Advisory Board to the US Department of Energy, Washington (DC), 1988, Exhibit 13.

improved energy efficiency. There are many reasons for differences among countries in energy consumption.

Considerations of geography and population density are major determinants. Denser populations, such as in Japan, tend to be more heavily concentrated in fuel-efficient apartment residences rather than in single-family houses. Furthermore, if a country's population is thinly sprinkled over a large land area, that country's population will tend to devote larger fractions of their output to the energy-intensive transportation sector. In 1970, for example, the United States devoted 22.2 percent of its energy consumption to the transport sector. The corresponding figures for the major western European countries and Japan were all less than 15 percent.[6] Differences in the composition of economic activity are also significant, inasmuch as there is large sectoral variation in energy requirements.[7]

Historical trends of resource availability and utilization

While such variables as population and land area can explain a substantial portion of the observed differences in energy consumption among countries, they can by no means account for all of the variation. To understand international variability further, it is necessary to account for historical differences in the availability and price of different energy sources across countries. In this respect, the American industrialization experience may be considered an extreme case, in the sense that it took place in an environment of unusual abundance. In particular, America has possessed an abundance of *energy resources*. To be sure, many of these resources were only slowly uncovered with the westward movement of population and gradual improvements in the technology of resource exploration. Nevertheless, when America launched into industrial development early in the nineteenth century, no doubt existed about the superabundance of certain resources – for example, timber and forest products and later coal. This windfall unmistakably shaped certain features of the American industrial experience, though historical trends do bear out the central role that technological change played in determining the relative value and relative use of different natural resources.

Early United States industrialization was marked by at least two distinct features that were, to a certain extent, consequences of the relative abundance of natural resources and the relative scarcity of other inputs,

---

[6] Joel Darmstadter, Joy Dunkerley, and Jack Alterman, *How Industrial Societies Use Energy*, The Johns Hopkins University Press, Baltimore (MD), 1977, p. 12.

[7] For a useful discussion, see Robert Wilson, "The Determinants of Energy Demand," *World Energy Issues and Policies*, ed. Robert Barro, Oxford University Press, Oxford, 1980.

notably labor. First, until at least the middle of the nineteenth century, the United States moved along a much more wood-intensive trajectory than Europe. For example, American sawmills utilized circular saws which had thicker blades and more widely spaced teeth than their English counterparts. Although American saws wasted large quantities of wood – in fact, they converted a large fraction of the log into sawdust rather than lumber – they were suitable for high-speed operation. The labor-saving characteristics of this technology represented an acceptable tradeoff in labor-scarce and resource-abundant America. In contrast, English sawmills were willing to trade off cutting speed for higher lumber yields.[8] Another example of America's wood-intensive trajectory can be found in the history of the iron industry. Americans remained committed to the use of wood long after the British had switched to coke. While the use of coke in the blast furnace was almost universal in Britain by 1800, nearly all the pig iron produced in America in 1840 was still made with charcoal. Even as late as 1860, only 13 percent of American pig iron was being made with coke.[9]

A second distinct feature of American development was the slow adoption of the steam engine for industrial purposes. Once again, an explanation can be found through examination of relative resource endowment. America possessed excellent alternative power sources in the form of abundant water power in New England, the primary center of American industry in the first half of the nineteenth century. Even as late as 1879, most of the primary-power capacity in New England manufacturing was water-based, although, for the United States as a whole, that share was barely over a third. Perhaps even more striking were the designs of the waterwheels that were employed. From an engineering perspective and by comparison with their European counterparts, American waterwheels in the early nineteenth century were highly inefficient. However, in an economy of scarce capital and abundant water power it made a great deal of economic sense to construct waterwheels that were cheap and easily constructed, such as the pitchback wheel, even though they captured only a small fraction of the kinetic energy of the falling water. Similarly, when steam engines were eventually adopted, Americans showed a distinct preference for the high-pressure stationary engine, whereas the British favored the low-pressure engine. Although high-pressure engines were less efficient in their utilization of fuel, their construction was less costly than low-pressure engines. Here again the Americans made selections that involved the substitution of energy for capital.

Finally, consider the very large domestic fireplaces that were commonly

---

[8] Nathan Rosenberg, "America's Rise to Woodworking Leadership," *Perspectives on Technology*, Cambridge University Press, Cambridge, 1976, pp. 32–49.

[9] Temin, *Iron and Steel*.

built in the United States in the early nineteenth century. Such fireplaces were indeed highly inefficient with respect to the amount of useful heat generated per cubic foot of wood. However, their large size drastically reduced the highly labor-intensive activities of chopping or sawing wood in order to accommodate the dimensions of smaller fireplaces or stoves. Stoves, which utilized wood supplies more efficiently but were more expensive and raised the costs of labor for wood preparation, eventually became popular whenever and wherever wood prices rose substantially. Both individual families and small manufacturing facilities took advantage of the relative resource abundance of America and the corresponding low prices placed on energy-producing materials.

Thus, due to an abundance of fuelwood and easy access to waterpower in its early history, America launched onto an industrialization path propelled by a very different pattern of energy use than that of western Europe. In particular, the American experience in the early nineteenth century was far less reliant on coal, the energy source most favored in western Europe. In 1850, more than 90 percent of all fuel-based energy in the United States was accounted for by wood and less than 10 percent by coal (see table 9.3).

As the rapidly expanding industrial establishment's needs increased the demand for energy in the second half of the nineteenth century, there was a contemporaneous shift in the composition of the energy sources that were relied upon. The increasing inadequacy and scarcity of additional water-power sources (especially outside of New England), the rising price of wood fuel and the discovery of rich coal beds west of the Appalachians brought about a rapid shift toward the use of coal. In fact, coal largely displaced wood by the early years of the twentieth century as the principal material source of energy. From a position of overwhelming dominance in 1850, wood declined until it was providing less than 10 percent of aggregate energy in 1915, whereas coal accounted for nearly three-quarters. By the time of the First World War, the transition out of wood was almost complete.

The dominance of coal in the United States, in comparison with the experience of the other industrialized countries, proved to be relatively brief. Coal accounted for a majority of American material energy sources only between 1885 and 1935. Between 1915 and 1955, coal sources declined from providing three quarters of aggregate energy to less than one-third. In part, the short reign of coal is explained by America's late shift out of wood. However, it is the emergence of oil and other petroleum products, whose rise was intimately linked to the rapid diffusion of the gasoline-powered automobiles, that led to the rather quick departure from coal as the dominant energy source. The incentives to use coal as a primary energy source were further eroded with the dieselization of the railroads and the conversion of household markets to petroleum-based heating. The diffusion of new technologies which were reliant on petroleum products, including natural gas, as an energy source contributed to the decline of coal as the dominant energy input. By 1955, petroleum sources, displacing coal, accounted for over 60 percent of the value of total aggregate energy production (see table 9.3).

Superimposed upon the growth in energy use and the long-term swings in interfuel choice was the rise of electricity as the most widely used form of *delivered* energy. The speed with which electricity was adopted by industry is easily demonstrated. Electric motors accounted for less than 5 percent of the total installed horsepower in American manufacturing in 1899. With the development of large steam turbines in the opening years of the twentieth century, the share of installed horsepower accounted for by electric motors leapt to 25 percent in 1909. Ten years later the share stood at 55 percent, and, by 1929, electric motors provided over 80 percent of total installed horsepower in manufacturing.[10] The advent of "fractionalized" power was made possible through the choice of electricity as the form of energy being used. Power could be made available in small, less costly units. This meant that manufacturers did not have to generate excess capacity in order to provide small or intermittent doses of power. This flexibility fundamentally altered the organization of work activity, directly and indirectly contributing to long-term productivity growth.[11] It is somewhat ironic to note that electric-power generation, whose growth was coincident with the fall of coal as the dominant resource, ended up as one of the major markets for coal after coal had been displaced as an input throughout the rest of manufacturing. Indeed, by 1973 fully 69 percent of all coal that was mined in the United States was sold to electric utilities.

Energy pricing and policies in an historical context

Thus, intensive energy use in the United States has a long history, deeply rooted in the recognition of an environment that has been richly endowed with potential energy sources. However, America's energy intensity can also be partially explained by looking at the prices that users face when purchasing energy. Since the Second World War, the general level of energy prices has been substantially lower than prices in other industrial countries (see figure 9.3 and tables 9.5 and 9.6).

As these data demonstrate, energy prices in the United States between 1953 and 1976 have been far below those of all the other countries listed.

[10] Landsberg and Schurr, *Energy*, pp. 52–53.
[11] Richard Du Boff, "The Introduction of Electric power in American Manufacturing," *Economic History Review* (December 1967).

Index: U.S. 1972 = 100

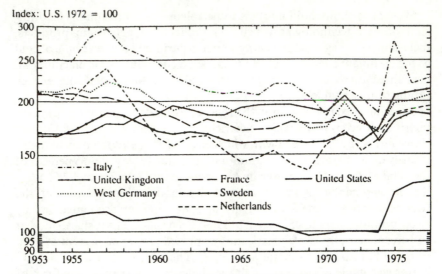

Fig. 9.3 Real prices of energy, 1953–1976. Index: US 1972 = 100. Reproduced from Joy Dunkerley, *Trends in Energy Use in Industrial Societies: An Overview*, Resources for the Future, Washington (DC), 1980, p. 56.

Not surprisingly, Canada has had the second lowest set of prices charged to final consumers. In contrast, energy prices paid by final consumers in Japan were consistently more than twice the level paid by American consumers during this period. Among the European countries shown in figure 9.3, there was a tendency for energy prices to converge among countries between 1953 and 1973 reflecting, as Dunkerley suggests, "the increasingly uniform composition of fuel supplies."[12] In 1973, before the Arab oil embargo, energy prices in western Europe were nearly 80 percent higher than prices in America.

In addition to sustaining lower prices, the United States was able to shield itself against the wide variability in prices experienced throughout the rest of the industrialized world. Despite a general downward drift between 1953 and 1973, the more striking observation in the European experience is the high volatility of prices over the period. Clearly European countries were more vulnerable to the impact of fluctuations in international petroleum prices.

In addition to facing lower, more stable prices, there was another factor that buffered American markets against the volatility of world prices. This same factor may, however, have made the American economy more

[12] Joy Dunkerley, *Trends in Energy Use in Industrial Societies: An Overview*, Resources for the Future, Washington (DC), 1980, p. 55.

Table 9.5. *Indexes of real energy prices paid by final consumers (United States 1972 = 100)*

Country	1953	1960	1970	1972	1973	1974	1976
United States	109	108	99	100	99	123	131
Canada	157	154	136	138	133	147	151
France	207	190	178	180	170	187	188
Germany	211	200	175	178	174	199	209
Italy	247	248	186	204	189	219	229
The Netherlands	209	165	160	154	164	188	196
United Kingdom	168	187	189	187	163	181	188
Sweden	167	170	162	162	173	207	215
Japan	269	267	204	211	196	229	272

Source: Based on Joy Dunkerley, Jack Alterman, and John J. Schanz, Jr., *Trends in Energy Use in Industrial Societies*, EPRI Research Project 864–1, Palo Alto (CA), Electric Power Research Institute, 1980. Reproduced from Joy Dunkerley, *Trends in Energy Use in Industrial Societies: An Overview*, Resources for the Future, Washington (DC), 1980, p. 57.

Table 9.6. *Real energy prices paid by industrial consumers, 1960–1976 (United States 1972 = 100)*

Country	1960	1966	1972	1973	1974	1976
United States	101	98	100	100	131	145
Canada	172	155	158	147	169	174
France	197	165	186	167	177	188
Germany	231	205	203	187	221	234
Italy	227	204	206	194	251	276
The Netherlands	163	151	168	188	217	230
United Kingdom	182	193	184	153	171	188
Sweden	181	180	187	202	256	272
Japan	241	225	221	205	254	318

Source: Based on Joy Dunkerley, Jack Alterman, and John J. Schanz, Jr., *Trends in Energy Use in Industrial Societies*, EPRI Research Project 864–1, Palo Alto (CA), Electric Power Research Institute, 1980. Reproduced from Joy Dunkerley, *Trends in Energy Use in Industrial Societies: An Overview*, Resources for the Future, Washington (DC), 1980, p. 98.

vulnerable to the oil-price shocks of the 1970s. In addition, it also played a crucial role in reinforcing the American thrust towards high energy intensity. The reference is, of course, to government energy policy.

Doubtless a more appropriate term is "policies." Before 1973, there was certainly no clearly defined and well-recognized government energy policy in the United States. Rather, energy issues were covered by a tangled web of *ad hoc* programs which lacked internal consistency. Indeed, in some cases government policies undertaken without any explicit intention to influence energy consumption nevertheless had significant, if unintended, effects. For example, President Nixon introduced controls over oil prices in 1971 as part of an anti-inflationary package. Nevertheless, the controls led to eight years of wrangling over such matters as distinguishing between "old oil" and "new oil." Complex and frustrating plans to shore up incentives for oil exploration and conservation were attempted while the price mechanism sent off conflicting signals to users. It is even possible that conservation and exploration were hindered by the very fact that government policy was confusing and unstable. The immediate effect of the freeze in the relative prices of gasoline and fuel oil was to exacerbate the heating-oil crisis in the winter of 1971–1972. President Carter eventually did deregulate domestic oil prices in 1979, but the existence of oil-price controls had seriously compromised the government's abilities and efforts to respond to the oil crises of the 1970s.

The unintended consequences of government policy have been observed in specific sectors of the economy as well. When the government's agricultural price-support program was strengthened by a system of acreage allotments to individual farmers, this increased farmers' incentives to maximize output per acre. One obvious way of raising output per acre was to add larger amounts of fertilizer to each acre. Since fertilizer is a highly energy-intensive product, the policy's result was to make American agriculture even more energy-intensive than it already had become as a result of mechanization.

If a single theme has united the various energy policies of the American government, it is the promotion and safeguarding of a stable supply of cheap and abundant energy. But even this statement requires some immediate qualification, since government solicitude for domestic oil producers led to oil import quotas that, at times, has raised domestic oil prices above the world market price. Oil and gas prices have been subject to extensive regulation, with particularly devastating effects upon the supply of natural gas. In the early 1970s, the pricing policy condoned by the Federal Power Commission had the anomalous consequence that gas sold on an interstate basis was priced lower than intrastate gas. As Kash and Rycroft point out:

FPC regulation had thus created an interesting conundrum. On the one hand, gas was a much cheaper source of energy than oil when supplied through the interstate framework. On the other hand, gas supplied to consumers within the producing states was more nearly comparable to the price of oil. Even with the addition of transmission charges gas might be cheaper on the East Coast than it was in Texas. At the same time the price paid for gas going into the interstate system was too low to permit oil-and-gas companies to search for new supplies of gas. Natural gas producers understandably preferred either to sell their gas within the producing state or, alternatively, to cap their wells.[13]

Government subsidies of energy supplies have been numerous and extensive, and can not be elaborated here.[14] One estimate, provided by the Center for Renewable Resources, suggests that the energy industry received more than 44 billion dollars in various kinds of federal government subsidies – direct agency outlays, tax breaks, loans and loan guarantees, and various federal support programs – in 1984 alone.[15]

In certain energy sectors, there have been long-standing government policies that encourage greater use of energy from specific sources. The government has often provided substantial funds and incentives for delivering energy in one very specific form – electricity. The Rural Electrification Administration played a major role during the 1930s in making electricity available to much of the rural population, and the Tennessee Valley Authority effectively transformed the upper South Central region by providing massive electric-power generation capabilities using a series of dams, water control projects, and other initiatives. Since the release of energy from the nucleus of the atom during the Second World War, the federal government has also spent enormous sums of money in pushing out the frontiers of atomic energy. The possible civilian applications for atomic energy, as overseen for many years by the Atomic Energy Commission, revolved around the provision of cheap electric power through construction of nuclear generation plants. It should be noted that the staggering level of support for nuclear research reflected the obvious interest in military and strategic payoffs from nuclear technologies. As a final example of this phenomenon, note that public utilities' aggressive support and encouragement of electricity-using appliances, a practice that continued until the mid 1970s, reinforced the role of government in increasing the consumption of energy in the form of electricity.

Thus, the high degree of energy-intensiveness of the American economy has been firmly rooted in an abundance of natural resources, a dynamic

---

[13] Don Kash and Robert Rycroft, *U.S. Energy Policy*, University of Oklahoma Press, Norman (OK), 1984, pp. 64–65.

[14] See Kash and Rycroft, *U.S. Energy Policy*, for a useful survey of the range of government energy policies.

[15] Center for Renewable Resources, *The Hidden Costs of Energy*, 1985, p. 3.

Table 9.7. *Gasoline prices and taxes in selected countries, 1987*

Country	Price[a] (including tax)	Tax
	(dollars per gallon)	
United States	0.94	0.29
Australia	1.47	0.65
West Germany	2.31	1.34
United Kingdom	2.39	1.53
France	3.06	2.32
Japan	3.34	1.47
Denmark	3.76	2.93
Italy	3.76	2.78

Note:
[a] Average price for April–June 1987.
Source: International Energy Agency, *Energy Prices and Taxes, Second Quarter 1987*, Paris (Organisation for Economic Co-operation and Development, 1987). Reproduced from Christopher Flavin and Alan Durning, *Building on Success: The Age of Energy Efficiency*, Worldwatch Paper 82, Washington (DC), 1988, p. 46.

technological capability that exploited the potential of those natural resources for energy purposes, and a complex array of government programs and policies that reinforced and encouraged energy utilization. America's experience has clearly been distinct from that of the other major industrial powers.

In fact, for reasons that were examined earlier, the United States has provided far weaker incentives for conservation or the improvement of energy efficiency than other industrialized economies. Unlike some European countries and Japan, the United States has never treated petroleum as a primary source of tax revenues, providing the government with a stable revenue base while providing strong incentives for energy efficiency in the important transportation sector (see tables 9.7 and 9.8). Thus, in considering America's prospects for improved energy efficiency against the background of history, one is tempted to recall Bernard Shaw on the subject of Christianity: what a shame it has never been tried!

Table 9.8. *Real prices of gasoline, 1960–1976 (United States 1972 = 100)*

Country	1960	1966	1972	1973	1974	1976
United States	121	117	100	100	125	118
Canada	129	124	114	113	122	115
France	298	270	235	221	273	242
Germany	266	194	175	172	193	193
Italy	436	286	314	283	298	215
The Netherlands	269	246	232	220	246	230
United Kingdom	255	251	230	221	271	190
Sweden	263	239	201	203	219	193
Japan	241	243	201	205	203	165

Note:
Because of the predominance of gasoline in total energy consumption, gasoline prices have been used as a proxy for all prices facing the transportation sector.
Source: Based on Joy Dunkerley, Jack Alterman, and John J. Schanz, Jr., *Trends in Energy Use in Industrial Societies*, EPRI Research Project 864–1, Palo Alto (CA), Electric Power Research Institute, 1980. Reproduced from Joy Dunkerley, *Trends in Energy Use in Industrial Societies: An Overview*, Resources for the Future, Washington (DC), 1980, p. 92.

Future prospects for energy efficiency

Of course, over the past twenty years, policies that promote energy efficiency have been attempted and some significant results have been achieved in reducing the ratio of energy inputs to gross national product. Extrapolating this experience into the future, however, involves large degrees of uncertainty and current evaluations for future prospects must be taken as tentative in the extreme. The historical experience with energy has been full of surprises – not only involving unexpected difficulties and constraints but also unanticipated opportunities as well. An essential ingredient for future success would seem to involve the development of policies and programs that allow for the possibility – indeed the likelihood – of future surprises. Maintaining sufficient flexibility in the energy system to allow for creative responses to such surprises seems a critical element of any successful policy.

In addition, it needs to be recognized that, until recent years, America has largely followed a pattern of adaptation in an environment where economic pressures pressed primarily in the direction of energy-intensive technologies rather than energy-saving ones. Reversing the direction of this long-term path obviously requires systemic change. Energy-efficiency policies are not likely to be successful without a considerable restructuring of economic incentives that will make it more worthwhile for individuals and organizations to pursue the stated goals of government policy. While the forces of the marketplace, alone and unfettered, are unlikely to provide satisfactory solutions to energy problems, such solutions are far less likely to succeed if they require people to behave *contrary* to incentives present in the marketplace. At the very least, individuals should be forced to internalize considerations of the relevant social costs as well as private costs of consuming energy. The historical record demonstrates a remarkable degree of technological dynamism in dealing with energy requirements. The challenge is to harness these technological capabilities for the fulfillment of economic and social welfare needs.

If harnessing is achieved, there is ample reason to believe that technologies that can be put at our disposal will be adequate for the task of establishing a new trajectory for future economic growth that will be less energy intensive or which, more likely, will generate energy from alternative, more abundant sources. Nevertheless, the mere assertion that, given the right incentive structure, a less energy-intensive trajectory is technologically feasible is, by itself, neither very comforting nor very interesting.

Energy-use patterns change slowly

The adjustments that will be required to move toward a genuinely new pattern of resource use, as opposed to adjustments that can be made within the present framework, will take a long time to achieve. The major transitions in energy use in the past – from wood to coal, from coal to liquid and gaseous fuels, the emergence of electricity – each took several decades. There are numerous reasons for the slow pace of a transition in patterns of energy use. Some of these reasons are unnecessarily suppressed by the mere choice of language. It has become a common practice to speak of "interfuel substitutions." Yet what has been involved historically has been much more than just "substitution" as economists ordinarily use the term. Interfuel substitution will not merely require a one-time alteration in factor proportions (a movement along an *existing* isoquant) in response to changes in relative prices. Transitions from reliance upon one fuel source to another have typically involved a highly time-consuming pattern of search, experimentation, pilot plant operation, and the design and eventual construction of extensive infrastructure as well as the specific new facilities. As a result, even when new technologies are available, it may take many years before the new fuels make a significant contribution to the nation's energy needs.

This slow adjustment response is reinforced, as indicated earlier, by an affluent society's existing stock of capital. Such societies are always, to a considerable degree, the prisoners of their own past investments in long-lived capital assets. Fuel-saving improvements are often highly expensive to insert into existing capital structures through retrofitting and, as a result, are not installed until capital is actually replaced. Consequently, technology is adopted and exercises its impact slowly, and any single improvement takes many years before it makes a significant impact upon the overall pattern of energy use. Thus, according to a calculation made in 1977, even "if solar energy captured 100% of the new-construction space heating after 1985, this would represent only about 6.5% of our total primary energy requirement by the year 2000."[16]

In addition, shifts from one fuel source to another have always been highly constrained by the imperfect substitutability among fuels in specific industrial contexts. Although sufficient time and capital outlays can make possible the substitution of one fuel for another in the generation of electric power, in many specific industrial applications such substitution is simply not feasible. The reason, which is too easily and too often neglected in highly aggregated approaches to the energy problem, is that there are significant characteristics of a fuel other than cost/BTU, and these characteristics are often an integral part of any particular industrial process. Thus, while there are numerous ways in which the energy efficiency of gasoline-powered automobiles can be improved, the substitution of a different energy source for gasoline – for example, electricity – is a far more formidable problem. In metallurgy, in spite of extensive searches, it has proven to be extremely difficult to find a good substitute for coal (or indeed, for very specific *kinds* of coal) in the blast furnace. An examination of the shift to coal in American industry in the second half of the nineteenth century reveals that, over a wide range of new industrial processes, wood was not a workable alternative to the new fuel. Similarly, the great ease of handling of liquid and gaseous fuels meant that, later in the twentieth century, coal was simply not a workable substitute for these new fuels in a wide range of industrial processing technologies, or even for home heating.

Energy use and life-cycle accounting

Even after confronting the complexity inherent in understanding the transition between fuels, arguments in favor of substitution are often based on an incomplete characterization of the benefits of current technology. For example, the use of electricity in industrial processes is often criticized as inefficient due to the large thermal losses involved. A closer examination

[16] Richard Balzhiser, "Energy Options to the Year 2000," *Chemical Engineering* (January 3, 1977), p. 88.

of electricity, however, reveals that it is a highly productive and, presently, nearly indispensable form of energy over a wide range of industrial processes. In addition, a complete accounting of the benefits of using electricity in industrial applications shows that, frequently, electricity is actually energy-saving. To highlight this point, consider the growing reliance in specific areas of metallurgy upon electricity as an energy source. This shift toward electricity is one of the most distinctive features of metallurgy in this century, an important outgrowth of the development of the electric furnace in the late nineteenth century.[17] Throughout the first half of this century, use of the electric furnace was confined to a limited number of specialty steels in which the furnaces produced only a few tons per heat. After the Second World War, however, the electric furnace was employed in larger sizes, predominantly to produce carbon steel. Capital costs are far smaller than those associated with other steelmaking technologies. Moreover, a particularly significant feature is its wide range of flexibility with respect to inputs. The electric arc furnace can operate with a 100 percent scrap charge and can be set up quite independently of blast furnaces and coke ovens. As a result, this furnace has become a highly attractive way of making relatively inexpensive additions to steelmaking capacity. Because of these features, the electric furnace offers the unique opportunity of bypassing the highly energy-intensive stages of mining, coke making and smelting. When scrap is available, the electric furnace is a highly energy-saving technology. In fact, "Producing steel by the blast furnace-basic oxygen furnace method consumes more than twice as much energy as electric furnace technology."[18] Given these circumstances, it is not surprising that, although the total output of raw steel declined substantially between 1970 and 1985, the share of that output produced by electric furnaces grew from 15.3 percent to 33.9 percent.[19]

Aluminum, the second most important primary metal in the American economy, also demonstrates forcefully the importance of specific characteristics of different energy forms, and, in particular, electricity. Aluminum is a commercial product that owes its existence to electricity. Although total energy requirements have been substantially reduced since 1970, attempts to substitute other energy forms for electricity have been totally unsuccessful, and there appear to be no short-term prospects for overcoming this dependence. From its commercial beginnings in the late nineteenth century, aluminum has been reliant upon cheap electric power. Huge quantities of

[17]   Nathan Rosenberg, "The Effects of Energy Supply Characteristics on Technology and Economic Growth," *Inside the Black Box*, Cambridge University Press, Cambridge, 1982, pp. 80–103.
[18]   Donald Barnett and Robert Crandall, *Up From the Ashes: The Rise of the Steel Minimill in the United States*, Brookings Institution, Washington (DC), 1986, p. 85.   [19]   *Ibid.*, p. 7.

electricity are required to separate the aluminum from the oxygen in the ore. After the bauxite has been converted into aluminum oxide (alumina), the aluminum oxide "is separated into metallic aluminum and oxygen by direct electric current which also provides the heat to keep molten the cryolite bath in which the alumina is dissolved."[20]

Thus, aluminum is not only energy intensive in its production but, more specifically, electricity intensive. Nevertheless, it is extremely attractive as an industrial material because it combines high electrical conductivity, high thermal conductivity, and strong resistance to corrosion. Most important for present purposes, however, is its high strength-to-weight ratio, a characteristic rendered more significant by the fact that aluminum is easily alloyed and becomes stronger and stiffer as a consequence. These character-istics offer excellent opportunities for saving energy. In fact, aluminum plays a major role in transportation equipment, e.g., aircraft and automo-biles, where its lightness has been responsible for significant savings in energy. This property of aluminum has been especially conspicuous in automobiles. The rise in gasoline prices and federally mandated mileage standards led to significant changes in automobile production, one of the most striking of which was a sharp increase in the use of aluminum. Thus, although aluminum is highly electricity intensive in its manufacture, a complete life-cycle accounting would show it to be, on net balance, energy saving.

Aluminum has another feature that strongly reinforces this point: it is readily recyclable using electricity-intensive methods. It is estimated that the recycling of secondary aluminum involves a saving of fully 95 percent of the energy that would be consumed in producing aluminum from the original bauxite.[21] It seems to be a reasonable conclusion that the utiliza-tion of energy in the particular form of electricity may turn out to be energy saving for the economy as a whole, and that judgments about energy efficiency need to be based upon life-cycle analyses and not upon inferences drawn from the particular form of energy employed at some specific stage in the production process.

This dependence upon the availability of energy in specific forms serves to underline several points in the pursuit of energy efficiency. First, it argues against any simplistic categorization of particular energy forms as being *economically* better or worse on the basis of irrelevant technological or engineering measures of "efficiency." It also emphasizes the point that economic judgments concerning energy efficiency need to be based upon the performance of entire operating systems and not single components of

[20] Carr, Charles, *Alcoa*, Rinehart and Company, New York, 1952, p. 86.
[21] U.S. Department of Commerce, Industry and Trade Administration, *1980 U.S. Industrial Outlook*, Washington (DC), p. 191.

such systems. Nor is it sufficient to examine only the energy efficiency involved in the manufacture of a product; equally important are the energy-using requirements of the product over the course of its own life cycle. Finally, it serves to identify an unavoidable source of difficulty in the pursuit of improved energy efficiency. Energy choices will continue to be constrained in the future by imperfect substitutability among different energy forms, and, at the very least, substituting between fuels takes a very long time. Energy policy therefore needs to be formulated at the micro as well as the macro level.

Alternative energy sources and flexible policy

The transition to improved energy efficiency or alternative energy sources is likely to be a slow process, as it has been in the past. A slow transition is almost inevitable, even if one does not take environmental concerns into account, a concern to which little attention was paid when making energy decisions in the past. This slowness of pace is, in effect, another way of recognizing that energy policy must be formulated with very long time horizons in mind.

The necessity of looking at long time horizons is further reinforced by the numerous technical as well as economic uncertainties that are unavoidable in the attempt to exploit alternative energy sources. Mere reference to the country's experience with nuclear power and synthetic fuels should be sufficient to underline the point that the uncertainties are both technical and economic. It must also be added that the various regulatory activities of government have served as an additional source of uncertainty in the energy sector. In view of the huge risks and large financial commitments involved in energy research, and the various reasons for the normally myopic outlook of private industry, there is a strong case for a more stable financial commitment to long-term energy research on the part of the federal government. In fact, however, recent experience has been highly volatile and erratic. Expressed in 1986 dollars, federal government funding of energy RD&D (research, development and demonstration) "rose from $2.3 billion in 1975 to a peak of $5.3 billion in 1979. Since then it has declined each year, reaching $2.3 billion again in 1986."[22] In the early 1980s, federal support for non-nuclear R&D declined precipitously. Moreover, between 1981 and 1989, the Department of Energy's expenditures for research on renewable power sources fell from $629.9 million to $108.4 million. Over the same period, research on conservation and improved energy efficiency fell from more than $800 million to $330 million.[23]

[22] International Energy Agency, *Energy Policies and Programmes of IEA Countries: 1986 Review*, OECD, Paris, 1987, p. 456.
[23] *New York Times*, August 6, 1989, section 4, p. 4.

In general, great uncertainties persist as to which energy sources will be most satisfactory in the long run, and which technologies will turn out to be the most efficient. In the face of this inherent uncertainty, there is strong support for the position that the government should not confine itself to championing any single alternative or even to a very small number of alternatives. An appropriate criticism of the federal government's postwar energy policy is not that it made a major commitment to nuclear power that subsequently turned out to be problem-ridden. Rather, the criticism is aimed at the single-mindedness of the focus on nuclear power that led to a comparative neglect of so many other possibilities. Research was systematically focused away from exploring those technologies that exploit resources that the country possesses in abundance, that might be less intrusive in their environmental impact, or might lead to straightforward conservation efficiency. It ought to be the policy of government in this sector to manage a much more diversified portfolio of long-term research commitments. It ought to be an explicit goal of government to emphasize research that holds out the promise of widening the range of fuel alternatives. It is important to establish a capacity for flexibility, particularly in view of the long lead times and great uncertainties that have characterized the energy sector in the past and are likely to continue to characterize it in the future.

10 Innovation in the chemical processing industries

RALPH LANDAU AND NATHAN ROSENBERG

Chemicals and allied products (Standard Industrial Classification 28) is the high-tech sector about which the general public probably has the least knowledge. Yet, judged by criteria that are generally regarded as socially and economically worthwhile, this sector should be ranked at the top of the high-tech scale. A common criterion for "high tech" is an industry's expenditure upon research and development (R&D). Chemicals and allied products are at the very top when industries are ranked in terms of the share of total R&D that is actually financed by private funds. With respect to the composition of R&D expenditures, a far larger share of such expenditures in this sector consists of basic research, and basic research and applied research together represent a much greater share of total R&D than is the case in any other industrial sector (see table 10.1). It is tempting to say that this sector has received so little public attention because its performance has, in certain respects at least, been so exemplary.

Clearly, chemicals and allied products have been heavily dependent upon the performance of scientific research. Having said that, it must be emphasized that such research is only the very beginning of the innovation process, and not the end of it. A laboratory breakthrough is, typically, very far from the availability of a commercializable product. Commercial success or failure in this industry, as in other industries, is largely a matter of what happens after a laboratory discovery. However significant the contribution of science to human welfare in general, the question of who will benefit most from specific innovations generated by science will depend on factors far removed from scientific research capability.

In chemicals, and especially organic chemicals, the development of new products depends on the findings of scientific experiments performed at the laboratory level. The initial stages in the development of new polymers, for instance, depend on the laboratory combination of individual molecules

This chapter originally appeared in *Technology and Economics*, National Academy Press, Washington (DC), 1991.

(monomers) to form a single composite molecule (polymers). Depending on the length, the shape, and the chemical properties of the individual monomers, one may create materials with different chemical and physical properties, such as plastics, resins, synthetic rubber and fibers, films, and foams. Of course the role of laboratory research becomes relatively less important at later stages of the development process when chemical engineering becomes the fundamental discipline for transforming the bench-scale reactions to production on a full industrial manufacturing scale. Yet the particular nature of the products and the production processes in chemicals accounts for the significance of scientific research at the early stages of the innovation development cycle, which sets closer ties between science and production than is the case in other industrial realms.

Furthermore, this preeminence of chemicals with respect to research performance is not a recent development. This sector has been the most research-intensive sector of the American economy throughout the twentieth century. If research intensity is measured by the employment of scientific personnel (scientists and engineers) expressed as a percentage of total employment, occasional surveys conducted by the National Research Council indicate that the chemical sector's research intensity was more than twice as great as any other sector between 1921 and 1946.[1]

An understanding of the present state of this industry, in terms of how individual countries rank with respect to performance and commercial success, requires some historical perspective. America's considerable success in this industry in recent decades has to be understood against the background of international differences in natural-resource endowments and the working out of what economists call path-dependent phenomena. Because the United States around the turn of the century already had an important domestic petroleum industry, and Great Britain, Germany, and France had essentially no petroleum supplies of their own, the United States readily, and at an early date, switched to a petrochemical base. The switch in resources was full of consequences, because experience with petroleum and petroleum refining led to the acquisition of many skills and capabilities that were, later, readily transferable to other chemical processing activities. This story, of the acquisition of skills and concepts that were acquired in petroleum, and their subsequent transfer to other large-scale continuous processing industries, is a central theme of the historical process by which America gained a position of world leadership. But this emergence had its base in differences in natural resource endowments and the consequences that flowed from that initial difference. This is where path-dependence became crucially important. The abundance of a particular

---

[1] See David Mowery and Nathan Rosenberg, *Technology and the Pursuit of Economic Growth*, Cambridge University Press, New York, 1989, pp. 64–71.

Table 10.1. *Percentage composition of the R&D expenditures in the six industries of the US economy where R&D is mostly concentrated*

	Chemicals and allied products			Nonelectrical machinery			Electrical machinery			Automobiles and other transportation equipment			Aeronautics and missiles			Scientific and professional instruments		
	BR	AR	D	BR	AR	D	BR	AR	D	BR	AR	D	BR	AR	D	BR	AR	D
1965	12.9	38.8	48.3	2.1	12.9	85.0	4.6	13.5	81.9	3.0		97.0	1.4	14.3	84.3	n.a.	n.a.	n.a.
1966	18.0	39.0	48.0	2.1	13.0	85.0	4.0	12.0	84.0	3.0		97.0	1.0	14.0	85.0	n.a.	n.a.	n.a.
1967	12.4	37.8	49.7	2.0	13.2	84.8	3.4	12.9	83.7	n.a.		n.a.	1.3	12.8	85.9	n.a.	n.a.	n.a.
1968	12.5	37.1	50.4	1.9	12.8	85.2	3.3	13.7	83.0	n.a.		n.a.	1.2	11.9	86.9	n.a.	n.a.	n.a.
1969	12.7	38.5	48.8	1.3	15.2	83.5	3.1	15.0	81.9	n.a.		n.a.	1.1	10.2	88.7	n.a.	n.a.	n.a.
1970	12.0	38.7	49.3	1.3	15.2	83.5	3.3	15.0	81.7	n.a.		n.a.	1.2	9.6	89.2	n.a.	n.a.	n.a.
1971	13.2	38.8	47.9	1.1	14.0	84.9	3.2	15.3	81.5	0.7	8.4	90.8	1.1	9.4	89.5	2.2	11.4	86.4
1972	12.9	39.5	47.6	1.2	13.6	85.2	2.9	16.3	80.8	0.6	7.9	91.6	1.1	8.5	90.4	1.9	11.7	86.4
1973	10.8	40.8	48.4	1.1	13.6	85.3	3.3	15.6	81.1	0.3	6.2	93.5[a]	1.0	10.1	88.9	2.4	10.5	87.0
1974	11.3	39.8	48.9	1.0	13.0	86.0	3.3	15.6	81.1	0.4	6.4	93.2[a]	1.0	11.6	87.4	2.2	11.0	86.8
1975	10.4	38.9	50.6	1.1	12.2	86.7	3.5	15.7	80.8	0.5		99.5[a]	0.8	11.2	88.0	1.2	9.6	89.2
1976	10.1	41.0	48.9	1.6	11.3	87.1	2.9	17.4	79.8	0.3		99.7[a]	0.9	10.5	88.6	1.7	11.6	86.7
1977	10.3	41.7	48.0	1.5	11.2	87.3	3.0	17.1	79.8	0.4		99.6[a]	0.8	10.7	88.5	1.6	13.0	85.4
1978	n.a.	n.a.	n.a.	n.a.	n.a.	n.a.	n.a.	n.a.	n.a.	n.a.	n.a.	n.a.	n.a.	n.a.	n.a.	n.a.	n.a.	n.a.
1979	9.1	41.6	49.3	1.3	13.1	85.5	3.0	15.4	81.6	n.a.	n.a.	n.a.	1.1	10.9	88.0	n.a.	n.a.	n.a.

1980	n.a.	n.a.	n.a.	n.a.	n.a.	n.a.	n.a.	n.a.	n.a.	n.a.	n.a.	n.a.	n.a.	n.a.	n.a.
1981	10.1	42.5	47.4	1.9	18.4	79.7	2.7	17.0	80.3	n.a.	1.1	12.4	86.5	1.1	99.8
1982	n.a.	n.a.	n.a.	n.a.	n.a.	n.a.	n.a.	n.a.	n.a.	n.a.	n.a.	n.a.	n.a.	n.a.	n.a.
1983		46.0	54.0	1.4	14.5	84.0	3.1	16.5	80.4	n.a.	1.1	25.0	73.9	n.a.	13.4
1984	8.4	37.4	54.2	1.6	14.0	84.4	3.0	16.7	80.4	n.a.	1.5	19.1	79.3	13.7

Notes:

[a] Does not include other transportation equipment. BR = Basic Research; AR = Applied Research;
D = Development. n.a. = Not available.

Source: Percentages calculated on data published by National Science Foundation, *R&D in Industry*, various years.

resource at a particular point in historical time set in motion a movement, the direction and momentum of which had consequences that persisted even when the forces that gave rise to that movement had receded.

On the other hand, an important aspect of the emerging discipline of chemical engineering is that it may also offer ways of exploiting alternative, lower-cost materials in the production of new or old products. The Haber/ Bosch process, the first great milestone of chemical engineering, involved a new way of producing a very old product – ammonia. But it did so by shifting the underlying German resource base from a limited resource – the by-product ovens of the iron-and-steel industry – to an immensely abundant base – atmospheric nitrogen.

There is an interesting counterpoint to these historical developments. On the one hand, the United States abundance of petroleum gave rise to a whole set of path-dependent phenomena by shifting United States industry to dependence on a resource, petroleum, that was available in abundance. On the other hand, the Haber/Bosch process, emerging in the second decade of the twentieth century, was a supreme instance of a country developing a new technology that enabled it to overcome the shortage of a critical industrial input – nitrogen. Thus, it is safe to say that, in these matters, history does indeed shape present capabilities very much, and many matters in which we have a current interest can be accounted for only by recourse to path-dependency types of explanation.

But neither is path-dependency the whole story, much less a simple story. What can be said is that Europe's lead in the chemicals industry, in the late nineteenth and early twentieth centuries, did not provide the most effective path for leadership in the chemical processing technology that later came to dominate the twentieth century. Whereas the United States was a distinct latecomer to the chemicals scene, its abundance of petroleum deposits and the experience that it had gained in continuous processing methods in exploiting these deposits, opened up a technology development path that provided an excellent entry into the chemical processing technologies of the mid twentieth century. Nevertheless, that can only be a part of the story: opening up a path in no way guarantees accelerated movement along that path. To put the matter in Toynbeesque terms, challenges sometimes generate vigorous responses; but sometimes they also overwhelm and prove to present insurmountable barriers.[2]

It is important to grasp the several separate dimensions along which productivity improvements are generated by innovations in chemical processing.

[2] See Peter Spitz, *Petrochemicals*, John Wiley and Sons, New York, 1988, pp. xiii, 26–29, and 57–60.

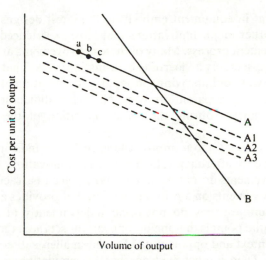

Fig. 10.1 Learning curves in innovation. Key: A = present plant and technology; a, b. c = movements down the learning curve of the present plant; A_1, A_2, A_3 = minor, continuous improvements embodied in new plants; B = learning curve associated with major innovation.

1. There are the major, Schumpeterian innovations that occur relatively infrequently but, when they do, they open up a wide range of significant new opportunities at substantially higher levels of productivity. The Haber/Bosch process is an excellent example of such a major innovation. But chemical innovations not only raise productivity in the conventional sense. They may also offer products that are not only of better quality but are more precisely configured and differentiated to cater more effectively to specific categories of consumer needs.

2. There is a flow of productivity and capacity improvements associated with the use of each of the major innovations. These improvements essentially involve a growing familiarity with a new technology once it has been introduced. Their impact is captured in the declining slope of learning curves or discussed in the vast "learning by doing" literature and popularized by the publications of the Boston Consulting Group (see figure 10.1). However, a smooth movement down these learning curves may be interrupted by subsequent major innovations that offer the possibility of moving to drastically new, cost-reducing technologies.

3. There is also a continual flow of individually small design improvements and modifications within the basic framework of individual Schumpeterian innovations (A_1, A_2, and A_3 of figure 10.1). These have the effect of offering superior technologies to firms that are prepared to make the

necessary investment in equipment embodying the latest designs and modifications of earlier major innovations that have experienced this subsequent improvement process. Many of these improvements are the outcome of what is essentially a "learning by using" process. That is to say, there are many ways of improving the design and operation of new equipment that become apparent only by observing difficulties or opportunities that emerge during the actual operation of the new equipment.[3]

Obviously, these small, continuous improvements in design and components become possible only after major, Schumpeterian innovations have occurred. Such improvements do not – cannot – take place in a vacuum. They are, rather, improvements on a prior innovation that provides a new framework of opportunities; they do not occur independently of such innovations. The essential point is that major innovations set the stage and provide the specific context and opportunities for the smaller, subsequent improvements process. There is much evidence that the cumulative importance of these individually small improvements is immensely important to productivity growth. Unfortunately, it is an aspect of the innovation process that has been badly neglected.

The overwhelming emphasis that has been placed, in recent years, on moving down the learning curve of an existing unchanging plant (category 2), fails to take account of the steady flow of incremental improvements in plant design (category 3) that, at some point, makes it economically attractive to introduce new facilities incorporating these later improvements. Thus, a more complete depiction of the competitive process in this industry is that there is a simultaneous movement on two fronts: (a) the technological frontier, originating with a major innovation, is being continually pushed out, as design and component improvements become available and offer competitive advantages to adopters of this latest technology. This is represented in figure 10.1 as learning curves shift inward toward the origin – A_1, A_2, A_3, etc.; (b) firms have the opportunity of moving down the traditional learning curve established by their existing plant and equipment. But it should now be apparent that it is a serious mistake to visualize the competitive process as if it were entirely a matter of squeezing out, as rapidly as possible, the cost reductions offered by such existing learning curves. This is because the ongoing changes in designs and

[3] These design and component improvements can sometimes be installed or retrofitted into existing equipment, but usually at a higher cost than when they are introduced at the stage of the actual manufacture of new equipment. In other cases new components can sometimes be installed during normal maintenance and replacement activities. See Ralph Landau (ed.), *The Chemical Plant*, Reinhold Publishing Corporation, New York, 1966. For further discussion of learning by using, see Nathan Rosenberg, *Inside the Black Box*, Cambridge University Press, New York, 1982, chapter 6.

components mean that the well-known learning-curve improvements take place on technologies that are, themselves, quickly becoming at least slightly obsolete. In this industry the rapid rate of technological change means that the economic life of a technology is commonly rendered obsolete long before its useful life is exhausted and, perhaps, also long before the firm has been able to approach the lower asymptote of this existing learning curve. Thus, a critical decision is to determine when it becomes worthwhile to commit to an investment that will replace the existing technology with the newest technology. There is an easy formal answer that is provided by economic analysis, which states that firms ought to continue to operate existing technology so long as it covers its marginal costs by doing so. This is, however, only a very inadequate short-run answer in the context of an industry undergoing rapid – and uncertain – technological change.

Thus, the fundamental tension in chemical processing plant is this: adopting the newest technology requires a huge financial commitment in physical and intangible assets of a long-lived nature. Once such an asset is acquired, learning-curve improvements make it possible to raise productivity, reduce costs, and perhaps also raise product quality from this equipment. At the same time, however, the steady forward movement of the technology frontier means that it is often possible for a later entrant to start with an equipment base which begins at a cost level that may be lower than that of the earlier entrant. Nevertheless, partially for the reason already mentioned, if the earlier entrant has had the opportunity to move rapidly down his learning curve and gain a commanding market share, the new entrant may not be able to dislodge him.

But even this statement understates the inevitable uncertainties and surprises that characterize the innovation process in chemical processing. On the one hand, as already suggested, technical improvements commonly occur before an innovative process has moved very far down its potential learning curve. This is particularly poignant since many promising new technologies are promising precisely because they offer the prospect of sharply declining learning-cost curves, but they must nevertheless begin their productive lives at cost levels that may be even higher than the present costs of technologies already in existence (in figure 10.1, the upper portion of learning curve B). Finally, sudden shocks, such as a sharp rise in energy costs, or the availability of a cheaper feedstock, can lead to a rapid redefinition of what constitutes an optimal technology. In an industry of long-lived and expensive assets, these uncertainties render the investment decision an especially painful process – one need only recall the years immediately following the oil boycott by the Arab members of OPEC in 1973.

As the chemical industry has grown and matured, it has given rise to an entirely new specialization: the discipline of chemical engineering, which simply did not exist a hundred years ago. The chemical engineer has become the critical factor in taking the products of the research process and developing feasible techniques for producing them on a commercial basis. It must be emphasized that the findings of laboratory research do not provide the information necessary for commercial production. Such production is not a matter of simple scaling up the tubes and retorts in which a new product was originally developed. That is often physically impossible and hardly ever economically sensible.

Nor is chemical engineering reducible to applied chemistry. It could be better described as the application of mechanical engineering to production activities involving chemical processing. The essence of chemical engineering, then, is a cluster of integrative skills that are applied to the design of chemical processing equipment. But there is much more to it than that. The chemical engineer has, at the center of his activities, the examination and synthesis of different technologies from the point of view of their comparative cost. The work and decision-making of the chemical engineer is inherently economic as much as it is engineering, since it involves the explicit consideration of innumerable tradeoffs in determining optimal design.

Moreover, it is clear from what has already been said that success in the commercialization of chemical processing innovations has depended critically upon the productivity gains realized through an improvement process that takes place after an innovation is introduced in the market. An integral part of this process of cumulative improvement, which deserves separate recognition and treatment, has involved the exploitation of economies of large-scale production and therefore a movement toward larger-scale plants.

Historically, success in the commercialization of new technologies in this sector has turned upon the ability to make the transition from small-scale, batch production to large-scale, continuous processing plants. The benefits of larger scale have been so pervasive in this sector that chemical engineers have developed and employed a "six-tenths rule," which is regularly invoked, that is, capital costs increase by only 60 percent of the increase in rated capacity.

A distinctive characteristic of the American chemical processing scene even in its earliest years was the continuous pressure toward the exploitation of larger size, and the alacrity with which American firms moved in that direction. One authoritative study, discussing the American situation shortly before its entry into the First World War, has referred to "the American attitude to the size of chemical works, which was, in short, to build a large plant and then find a market for the products."[4] It would seem plausible to infer that such an attitude developed at the time because the relevant markets were, as a matter of fact, both large and growing rapidly.

As the industry shifted to petroleum feedstocks in the interwar years and mastered the problems of large-scale, continuous process operations, the optimal size of plant often grew to exceed the market requirements of even the largest of western European countries. Since the European industry had relied much more heavily in its earlier years upon coal as the basic raw material, the transition to larger scale was impeded by skills, attitudes, and educational preparation that had been developed under that coal-based industrial regime. European developments were also influenced by the determination of each country to maintain a capability for satisfying the requirements of its own domestic market.

Even in countries with a relatively large population, such as France and Great Britain, chemical firms planning new projects in the postwar period found it difficult to build a large enough plant that would have reasonably attractive economics. Substantial exports were needed to build such plants, but the products in question would not necessarily be saleable in adjacent European countries, since potential purchasers were still averse to being dependent on supply from across the border.[5]

Building larger chemical processing plants is, however, much more than merely having assurance of access to sufficiently large markets. Such larger plants are necessarily also a product of technological innovations that make them feasible. In this respect it is much more common than it ought to be to assume that the exploitation of the benefits of large-scale production is a separate phenomenon independent of technological change. In fact, larger plants typically incorporate a number of technological improvements, based upon the wealth of experience and insight into better plant design, that could be accumulated only through prolonged exposure to the problems involved in the operation of somewhat smaller plants. The building of larger plants must, as a result, often await advances in the technological capabilities in plant design, equipment manufacture, and process operation. Thus, the benefits of scale cannot be attained until certain facilitating technological conditions have been fulfilled.

Both as a conceptual matter and as a practical matter, it is not easy to disentangle the benefits of larger-scale production from those achieved through introduction of improved equipment, improved design, or better "know-how," that is, better understanding of the technological relationships that are eventually embodied in the larger plant. Such later plants

---

[4] L.F. Haber, *The Chemical Industry 1900–1930*, Oxford University Press, Oxford, 1971, p. 176.

[5] Spitz, *Petrochemicals*, p. 348. See also Ralph Landau, "Chemical Engineering in West Germany," *Chemical Engineering Progress* (July 1958).

typically incorporate a large number of cumulative improvements and conceptual insights.

The discussion of scale raises a final set of considerations. Scale factors have been important not just at the level of the individual plant and its optimal output, compared to the size of the available market. A central additional question is whether the market is large enough to support specialist plant contractors and designers who will eventually be responsible for delivering the plant and the equipment. This is a critical and badly neglected consideration, because the chemical sector has developed a unique set of specialist firms and organizations which have, in turn, played a major role in the innovation process. These specialists now operate on a world scale for a world market, and commercial success and failure must inevitably be addressed in terms of that world market and the ability of various specialist firms to prevail against competition in that market.

Specialized engineering firms (SEFs) came to play a critical role in the chemicals sector during the years following the Second World War. Chemical firms had subcontracted functions like procurement and installation to the SEFs even before the War, when design and process development was essentially carried out in-house. Chemical companies typically carried out their own process design, and used external contractors to handle construction, piping and mechanical work, electrical work, and other separate facets of the project. Petroleum companies typically farmed out most of the detailed design as well to SEFs to design, engineer, and develop their manufacturing installations. In the 1960s, nearly three-quarters of the major new plants were engineered, procured, and constructed by specialist plant contractors.[6]

There were various specific advantages accruing to SEFs in designing and developing chemical production processes. First, during the 1920s and 1930s, while large chemical companies had concentrated mainly upon product innovation and development, SEFs had acquired an ability to handle sophisticated process design and development work. In this, they had benefitted greatly from their experience in the petroleum sector, which had faced, earlier than the chemical industry, problems of large-scale processing refining. The unique capabilities derived from this earlier involvement in design and development work for the petroleum sector constitutes a critical instance of the role of path-dependent phenomena, referred to earlier. As the world moved into the petrochemical age, some countries were better situated by their own past for dealing with the new design and production problems of the new chemical industry. History indeed matters.

[6] C. Freeman, "Chemical Process Plant: Innovation and the World Market," *National Institute Economic Review*, 45 (August 1968).

A further important source of advantage to SEFs came from their opportunity for exploiting economies of specialization and certain forms of learning by doing. Once a major new process technology was developed, or the scaling up of a given production process was carried out, SEFs could reproduce that new technology, or larger-scale production process, for many clients. Such economies could not be accumulated by the chemical manufacturers themselves, precisely because they could produce that technology only for their own, limited internal needs, whereas SEFs had a much more extensive experience with designing that particular plant many times for different clients. Moreover, as they worked for many different clients, they accumulated useful information related to the operation of plants under a variety of conditions. This represented an opportunity for accumulating knowledge and specialized skills which were not available to the chemical producers. SEFs thus acquired the capability to design better plants for other potential customers.

The role of SEFs had important consequences with respect to competition among chemical manufacturers on a global scale. The most significant was their development of the complete technology and plant designs for the basic building blocks of the chemical industry, for example, olefins and aromatics. American-designed ethylene cracking plants appeared all over the world, and these in turn required technologies for the manufacture of key intermediates for the chemical industries of many nations. Such technologies were supplied by SEFs and manufacturers in other countries who sought to generate additional revenues outside their own domestic markets. Latecomers to a particular chemical technology could benefit from their relations with SEFs, which were able to provide them with the process know-how that they had accumulated, at least in part, through their previous relations with earlier entrants (thus, in terms of figure 10.1, latecomers were likely to be supplied with plant that incorporated the design improvements designated by broken lines A_1, A_2, and A_3). Moreover, the availability of such technology from SEFs also encouraged many new entrants into the industry from related sectors such as petroleum, paper, food, metals, and the like. A result was intensified competition, including periods of overbuilding and excess capacity.

In the postwar period, then, the world chemical industry was powerfully shaped by successive waves of diffusion of new technologies, including both product and process technologies. Although the sources of chemical innovation were diverse, a major factor was the role played by American specialized engineering contractors. More specifically, the division of labor between SEFs and the chemical manufacturers had important consequences for the diffusion of new technology, both at domestic and international levels. SEFs licensed extensively to chemical firms all over the world. As a result, they served as major carriers of technological capabilities, including highly elusive but significant "know-how," that is, essential knowledge of a noncodified sort that was, nevertheless, vital to successful plant operation and performance.

The vital role played by SEFs in designing and diffusing new technologies in the chemicals sector underlines a point that it is useful to make in closing. That is, the competitive process, even in high-tech. industries, needs to be examined in terms of a range of activities located "downstream" from the scientific research process. Economists have not, so far, done a very thorough job of this. They have, on the whole, treated technological innovation in a highly abstract way as a collection of activities going on inside a black box, the contents of which are never subjected to systematic examination. When the inputs into that black box are unpacked, it turns out that R&D expenditures are, in fact, not primarily spent on scientific research, but on development which, in the United States has, for many years, constituted more than two-thirds of all R&D spending. Alternatively, even where scientists dominate the initial stages of new product development, the later stages, and eventual commercial success, are likely to be dominated by engineering, design, and technological capabilities.

If these "downstream" activities seem to be lacking in glamor and to be, in fact, rather pedestrian, no doubt they are, at least from certain perspectives. But that perspective is likely to belong to the academic or the intellectual, who is interested in "the big picture" or in large conceptual breakthroughs. It is essential to understand that the marketplace renders judgments that are based on modest improvements and the cumulative effect of individually small, pedantic modifications in product or process design. Small, incremental improvements have brought the semiconductor industry from a handful of transistors on a chip to more than a million such transistors; in telecommunications, it has brought the channel capacity of a $\frac{3}{8}$-inch coaxial cable to more than an order of magnitude increase over an earlier level; and in the computer industry the speed of computational capability has been increased, by individually small increments, by many orders of magnitude. In high-tech as well as in low-tech industries, an unkind Providence seems to have ordained that commercial success is likely to favor particularly the possessors of a varied assortment of grubby skills.

11 Telecommunications: complex, uncertain, and path-dependent

Telecommunications devices have become ubiquitous features of the postmodern industrial society, and dependence on the ability to process and transmit information continues to grow rapidly. Further, the telecommunications industry is currently undergoing rapid and far-reaching technological change. Understanding the forces that shape the rate and direction of inventive activity in telecommunications, then, is compelling from the point of view of the historian of technology as well as the policy-maker. Unfortunately, the difficulties in the prediction of innovations are quite daunting. Even if it were possible to make authoritative predictions about the future path of technological change, which it is not, the question of the ultimate social and economic impact of these changes is another matter entirely.

When a product is already a commercial success, its continued commercial success is dependent upon economic and social variables, and perhaps upon other environmental variables as well. For example, fifteen years ago, at least one authoritative source predicted a "spectacular boom" in Citizens' Band (CB) radios.[1] In fact, the market grew rapidly for such radios, but then suddenly and unexpectedly fizzled. Clearly, we need to recognize, at the outset, that technical success is only a necessary and not a sufficient condition for commercial success. Furthermore, it is hazardous to extrapolate from early commercial successes to future growth and success.

Having laid out these cautionary notes, and as long as expectations are not set unrealistically high, there is a great deal of significance that can be said about the forces that have shaped technological change in the telecommunications industry. Historical analysis makes it possible to isolate and identify at least some of the major forces that shape and

This chapter has benefitted immensely from the able assistance of Scott Stern. Valuable comments were also provided by Prabhakar Krishnamurthy and Joshua Gans.
[1] James Martin, *Future Developments in Telecommunications*, Prentice-Hall, Englewood-Cliffs (NJ), 2nd edn, 1977, p. 385.

constrain the technological future. In so doing, we may be better prepared for dealing with the impact of future changes in the industry and for evaluating the options and tradeoffs that these unexpected changes will present.

A large part of what follows will inevitably center upon attempting to provide answers to the following questions: what are the distinctive features of the telecommunications industry? Which of these features should play a large role in the way we structure our thinking about its future course of development? This chapter examines some of the most distinctive features of the telecommunications industry, such as its inherently systemic nature, explores some of the historical consequences of these features, and attempts to enrich the understanding of the bounds of the rate and direction of future technological change and their economic consequences.

Definitions

It is essential to appreciate that telecommunications, as an industry, has come to encompass a vast range of activities drawing upon a wide variety of techniques. In the most general terms, telecommunications systems "use electricity and electromagnetism to transmit messages or information."[2] Telecommunications systems are composed of a well-defined sender, some transmission device, and some population of receivers. Currently, the economically relevant devices for transmitting information are the telephone, the television, the radio, and, in recent years, the computer and the facsimile machine. Telecommunications systems can consist of one-way or two-way transmission mechanisms, as well as communication that involves two parties at a time or many parties. Communication networks may be local, or, literally, global. There can be free access to the network or network sponsors can restrict access to paying subscribers. Thus, the activities that are encompassed by telecommunications are quite large and varied. The number of permutations of possible institutional structures will be one of the many complications that deserves consideration.

One important qualification should be made. Telecommunications does not presently include the range of activities that encompasses the manipulation of electronic information, namely data processing. Nevertheless, in some ways, these two fields have broad-based complementarities and similar theoretical principles, and the activities within each field have in fact become more and more similar over the last twenty years. Thus, the distinction between telecommunications and data processing has become harder to draw. In 1992, Xerox introduced software that allows computers

---

[2] H. S. Dordick, *Understanding Modern Telecommunications*, McGraw-Hill, New York, 1986, p. 27.

to be operated remotely by means of a facsimile machine.[3] Essentially, it is now possible to manipulate and transmit documents by sending a written message to a computer using a facsimile machine. The transmission of information obviously falls under the aegis of telecommunications, while the possibility of electronic manipulation of information is more akin to data processing. As a result, the technological barriers between telecommunications and data processing have been considerably weakened over time. The breakdown of these barriers can be more adequately understood through an examination of the determinants of inventive activity in the telecommunications industry.

Unique features

To understand the rate and direction of technical change, one must have an appreciation of the following features of the telecommunications industry:

the importance of path dependence, a concept that amplifies other unique features of this industry;

its systemic nature, reflected in the importance of long-lived capital equipment, a need for compatibility standards, and the rise of Systems Engineering approaches to problem-solving;

the role of research and development, particularly the importance of basic research and the interface between corporate and university research;

and the role of government policy, which both regulates industry structure and coordinates the standardization of technological choice.

Path dependence: the unlikely becomes inevitable[4]

Path dependence is a concept that, at the very least, magnifies each of the other effects discussed in this chapter. Path-dependent processes are those phenomena whose outcomes can only be understood as part of a historical process. Early pressures and decisions can "lock-in" a certain technology or market structure for a far longer period of time than may be socially optimal. There are usually several technological options available to a decision-maker, and it is often very difficult and costly to reverse technology decisions once they have been made. This is particularly true in telecommunications where future investments must remain compatible with the currently chosen system, as capital in telecommunications is unusually long-lived.

---

[3] John Markoff, "Is the Elusive Paperless Office about to Become Reality?" *New York Times*, March 24, 1992.

[4] For a more general discussion of path dependency, see chapter 1, above.

The ability to evaluate current technological options is complicated by an inability to predict the future *evolution* of each technology before its adoption. Indeed, future innovations and decisions are dependent on today's choice. The payoff and costs of tomorrow's innovation are dependent on the current adoption decision. Obviously, the potential payoff to an innovation is increased if the innovation is compatible with the current system. Thus, once a system is adopted, innovations that are compatible have higher worth. Further, learning and standardization can decrease the relative costs of innovation that is compatible with the current system. In part, this is because risks become smaller and there is more experience with the technology which is being advanced.

Thus, there will typically be a great deal of uncertainty about the type of telecommunications technology which might become available in the future. However, many decisions cannot be postponed indefinitely. These decisions, being difficult to reverse because of the need to ensure compatibility, will change the calculus of future decision-makers. Therefore, early, small decisions can have a profound and lasting effect on the future evolution of the network.[5] In many cases, another path may have been just as *feasible*, if not superior to the path chosen. The path actually taken is largely a matter of chance occurrences and limited information early on. The evolution of the system might largely depend on the choices of early information-poor decision-makers.

Path dependence is a powerful concept which can be used to explain many of the complications that arise in the analysis of technical change in the telecommunications industry. Like a mountain climber who takes the wrong route of descent from a peak and finds himself above a sheer cliff with no way to proceed further, telecommunications network technology can be locked into an inferior path of development. An excellent example of the deleterious effects of premature standardization is found in American color television, both in its initial adoption decision and with respect to the current debate over High-Definition Television (HDTV). The Europeans, who introduced color television somewhat later than the United States, employ systems that are not only incompatible with American technology but are clearly superior. European systems (such as PAL in Germany and SECAM in France) offer higher picture resolution and better color than standard American technology. However, a switchover by American broadcasters to the European system was unfeasible: millions of consumers would need to buy new television sets or costly adapters capable of receiving the new broadcasts. Thus, reversing past technological develop-

---

[5] W. Brian Arthur, "Competing Technologies, Increasing Returns, and Lock-in by Historical Small Events," *Economic Journal* (1989), pp. 116–131.

ments may be possible only at an extremely high cost. Ironically, the alternative, untrodden paths are largely hidden from the view of those involved. Adoption of a system can preclude further research that might show the viability of alternative, and possibly superior, approaches. Had all foreign countries quickly and uncritically adopted American standards, it is conceivable that no one would ever have realized the feasibility of a superior color TV system. However, had the realization eventually been achieved, it would have proven too costly to make the switch.

Given that broadcasting technologies have already been shown to be highly path-dependent, the complicated analysis necessary to inform the policy debate over HDTV is not surprising.[6] Broadcasters and policy-makers are aware of the dangers of premature standardization of an HDTV technology. However, until a decision is made, consumers' options are limited with respect to the current technological potential, and HDTV manufacturing profits might accrue to firms in those countries that adopt a standard early on. Some industry spokespeople claim that early United States adoption of HDTV is necessary to induce United States firms to become leading international manufacturers of the technology. The power of this argument might be limited, however, as soon as one considers the success of foreign firms, primarily Japanese concerns, in capturing the United States television market under the current standard. Clearly, the standardization necessary for broadcasting technology highlights the path dependency that pervades analysis of telecommunications technology. Indeed, as one examines the systemness requirements of a telecommunications network, or the continuing importance of R&D, one should always be mindful of the complications that arise from path-dependence. Early decision-makers, in information-poor environments, may make small decisions that have large, unintended future consequences, locking them into possibly suboptimal paths.

Systemness: historical roots and consequences

Efficient telecommunications production is inherently systemic in nature. Communication requires a minimum of two participants who communicate through a medium. It is easy to recognize the "network" externalities that are so pervasive in telecommunications, particularly in telephones. The greater the number of participants in the system, the more uses any one individual may be expected to have for that system. At the extreme, no one has an incentive to be the sole member of a telecommunications systems

---

[6] For an introduction to this policy debate, see J. Farrell and Carl Shapiro, "Standard Setting in High Definition Television," *Brookings Papers on Economic Activity: Microeconomics*, 1992.

network. What is harder to recognize about the systemic nature of telecommunications is the critical tradeoffs between individual flexibility and the compatibility and standardization necessary to maintain the system over time.

One of the distinctive features of modern industry is the complicated interdependencies in production. The highway system, airplane manufacturing, and electric-power production are all economic goods that possess a high degree of "systemness." However, the telephone industry clearly lies at the extreme end of the systemness spectrum. In the telephone network, changes in the composition, design, or operation of one part of the network can dramatically affect the rest of the network. A telephone system's primary distinctive feature is to function as a network with simultaneous utilization by many users. Recognizing the importance of systemness is a key to understanding some of the factors that affect the introduction of new services. Features such as Voice Mail, Automated Operator Services, and a common pathway for electronic mail transmission (BITNET and INTERNET), as well as cost-reducing, network-enhancing innovations such as Customer Premise Equipment (CPE), electronic switching, and fiber-optics technology all needed to pass similar requirements before widespread diffusion. Each of these innovations could only be adopted when an *economically* feasible method for integration within the system could be found.

Integrated Services Digital Network (ISDN) technology, currently in the early stages of diffusion, has clearly received a lot of attention due to its goal of increasing personal flexibility without the loss of system-wide network economies. According to American Telephone and Telegraph (AT&T), ISDN technology will provide for the "graceful evolution of today's telecommunications network towards a powerful, unified, network fabric featuring universal ports, dynamic allocation of bandwidth and other resources and adaptive, logically provided services."[7] Essentially, ISDN provides a method for integrating, through the use of standardized protocols and sophisticated software, the various mini-systems that make up the telecommunications network. ISDN provides end-to-end digital connectivity. However, the telecommunications community has hotly debated the need for and economic viability of ISDN. For some time, ISDN was referred to as a "solution looking for a problem."[8] Early criticisms throughout the 1980s were coupled with a slow adoption rate for ISDN systems. While nearly all telecommunications specialists agreed on the potential for long-term benefits, considerable doubt existed about the "need" for quick and uncritical adoption. As ISDN has become more

---

[7] Quoted in Tony Newstead, "ISDN: A Solution in Search of a Problem?" *Telecommunications Policy*, 5. 10 (March 1986), p. 2.   [8] *Ibid.*, pp. 2–5.

widespread, however, some of the specific benefits from this technology have become more clear. In particular, the ability to maintain system-wide compatibility along with the introduction of flexibility for each user decreases the hurdles faced by new innovations. Early observers of ISDN argued that, while elegant, ISDN did not itself provide any new services that could not be handled by the traditional system. The main long-term payoff to IDSN, namely the less stringent requirements for adoption of new, unexpected innovations, is only now beginning to become apparent. In a meaningful way, ISDN *is* "the proverbial egg (the network) for a future chicken ([new] applications)."[9]

A further implication of systemness is that the replacement of capital equipment such as a switch box must be accomplished with a minimum of "down time" for the network. One of the essential features of the telephone industry in particular is the need for constantly maintained service from the point of view of customers. Short disruptions of service by AT&T are always followed by a general public outcry, including threats to switch service to more "reliable" carriers.[10]

It should be noted that mass-media telecommunications such as radio and television are subject to their own systemness idiosyncracies, but to a lesser degree. In particular, most current technology for mass media is one-way, and there is a certain degree of separateness across geographic markets not found in the telephone industry. A more precise understanding of the economic effects of systemness of technological change can be inferred from a historical perspective of how these complex telecommunications systems evolved.

Historical roots of systemness in telephony

For example, one of Alexander Graham Bell's earliest and most important insights pertained to the benefits of a systemic approach to the development and diffusion of telephone technology. As early as March 25, 1876, Bell conceived a telephone network not dissimilar to a sewer or drainage system, that is, connecting every house and providing universal service.[11] It is difficult to appreciate how radical this concept must have seemed at the time. Even after two-way communication had been properly established, a large number of complementary innovations were required to make a network service possible. Indeed, during the most fragile years of the

[9] Eli Noam, "The Future of the Public Network: From the Star to the Matrix," in *Perspectives on the Telephone Industry*, ed. James Alleman and Richard Emmerson, Harper & Row, New York, 1989, p. 13.

[10] Cf. G.W. Meyer, "AT&T's Bad Connections," *New York Times*, September 9, 1991.

[11] Sidney H. Aronson, "Bell's Electric Toy: What's the Use?" in *The Social Impact of the Telephone*, ed. Ithiel de Sola Pool, MIT Press, Cambridge (MA), 1977, p. 22.

telephone's early existence, a central switching technology had not yet been invented; point-to-point private line service was the primary product that Bell Telephone Company leasing agents were selling. Bell's desire to connect areas through a central switching box seemed overambitious and imprudent. Thomas Sanders and Graham Greene Hubbard, Bell's financial backers, understandably wanted to earn quick returns on their investment. Sanders was a generally conservative businessman who had uncharacteristically sunk nearly all his liquid assets into Bell's venture, while Hubbard, Bell's future father-in-law, believed the telephone could provide a modest financial reward. To protect their investment, Hubbard and Sanders tried to generate revenues through the sale of "private-line" service and theatrical demonstrations of point-to-point service.

The famed first conversation between Bell and Watson occurred in March 1876, and by June 1877 there were only 230 telephones installed, almost exclusively replacing point-to-point telegraph facilities. During the summer of 1877 telephone use started to explode. By the end of August, over 1,300 units were installed, quadrupling installations in less than three months. Indeed, Hubbard and Sanders tried to pressure Bell to generate revenues through leasing arrangements on machines which quickly became obsolescent.

However, this desire to generate quick revenues actually increased the rate of complementary technological innovation in the early years of the industry. To save on promotional and construction expenditures while maintaining a fast diffusion rate, Sanders and Hubbard decided that early telephone-leasing agents would be responsible for selling, installing, and maintaining each new local system. Given the novelty and unreliability of the early devices, a technical background was quite helpful in order to be a successful leasing agent. Thus, small, local telegraph owners such as George Coy of New Haven became leasing agents. Their income was dependent on finding a cost-minimizing method of installing and maintaining service. Given this financial incentive, they found it profitable to experiment with the new technology. In this way, Coy became the first operator of a commercial exchange system. Though the central Bell offices would deliver a more sophisticated and standardized telephone exchange fairly quickly, the work of leasing agents seems to have played no small part in demonstrating the viability and increased profitability of providing a centralized switching service.[12] As a result, early incremental innovation in the telephone was spurred and shaped by early users' experience with the new technology.

Thus, Bell himself was confident that the true potential of his device

[12] Robert W. Garnet, *The Telephone Enterprise*, The John Hopkins University Press, Baltimore (MD), 1985, p. 23.

could only be accomplished through establishment of a telephone system which provided a central switching box for interconnected service. Financial concerns, however, dictated that a point-to-point system be sold initially, given the lack of complementary switching technology that would allow for the creation of a network. However, this aggressive early diffusion policy actually led to learning-by-using that was unexpected from the point of view of the central Bell management. This learning-by-using focused the early inventive activity in particular directions which turned out to be useful for the long-term needs of the network.[13]

Further, the relatively early adoption of a network technology and the ability to deter competition by providing exclusive networked service pointed to a path for research that reinforced the systemic aspect of early telephone systems. Large investments in switching technologies had to be incurred as fixed costs that were relatively insensitive to the number of adopters. After this investment, the marginal cost associated with installing an additional line was relatively small. And, while the cost-savings involved with a central switching system were quite impressive, these early choices effectively precluded research on how to make the system more flexible from the viewpoint of any specific user. Thus, early technological, financial, and strategic choices in the Bell System's history effectively "locked in" a research program biased towards a systemic approach to telephone technology. Theodore Vail, the influential head of AT&T in the early part of the century, articulated the vision of "universal service" that would ensure that all American homes would be connected to the Bell System. Studying the early history of telephone innovation and adoption reveals that the feasibility of Vail's plan was highly dependent on decisions made by Bell management in 1880 and not 1920. Further consequences of systemness are the precise compatibility requirements that arise and the complicated tradeoffs that emerge. Adoption of one technology might preclude or usurp other established technologies. The effect of adoption on the system might be difficult to foresee, and the difficulty of installation might be formidable.

The role of Systems Engineering

Given these very precise compatibility requirements, it is probably no coincidence that the discipline of Systems Engineering originated and experienced its most extensive development within the Bell System.[14] As the industry grew in size, interdependence, and complexity, and as the individual components drew upon increasingly specialized bodies of

[13] Nathan Rosenberg, "Learning-by-Using," in *Inside the Black Box*, Cambridge University Press, Cambridge, 1982, pp. 120–140.
[14] "Systems Engineering," *Encyclopedia Britannica*.

knowledge, it became imperative that more sophisticated methods be employed for evaluation and planning that would explicitly take into account the numerous interdependencies within the network. Efficient performance of an entire communications system requires scrupulous attention to each interface to assure compatibility among separate components of the system. It is in fact the essence of a technological system that the performance of components can only be evaluated meaningfully within a larger context that explicitly takes into account the nature of their interaction with other components.

The collection of methodologies and techniques that is now called Systems Engineering had its main development under the impact of the electronic revolution that began with the invention of the transistor at Bell Labs. shortly after the Second World War. It was correctly perceived at the time that the new wave of components and expanded technological capability would have profound implications upon the telephone system – a system that was already expanding rapidly because of increased public demand for telephone services. It was obvious that a wide new range of choices would be opened up, and that many of the established interfaces would be drastically reshaped and many new interfaces would be created. The possibility of offering new services, such as Touchtone, Automated Operator Services, and Direct Long-Distance Dialing, involved dealing with a new collection of compatibility problems and interdependencies. But individual technical choices could be made intelligently only if the numerous interdependencies were incorporated into the decision-making process. Economic efficiency could be ensured only in an analytical context where the economic implications of technical alternatives were carefully spelled out.

Thus, Systems Engineering owed much of its development within the telephone system to the fact that choices and tradeoffs in this industry attained levels of complexity that had not been attained elsewhere in industry. Systems Engineering has served as a set of analytical techniques for integrating economic considerations with the overall evolution of the telephone system as it confronted an expanding set of technical alternatives. On the one hand it served as a method for articulating the needs of the final consumer and the concern with cost minimization. Without the analytical capability offered by Systems Engineering, there was the serious danger that the telephone system might slip from choices that optimized the performance of the entire system. Instead, choices might represent optimization for separate parts of the larger system, but not for the system as a whole, that is, suboptimization. Moreover, Systems Engineering played an increasingly prominent role in providing guidance to research activities by identifying possible problems and constraints that would be thrown up by the continuing evolution of the entire system, or by identifying potentially high payoffs from advancing specific points on the technological frontier. In some ways, the development of Systems Engineering served as a formal response to the path-dependent nature of technological choice and the necessity of technical compatibility throughout the system.

Thus, Systems Engineering grew rapidly in the years since the Second World War because it facilitated several forms of interaction that were becoming increasingly prominent within a complex and evolving technological system. In fact, it may be taken as an interesting index of the intensely systemic nature of telecommunications that the evolution of this industry gave rise to Systems Engineering in the first place.

Systemness in radio and television

It is necessary, of course, to distinguish between different sectors of the telecommunications industry. What is true of telephones is not equally true in all other sectors. Radio and television have a much smaller degree of "systemness" than the telephone. In radio and television there is a single transmission source. There are, to be sure, many receivers, but the traffic is only one way. The development of the telephone system was heavily focused toward technological possibilities that allowed each device to communicate with every other device. This feature makes for a quite complicated system. Early development of radio, on the other hand, was focused on point-to-point communication. This focus persisted for a much longer period of time than the similar period for the telephone. The relative lack of systemness in modern broadcast technologies can be understood as resulting from a specific historical process of innovation and research focus guided by the particular economic forces that diffused this technology.

Marconi's invention of the "wireless" was originally perceived as a technology for ship-to-shore communication. For the first twenty years of wireless technology, research was focused on providing point-to-point communication. In fact, a major goal of early research projects was to reduce the bandwidth of a particular transmission, allowing for the transmission of a greater number of distinct messages.[15] Early adopters of Marconi's system included the military, news organizations, and shipping lines. The needs of these buyers were influential in the research decisions of the young technology. For many years, research efforts were focused on providing an increasingly sophisticated technology for ship-to-shore communication. Economic pressures compelled early radio technology to be flexible in the changing environment. Essentially, it was important that no

---

[15] W.J. Baker, *A History of the Marconi Company*, Methuen & Co., London, 1970.

innovation supersede prior purchases. For example, Marconi's financial backers were concerned that Transatlantic Service would swamp ship-to-ship communication, and the Board did not give a financial go-ahead to experimentation until they were reassured that there were enough distinct frequencies such that early adopters would not be disadvantaged by the proposed new technology. In this way, early research was focused on innovations which, at the least, did not enhance the systemic aspect of radio telecommunications. This early emphasis lingered in the arrangements instituted after the widespread adoption of radio as a societal entertainment device. One-way communication, the ability for receivers to possess a wide variety of technologies capable of deciphering radio waves, and the viability of locally unconcentrated radio markets, all reflect the fact that this industry is less systemic than the telephone industry. Thus, early events and economic pressures in the radio industry shaped the present observed level of systemness.

One of the most important, and most unique, features of the telecommunications industry is the inherent systemness involved in any communications network. The systemic nature of this industry will continue to interact with dynamic technological change for the foreseeable future. It is increasingly observed that computer technologies are allowing for greater and greater flexibility throughout the telecommunications industry. For example, ISDN's popularity reflects the desire for all telecommunications users to have the capability to interact with each other (regardless of the type of sending medium). ISDN provides a technology that can serve as a flexible highway for information. One of ISDN's primary benefits lies in the fact that it decreases the need for new innovations to be compatible with the entire telecommunications network. It should be noted that massive advances in computing technology were necessary before the telephone network could begin the slow process of reducing systemness, as highlighted by the adoption of ISDN technology. In other areas of telecommunications, such as television, much recent history has pointed instead toward an increase in the level of systemness. As already discussed in the early history of the radio, early research on wireless broadcasting was focused on point-to-point communication. The effects of this early emphasis still lie with us today. Indeed, it is only recently that systemic communication between radio and television broadcasters and listeners/viewers has begun to become a technological reality. In particular, the 20-year-old experiment with cable television is only now transforming the technology of television broadcasting, allowing for two-way communication.

While home-shopping capability has been discussed as a technological possibility since the early 1960s, emergence of cable television as a profitable venue for retailers has been a recent phenomenon.[16] The "cheap" broadcasting space afforded by broadcast deregulation led to the viability of "commercial" channels. Programs are entirely devoted to selling products, which can be ordered by calling a toll-free number. As home shopping emerges as a profitable marketing strategy, cable operators have increasingly experimented with completing the loop between broadcasters and consumers. In the most sophisticated systems, cable operators install home-based computers which can be linked to a shopping network and a host of other interactive services. In order to capitalize on the unserved market of home consumers, cable operators are beginning to utilize a systems approach. It seems that cable firms expect that the most profitable method for exploiting the consumer niche afforded by home shopping will be to offer a technological bundle, a system that fully internalizes the necessary information transmissions for purchase to occur. Thus, advances in digital computer technology are affecting telecommunications systems quite diversely, with the critical variable being the historical development of the system over the past century.

Research and development

What should be plainly obvious in this discussion is the prominent role of observable technological change in the telecommunications industry. Whether measured in terms of R&D expenditures or the employment of scientific personnel, telecommunications is one of the most research-intensive and technologically dynamic sectors of the American economy. Two firms, AT&T and IBM, have dominated industry research. AT&T has been a technological leader since its inception in the nineteenth century, accelerating its commitment to research after the founding of Bell Labs. in 1925. IBM, on the other hand, emerged as an information technologies trailblazer after the Second World War, as the world's leading computer designer and manufacturer. The research output of these two organizations alone comprises a nontrivial portion of scientific advance in this century.[17] If United States industries are ranked by company R&D expenditures for 1989, electrical equipment, which includes communication equipment, would rank third, and communication equipment, if viewed as a separate industry instead of as a subcategory of electrical equipment, would rank

---

[16] Loy Singleton, *Telecommunications in the Information Age*, Ballinger Publishing, Cambridge (MA), 1983, pp. 45–46.

[17] AT&T and IBM have employed a large number of renowned researchers, many of whom have earned a Nobel Prize for their efforts. As early as 1937, C.J. Davisson of Bell Labs. was awarded a Nobel Prize for his authoritative demonstration, back in the 1920s, of the wave nature of matter.

Table 11.1. *Corporate-funded R&D by industry – 1989*

Rank	Industry	Corporate-financed R&D (in millions in US dollars)
1	Transportation equipment	15,100
2	Machinery (includes computing machinery)	13,216
3	Electrical equipment (includes communication equipment)	11,546
4	Chemicals and allied products (includes drugs and medicines)	11,449
5	Office, computing, and accounting machines	10,533
6	Communication equipment	5,842
7	Professional and scientific instruments	5,638
8	Drugs and medicines	5,206

Source: Compiled from Appendix 6–18, *Science and Engineering Indicators*, National Science Foundation, 1992.

sixth (see table 11.1). Further, even the most casual observer can note the continual transformation and speedy obsolescence of equipment in communications technologies, a characteristic that sits uncomfortably, cheek-by-jowl, with the great durability of the equipment. Indeed, telephonic technologies, now over a hundred years old, have probably not even *begun* to approach maturity.

Two distinct qualitative features of the innovation process in telecommunications will be stressed here. First, the continuing importance of basic research in telecommunications cannot be underestimated. Second, the persistent inability to appreciate the long-term consequences of innovation needs to be explored. Tying these two points together, the ever-present tension between standardization of the present technology and the possibility of superior technology on the horizon will be discussed with respect to the history of fiber optics in the telephone system.

Basic research: source of perennial uncertainty and change

In many cases, problems in telecommunications have given rise to and been informed by basic research and relatively "new" science. In fact, basic research in telecommunications firms has led to the development of a number of new or improved technologies. One distinctive property of basic research, of course, is that its outcome is highly unpredictable. Thus, even when one eliminates all the complications of technology forecasting that are contingent on economic considerations, it is extremely difficult to predict the rate and direction of technological change in an industry that relies so heavily on basic research for new technology, as does telecommunications.

A detailed technological history of the telecommunications industry, which obviously cannot be undertaken here,[18] would be organized around a small number of technological discontinuities and their major effects in redefining the set of possibilities open to the industry. Many of these major innovations had their origin in the basic research activities conducted within the industry. Confining ourselves to the post Second World War period, the invention of the transistor at Bell Labs. in 1947 serves as the archetypal example of the importance of basic research. The story that accompanies the development of the transistor highlights the forces and spillover effects between university-sponsored basic research, corporate basic research, and the positive feedbacks between economic payoffs from basic research and funding of basic research. The transistor was invented at Bell Labs. in late 1947 by a research team headed by William Shockley and including Walter Brattain and John Bardeen. The factors that were critical in the development of the first transistor included the economic priorities of Bell Labs., the background in solid-state physics as it had developed at the end of the Second World War, and the understanding by Bell Labs. and Shockley of the natural complementarities that can exist between applied corporate research and basic science.[19] The Bell System faced a particular challenge in the years immediately following the Second World War, namely the need to improve the quality, reliability, and efficiency of long-distance transmission. This service became increasingly critical as the utilization of long-distance service expanded. Without this particular impetus focusing research at Bell Labs., it is easy to conjecture that the development of a workable transistor would have been long delayed. Mervin Kelly, director of Bell Labs. at the time, pursued the goal of improved Long Lines service by steering William Shockley's research program on the general properties of semiconductors in a slightly new direction. Shockley worked with Kelly to design a research program that

[18] Brock's work, *The Telecommunications Industry*, Harvard University Press, Cambridge (MA), 1982, provides a valuable introduction to the industry, although its main focus is not on technological considerations. By far the most detailed technological history through the late 1970s can be found in the nine-volume work, *A History of Science and Engineering in the Bell System*, compiled by Bell Labs.

[19] A thorough history of the transistor can be found in *A History of Science and Engineering in the Bell System*, vol. VI. For an insightful economic analysis, see also *The Rate and Direction of Inventive Activity*, ed. Richard Nelson, Arno Press, New York, 1962.

would test the existence and explore the viability of germanium as a conducting material. Kelly was convinced that exploring the properties of semiconductors would ultimately advance transmission technologies, that is, possibly replace the notoriously unreliable vacuum tube.

Shockley's education at MIT, where he completed his PhD in 1936, was instrumental in providing the background necessary to formulate the research program in an efficient manner. MIT was among the two or three research universities that devoted substantial resources to exploring solid-state physics in the 1930s. Shockley's awareness of the underlying scientific principles and questions of solid-state physics avoided possible costly delays in research. It should be noted that before the development of the transistor, solid-state physics was a relatively underdeveloped subdiscipline, though it had been increasing in importance after 1930. Indeed, Bell Labs. offered one of the few well-funded venues where Shockley could continue such research after his graduation from MIT.

Before 1947, research investment in the physics of materials was quite risky and the scientific payoffs to research on solid-state theory were uncertain. The invention of the transistor undoubtedly altered the incentives for additional commercial research by AT&T. However, the obvious economic payoffs from more efficient semiconductors also changed the perception of the scientific payoffs to be realized from work in solid-state theory. Within a short number of years, nearly all major American physics research programs included research on the basic scientific properties of semiconducting materials.[20] Indeed, Shockley's team not only applied scientific theory to yield broad-based economic benefits; Shockley, Brattain, and Bardeen also shared the Nobel Prize in Physics for their part in the advancement of scientific knowledge.

Thus, development of the transistor was facilitated by university research and training. This knowledge was acquired without the specific intention of applying it to the particular research undertaken at Bell Labs. Given this background of university research, the excellent resources, standards, and focus of Bell Labs. dramatically increased the efficacy of Shockley's research program. The implicit partnership in basic research between MIT and Bell Labs. resulted in a long-term shift in the priorities of each institution. Due to the sustained investment in William Shockley's research program, the economic and scientific payoffs from understanding the properties of semiconductors multiplied.

The interrelationships between university and corporate basic research highlighted here are not unique to the development of the transistor.

[20] Diffusion of solid-state theory was in fact spurred by Shockley. Bell Labs. undertook a vigorous program of informing the scientific community of its discovery, highlighted by Shockley's classic, *Electrons and Holes in Semiconductors*, D. Van Norstrand Co., Princeton (NJ), 1950.

Instead, this history is only one of a host of major technological innovations that occurred within the corporate telecommunications laboratory but was informed by work at the university level. Indeed, important advances in laser technology, also at Bell Labs. around 1958, closely mirror the experience with the semiconductor. As discussed below, the economic payoff to AT&T resulting from development of the laser was delayed due to the need for complementary innovations in transmission technology. Nevertheless, it is also true that the basic research that led to the development of the laser restructured the priorities of university-sponsored research on optics. Basic research in telecommunications has consistently redirected the pursuit of knowledge by both private and academic researchers. Indeed, understanding technological change in telecommunications requires an understanding of how basic research breakthroughs create discontinuous changes in the value of the choices available to firms and scientists.

The inability to perceive the consequences of technical change

The history of the telecommunications industry is in fact the history of these technological discontinuities and their unexpected impacts. Two central elements of this industry, the telephone and the radio, are classic examples of new sets of possibilities that contemporaries singularly failed to anticipate.[21] Western Union was given the opportunity to purchase Bell's telephone patent in 1877 for $100,000, but turned it down! Although the reasons for the refusal are not completely clear, it seems apparent that the telephone was not perceived as a good substitute for the telegraph.[22] This unilateral offer to Western Union was made by Gardiner Hubbard, not Alexander Bell himself. As mentioned earlier, Bell articulated the possibility of universal service as early as March 1876. It was Bell's financial supporters who could not envision the kind of systematic and societal change that would result from the telephone's introduction. Even as the telephone became recognized as an important innovation, telegraph interests were slow to recognize the discontinuity that had occurred. In fact, "Western Union was willing to withdraw from the telephone field in 1879 in exchange for Bell's promise to keep out of the telegraph business."[23]

[21] It is a closely related point that major inventions are frequently the work of outsiders – people whose conceptual frameworks and training are not defined by and limited to the prevailing technology. Thus, three of the greatest inventors in telecommunications were not technologists by training. Samuel Morse was a portrait painter before he invented the telegraph in 1835, Alexander Graham Bell was a teacher of the deaf, and Guglielmo Marconi had little formal training in technological subjects of any kind. Clearly, expertise in the *existing* technology is not a great advantage when technological discontinuities are involved.   [22] Brock, *The Telecommunications Industry*, pp. 87, 92, 123.

[23] W. Rupert Maclaurin, *Invention and Innovation in the Radio Industry*, The Macmillan Company, New York, 1949, p. 24.

The inability to perceive the entertainment and commercial applications of radio was even more pronounced. In contrast to Bell, Marconi did not correctly anticipate the major societal purpose for which his invention was eventually used. Instead, he thought of radio as primarily a device for communication under circumstances where conventional wire technology was not feasible – ships at sea, remote and inaccessible locations, etc. Marconi pursued wireless technology energetically without a clear sense of the new possibilities that would be opened up by his invention. Again, most of the decision-makers in the telegraph industry persisted in their myopia. The British Postal monopoly, European governments, and even the telegraph monopoly of Newfoundland, all hindered Marconi's efforts to broadcast messages between and within countries.[24] It was not until the end of the First World War, under the leadership of David Sarnoff at Radio Corporation of America (RCA), that the radio was transformed into the first mass telecommunications device, bringing along with it widespread societal change. A Postal Telegraph executive succinctly expressed the limited vision of insiders in the case of the radio: "We were *telegraph* men, and we did not think about alternative methods of communication."[25]

The third great technological discontinuity that makes up the present-day telecommunications industry, the computer, again illustrates the difficulties in anticipating the great potential of a new technological capability. The computer was regarded by its inventors as a purely scientific device, useful for very tedious mathematical calculations, such as solving differential equations. Even Thomas Watson, Sr., an executive with extensive business experience, foresaw no commercial demand for the computer. He believed that a single computer, already in operation at IBM's New York headquarters, "could solve all the important scientific problems in the world involving scientific calculations."[26] As of 1950, private industry's view of the demand for computers was that "the only demand was from government agencies such as the Bureau of the Census, NACA, the Ballistics Research Laboratory, the Naval Proving Grounds, the Coast and Geodetic Survey, the Weather Bureau, the White Sands Missile Range, and the like."[27] Thus, throughout the history of telecommunications, there has been a systematic inability by contemporaries to foresee the future uses and improvements in inventions which engender a discontinuous expansion of the technological frontier. The reasons for this

---

[24] Baker, *Marconi Company*, pp. 44–85.
[25] Maclaurin, *Invention and Innovation*, pp. 24–25. Italics in original.
[26] Barbara Goody Katz and Almarin Phillips, "The Computer Industry," in *Government and Technical Progress*, ed. Richard Nelson, Pergamon Press, New York, 1982, p. 171.
[27] *Ibid.*, pp. 171–172. See also Paul Ceruzzi, "An Unforeseen Revolution: Computers and Expectations, 1935–1985," *Imagining Tomorrow*, ed. Joseph Corn, MIT Press, Cambridge (MA), 1986.

inability to perceive the long-term effects of technological change are varied, but some important regularities can be pointed out that should usefully inform a discussion of the future of telecommunications.

First, there is a need to place major changes in technology into a systems context. When a new technology becomes available, it is extremely difficult *not* to perceive it and to define its potential as a supplement to the existing technological infrastructure. Contemporary systems exercise a powerful influence in shaping the reaction to technological novelty. New technologies are usually defined as if they were to perform a role within the existing system, and there is indeed a natural tendency to seek out such roles by identifying specific locations in the existing system where the new technology may have certain advantages. Thus, when railroads were introduced in the United States in the 1830s and 1840s, it was believed that they would be inserted into the existing canal network in locations where canals have severe disadvantages, such as hilly or mountainous terrain. To some extent, this actually happened. Moreover, when the railroad finally established its own network, it did not entirely displace the old canal system, much of which continued to function for some years, and some of which still does.

The telecommunications industry offers similar experiences. The telephone was regarded by many as, at best, a supplement to the telegraph, and this had much to do with Western Union's limited interest in it. The fact that it provided instant voice communication seems not to have been a decisive consideration. Similarly, the wireless telephone, when it became feasible in the second decade of the twentieth century, was relegated to the same role as the wireless radio. J.J. Carty, Chief Engineer of the New York Telephone Company, stated in 1915: "The results of long-distance tests show clearly that the function of the wireless telephone is primarily to reach inaccessible places where wires cannot be strung. It will act mainly as an extension of the wire system and a feeder to it."[28]

The announcement of the transistor highlights the misperceptions that are being described. The popular press totally underestimated the potential impact of the transistor; the *New York Times* relegated the announcement to an inside page in a small, regular column entitled "News of Radio." On the other hand, the technical press was immediately responsive to some of the potential applications of the transistor, claiming that "the Transistor is destined to have far-reaching effects on the technology of electronics and will undoubtedly replace conventional electron tubes in a wide range of applications."[29] Though technically competent individuals were aware that the effect of the transistor would be large, they perceived that the

[28] Maclaurin, *Invention and Innovation*, pp. 92–93.
[29] Quoted from *Electronics* (September 1948), in *Engineering and Science in the Bell System*, vol. VI, Bell Labs., p. 16.

primary application of the transistor would be the replacement of vacuum tubes. Speculation centered around how the transistor would increase efficiency in the existing system, rather than how the transistor would alter the system or create entirely new systems. Today, the successor to the transistor (the integrated circuit) is crucial to the operation of every stage of telephone service. Production of an electronic signal, complex routing through the network, and decoding and amplification to the receiver are all entirely dependent on miniaturized IC technology.

Of course, there is an additional reason why it has been so difficult to perceive new technologies as harbingers of new systems. Separate from the systems point, but compelling in its own right, new technology is often a very poor performer in its earliest stages and initial capabilities are often quite limited. Eventual diffusion is a reflection of the trajectory of subsequent productivity and performance improvements.

Thus, commercial telegraph operations in the United States are ordinarily regarded as having commenced with the opening up of the "Philadelphia–New York Line" in January 1846. However, the speed of transmission was substantially reduced by the fact that the telegraph did not yet cross the Hudson River. Telegraph messages were sent from Philadelphia to Newark. The actual delivery of a message required a ferry trip across the Hudson.[30] Similarly, Bell's original telephone was a very modest instrument. It could not very effectively transmit and receive, and the quality of sound was very poor. Moreover, it could transmit only over a maximum distance of about twenty miles at a time when the telegraph network crossed the entire continent.[31] As discussed earlier, establishment of a network required complementary inventions such as the telephone exchange, itself a product of experimentation by leasing agents. Thus, it was not unreasonable to regard the telephone of April 1876, as no more than a feeder to the telegraph. The failure was a failure to anticipate the future improvements that would transform a poor and primitive instrument into a sophisticated and reliable device. However, we should not feel too smug or superior over the failure of earlier generations to accomplish this. It is, at the very least, not obvious that we are doing a better job today. As one authority on the industry has remarked:

Although he might possibly have realized that they were conceivable in theory, a reasonable forecaster in 1940 would not have predicted the computer; in 1945 he would not have predicted the transistor; in 1950 he would not have predicted the laser; in 1955 he would not have predicted the use of pulse code modulation, large-scale integration, solid state switching, computer time sharing, on-line real-time

---

[30] Brock, *The Telecommunications Industry*, p. 64.
[31] *Ibid.*, pp. 90–91, 123. Also Aronson, "Bell's Electric Toy".

systems in commerce, direct-access data banks or synchronous communication satellites; in 1960 he would not have predicted holography or satellite antennas on the rooftops; in 1965 he would not have predicted the hand-held calculator or the spread of microcomputers.[32]

Fiber optics: a case study in telecommunications innovation

The importance of basic research and the systematic biases that accompany breakthroughs in innovation should now be relatively clear. Indeed, the history of fiber optics neatly encapsulates several points of interest, while providing a framework for analyzing how R&D breakthroughs are related to difficult technology policy questions regarding standardization.

Somewhat separate from the breakthroughs described above, a sequence of technological discontinuities has transformed the technology of transmission in telecommunications a number of times in the last century. The major events here center around the great advances in microwave technologies that came out of the Second World War,[33] the introduction of communication satellites, partially a by-product of the Space Program, and the recent emergence of fiber optics as the apparent technology of choice in transmission. The development of fiber optics was made possible by a particularly unpredictable *combination* of breakthroughs involving optical fibers and laser technology. The extent to which this represented a major discontinuity in telecommunications is aptly conveyed by the fact that the patent department at Bell Labs. was initially unwilling even to take out a patent on the laser, on the grounds that such an invention had no possible relevance to the telephone industry. In the words of Charles Townes, who subsequently won a Nobel Prize for his research on the laser, "Bell's patent department at first refused to patent our amplifier or oscillator for optical frequencies because, it was explained, optical waves had never been of any importance to communications and hence the invention had little bearing on Bell System interests."[34]

Obviously, a glance at the makeup of the capital structure of the contemporary telecommunications system might make Bell Labs. patent office appear inept. But, that would be unfair. In fact, the attractive properties of commercial fiber-optics technology were not at all clear until the very recent past. The lack of electromagnetic interference, conservation of heat and electricity, and the enormous expansion in bandwidth that fiber optics provides[35] are all features whose utility only became apparent with

---

[32] Martin, *Future Development*, pp. 12–13.
[33] Brock, *The Telecommunications Industry*, pp. 180–183.
[34] Charles Townes, "Quantum Mechanics and Surprise in Development of Technology," *Science* (February 16, 1968), p. 701.
[35] Note that the light spectrum is approximately 1,000 times wider than the radio spectrum.

the decision by new long-distance firms such as Microwave Communications Inc. and Sprint to invest in the new technology. The speed with which fiber optics established itself as the most attractive technology of transmission cannot be better communicated than by the observation that an excellent book on the industry, published as recently as 1981, provides no discussion whatever of this new technology.[36]

Further, fiber-optics technology displaced a previous transmission technology breakthrough that was confidently expected to hold central importance in modern long-distance service – the communications satellite. The large bandwidth and huge channel capacity offered by fiber optics resulted in drastic reductions in long-term demand for communications satellites. As recently as the early 1980s, communications satellites were considered to be a technology in their earliest growth phase. Prior to the breakup of AT&T, communications satellites were viewed as central elements in the modernization of exchange-to-exchange transmission (Long Lines).[37] However, the establishment of long-distance nationwide fiber-optics networks both transformed the structure of the long-distance market and relegated communications-satellite technology to a secondary, but still visible, role. There remains, of course, a number of uses where it is difficult to conceive of fiber optics displacing communications satellites. The popularity of car phones is an obvious example; the newly emerging use of satellites as a navigational guide for airplanes and ships is another. Just as the vacuum tube found niche uses that even the most sophisticated transistors have not displaced, communications satellites represent a powerful and useful technology whose usefulness in the telecommunications system is unlikely to be totally eliminated by the revolution in fiber optics.

In spite of its clear superiority as a transmission medium, it will be a long time before fiber optics actually dominates transmission in telecommunications. For the industry to function well, its individual components must be built to very high standards of reliability. As a result, telephone equipment has a very long life expectancy. Thus, existing households and businesses are already served by wire that is expected to last for many years. While new construction will utilize the new fiber-optics technology, it would be incredibly expensive to replace all existing copper wiring with optical fiber.[38] The "last mile" will not utilize the latest technology until yesterday's technology is not merely obsolescent but in need of replacement.

[36] Brock, *The Telecommunications Industry*.
[37] Singleton, *Telecommunications in the Information Age*, pp. 77–87.
[38] "Even if the cost of optical fibers falls drastically, fibers would not cause the instant revolution that communication satellites did. Launching a satellite and constructing earth

The point to be made here is one with the broadest policy implications. The telecommunications industry is experiencing technological change of a truly breathtaking nature. Scientific research in a number of disciplines rapidly pushes out the technological frontier. The photonics revolution has been under way since the introduction of laser technology in the 1960s, computer technology continues to expand exponentially, and some of the deepest systemic changes from the transistor revolution are only now beginning to become apparent. The great technological dynamism of this industry, however, is tied to a gigantic investment in telecommunications physical capital and infra-structure of an exceptionally long-lived sort. Telephone plant and equipment has in the past been designed and constructed with the expectation of a normal operating life of forty years. The important policy issue lies in the inherent conflict between a vast financial commitment to long-lived plant and equipment and the present availability of superior technologies – to say nothing of the uncertain *prospect* of as yet undeveloped technologies of even higher performance.

When technological change is rapid, even the most "rational" decision-maker is uncertain when to invest.[39] Waiting for tomorrow's superior technology delays today's modernization program. Moreover, the decision to adopt a technology in telecommunications often requires a commitment to a *standard*. This standard must be compatible with the current system, and future investments must be compatible with the chosen standard. Adopting standards can lock in certain systemic paths of development. Indeed, industry observers as well as regulators often fail to appreciate the importance of those narrow "windows of opportunity" that allow for optimization of the current system and simultaneous adoption of a superior dynamic path.[40] In telecommunications, an industry whose costs are composed of long-lived capital, adoption decisions have extremely far-reaching consequences which must, nevertheless, be undertaken in an information-poor environment.

It is symptomatic of this problem to note that Martin, in his influential 1977 book, closed his section on "Rate of Return Regulation" with the following comment: "The worst aspect of the rate-of-return regulation is

stations establishes communication to remote areas very quickly ... [In contrast] the full exploitation of lightwave communication will mean routing fibers to millions of locations most of which are already served by existing wire pairs. This will take time, and it would be very expensive even if the fibers themselves were to cost nothing." From H. Inose and J. Pierce, *Information Technology and Civilization*, Freeman Publishing, Boston (MA), 1984, pp. 45–46.

[39] Nathan Rosenberg, "On Technological Expectations," in *Inside the Black Box*, Cambridge University Press, Cambridge, 1982, pp. 104–119.

[40] Paul David, "Some New Standards for the Economics of Standardization in the Information Age," in *Economic Policy and Technological Performance*, ed. Partha Dasgupta and Paul Stoneman, Cambridge University Press, Cambridge, 1987.

that it tends to discourage projects which could bring a massive saving in capital equipment costs, as could the use of large telephone company satellites today."[41] In fact, we *now* know that huge investments in satellites would itself have been a "mistake." The development of fiber optics as a transmission technology over the past fifteen years has provided a far cheaper alternative, for most telecommunications purposes, than communications satellites.

An added twist to the inherently difficult adoption-decision calculus concerns a feature of innovation that pervades telecommunications and is particularly evident in transmission technologies and the recent history of fiber optics. Research has increased the capabilities of the already installed transmission base, in addition to leading to the development of new and more productive technologies. Every major transmission system – coaxial cables, microwaves, satellites, fiber optics – has been subject to vast improvements in message-carrying capabilities, with relatively minor modification of the existing transmission technology. In some cases, there have been order-of-magnitude increases in the message-carrying capability of an existing channel, and often such productivity improvements have led to the postponement of the introduction of newer generations of transmission technologies. For example, time-division multiplexing allows an existing pair of wires to carry twenty-four voice channels or more, rather than the single channel that it originally carried. The same pattern is observed in fiber-optics technology. Improvements in the 1980s allowed fiber-optic cables to carry vastly increased flows of information. When AT&T began field trials with fiber optics in the mid 1970s, information was transmitted at 45 MbPS (megabytes per second). By the early 1990s, the standard for new fiber cables has reached 565 MbPS, with reliable sources predicting capacities of nearly 1,000 MbPS in the near future.[42] This increase in capacity has led to observable improvements from the point of view of network users. Fifteen years ago, the standard modem baud-rate was 300. Today it is 2,400, using the same telephone lines. The simultaneous advance in new transmission technology and the upgrading of old technology underlines the pervasive complexity flowing from research in the telecommunications industry.

Policy implications: some speculations on divestiture

An understanding of the broad properties of technological change in telecommunications can serve as a useful tool to reassess the rationale and

---

[41] Martin, *Future Development*, p. 360.
[42] Michael Hordeski, *Microcomputer LANs*, TAB Books, Blue Ridge Summit (PA), 1991, p. 288.

possibilities for government regulation and government cooperation with private firms in a telecommunications network. The existence of regulation in telecommunications is not in question. It is the form and the extent of government involvement and uncertainty over the efficacy of different policy choices that induce heated debate. Certainly, the epochal event in telecommunications regulation was the divestiture of the Bell System in 1983 under the Modified Final Judgement (MFJ).[43] The AT&T breakup included the establishment of autonomous local exchange monopolies and a separate, more competitive, long-distance market. Observations concerning the rationale behind divestiture and post-divestiture policy can illuminate the importance of paying closer attention to the idiosyncratic elements of technical change in telecommunications. Many observers have analyzed the last ten years of telecommunications service in order to answer the question, "Was divestiture a mistake?" This question will not be addressed here: it is tempting to say that it is still too soon to tell, but the deeper truth is that an answer is probably unknowable.

Instead, divestiture can be more usefully analyzed as an attempt by government to take advantage of a perceived window of opportunity to redirect the path of the telecommunications industry. There was a widespread perception that the availability of telecommunications satellites was about to revolutionize long-distance communication and that satellites would occupy a primary role as a switching-and-transmission technology. Given this belief, the relief sought by the Justice Department on behalf of consumers and entrants such as MCI seemed quite compelling. As cable transmission technologies became less prominent, the systemic nature of long-distance telecommunications would decrease. Indeed, a perceived discontinuous decrease in systemness seemed to substantially undercut the force of AT&T's primary defense of legal monopoly, namely the cost-effectiveness of central control over a breathtakingly complicated and interdependent system. However, "to the extent that the Bell System was broken up to usher in the age of microwave radio, the government forced a permanent shift in market structure to take advantage of a temporary technical opportunity – which has already been superseded [by the preeminence of fiber optics]."[44] As a criticism of the Justice Department's rationale for divestiture, Temin's argument makes sense. But, at a deeper level, how was the government to know that satellite technologies would be largely superseded by a superior cable technology that has, for the most part, *reinforced* systemness?

Telecommunications policy is heavily focused towards weighing the

[43] For a thorough examination of the history that preceded the breakup of AT&T, see Peter Temin's insightful book, *The Fall of the Bell System*, Cambridge University Press, Cambridge, 1987.   [44] *Ibid.*, p. 347.

tradeoffs between currently available technologies under alternative regimes. In the case of the AT&T break-up, the perception that superior satellite technologies were being adopted "too slowly" due to national monopoly coupled with the belief that government action could substantially increase the adoption rate was important in the sanctioning of pro-competitive institutions in the long-distance market. In fact, the recent explosion in the use of satellite-based cellular technologies, and the effect of decentralized cellular suppliers on the viability of *local service* monopolies, suggests that the market viability and competitive effects of competing technologies have not yet been determined.[45] Indeed, the current debate is prudently centered on the viability of a "public network," the cornerstone of basic residential service, within the emerging decentralized matrix of telecommunications services.[46] There exists little doubt that these issues are important. However, the broad policy issue that has persistently not been addressed is the inherent uncertainty facing the policy-maker. Unusually complex analysis is necessary merely to predict a possible range of outcomes that might emerge from a policy decision.

Regulators should not pretend to be able to predict the future level of systemness or the viability of a specific technology in something as complex as the telephone network. Even when the path of technological adoption is clear, the effect of the policy-maker is still often uncertain. Briefly, windows of opportunity are usually only observable ex-post. In an industry as complex as telecommunications, regulators should not be overconfident in their ability to "manage" technological change. Further, regulators should guard against the tendency to hop onto any particular technological bandwagon, using government resources to promote technologies that might be pre-empted far more quickly than anticipated. This is not to say that the government's role should necessarily be limited or that some invisible hand will lead an unfettered industry down the optimal path. Instead, policy should be constructed to ensure that the technological path *is as flexible as possible,* that resources are channelled toward those institutions which consistently provide large social benefits, and that viable economic opportunities are available to those who push out the technological frontier. Peter Temin has succinctly stated one of the main implications of this view: "To be fully rational, the government should support the kind of basic research that has been done at Bell Labs."[47] Whether or not divestiture was a mistake will never be known – no one will ever observe the path of the industry in which AT&T remained a monopolist. However, the

[45] See "The Big Break," *The Economist* (November 14, 1992), pp. 75–76.
[46] For a perceptive discussion of the path that technological change and adoption have taken since divestiture, see Noam, "The Future of the Public Network."
[47] Temin, *The Fall of the Bell System*, p. 360.

diminished role of Bell Labs. as a national resource for basic research reflects an insufficient appreciation for the role played by such private-sector research as a determinant of long-run economic growth.

Conclusions

The discussion in this chapter has placed heavy emphasis upon the importance of technical change in telecommunications. As should now be apparent, the telecommunications industry exploits a technology that has a number of very distinctive and somewhat neglected features. Nevertheless, it cannot be emphasized too strongly that the direction taken by this industry does not turn just upon the availability of improved technologies and their performance, but upon how these finally translate into economic terms. This is turn raises questions of how the new technological capability can be packaged into new goods or services and what potential buyers will be prepared to pay for these things.

Immense communication and information-processing capability are being placed at the disposal of American society. The management and exploitation of this expanding capability is a central policy issue. Even if further technological improvement were to be completely halted, there is now a sufficient technological capability to do a great many things that are not yet being done. In this sense the existing technology can be usefully thought of as consisting of building blocks. What will be constructed with these building blocks, and what shapes these products will assume, is not something that is inherent in the underlying technology. Similarly, the kinds of information that will be communicated and processed will turn upon decisions at the social and political levels, but also upon the willingness of the public to pay for a particular service. Consider Picturephone.[48]

AT&T had developed a Picturephone by the early 1960s that was purportedly the product of several hundred million dollars in R&D expenditure. There were some technical problems, including a picture quality that left something to be desired. Nevertheless, the technology was developed to the point of full practical applicability, and further improvements were to be expected. However, the product was a total failure. It seems to have been subjected to astonishingly little market research. When people were asked at the 1964 World's Fair if they liked the Picturephone on display, the responses were strongly positive. But no systematic attempts were made to establish how much people were prepared to pay for it – and the cost was very high. The basic charge for a Picturephone line in Chicago

[48] Prescott Mabon, *Mission Communications: The Story of Bell Laboratories*, Bell Labs., Murray Hill (NJ), 1975.

in the early 1970s was $50 per month, plus $25 per month for the set, plus a high per-minute charge, since transmission of moving pictures requires substantial bandwidth. In present-day prices, someone using the Picture-phone for one hour per month would be paying more than $200 per month for the service. It is hardly surprising that a mass market did not emerge. However, the recent reintroduction of the Picturephone has been relatively more successful, though still below the glossy expectations of Picturephone enthusiasts at the World's Fair. The last thirty years have led to comple-mentary changes in technology that have allowed for a relatively modest but profitable and cost-effective market for video point-to-point communi-cation. Particularly, business teleconferencing, while still leaving a lot to be desired, has become a relatively popular way of conducting meetings that would otherwise require air travel.

The history of the computer is a case where the errors were of the opposite sort. There is no doubt that the possibility for technical improve-ment in computers was drastically underestimated. Additionally, there was a persistent and widespread failure to appreciate how much calculating people would want to do when the *cost* of calculation declined by several orders of magnitude. A general inability to predict the uses to which precise calculating capability could be applied led to a singular failure to anticipate the possibilities of computing technology. Howard Aiken, one of the great pioneers of the computer in the 1930s, continued to conceive of it as essentially a scientific instrument suitable for only a very narrow range of purposes. In 1956 he stated: "if it should ever turn out that the basic logics of a machine designed for the numerical solution of differential equations coincide with the logics of a machine intended to make bills for a department store, I would regard this as the most amazing coincidence that I have ever encountered."[49] No doubt many people today will be most amazed at Aiken's amazement. Once a technology had been developed that was capable of performing mathematical calculations very rapidly, it would not seem to require extraordinary talent to design computers and to develop special programs for a bewilderingly large array of data-processing applications, including bills for department stores. Oddly, this does seem to be exactly Aiken's failure: an inability to make the intellectual transition from the level of improving technological performance to the ways in which this capability could be mobilized in other social contexts for the satisfac-tion of human needs.

How this capability will be exploited, and just what human needs will be addressed, are of course the enduring social questions posed by the

---

[49] Howard Aiken, "The Future of Automatic Computing Machinery," *Elecktronische Rechenmaschinen und Informationsverarbeitung*, Vieweg, Braunschwing, 1956, pp. 32–34. Quoted in Ceruzzi, "An Unforeseen Revolution", p. 197.

telecommunications industry. Henry Thoreau stated the issue with an awesome succinctness when informed of the marvellous powers of the telegraph back in the 1840s: "They tell me that Maine can now communicate with Texas. But does Maine have anything to say to Texas?"

Thoreau's formulation can serve as a useful parable for the future of this industry.

12 Understanding the adoption of new technology in the forest products industry

NATHAN ROSENBERG, PETER INCE, KENNETH SKOG AND
ANDREW PLANTINGA

Many times in this century, serious timber shortages have been forecast for the forest products industry. Although the economic scarcity of some wood materials is apparently increasing (the real price of sawlogs has been rising for a long time)[1] other wood materials seem unaffected (pulpwood prices have remained relatively stable over the last four decades).[2] Thus, although numerous wood-saving technological improvements are reportedly "on the shelf" and others are being adopted rapidly by the industry, slow adoption rates for some major innovations undoubtedly reflect an appropriate response to economic conditions rather than conservatism.

This chapter addresses the following questions: what are some of the principal and unique influences on technological change in the forest products industry that must be understood to anticipate future rates of adoption of new technology? Do these influences currently elicit appropriate rates of technology adoption?

The chapter has five major sections: (1) the importance of innovations imported from other industries (interindustry flow) and other countries; (2) the effect of raw material shortages; (3) the effect of the economic performance of innovations; (4) problems presented by the heterogeneous nature of wood raw material; and (5) problems presented by the heterogeneity of finished products. It is taken as axiomatic that the impact of technological change is not felt at the stage of invention or innovation, but only when improved technologies are actually used in production. For this reason, we pay particular attention to the determinants of the adoption of new technologies.

This paper originally appeared in *Forest Products Journal*, 10, no. 10 (October 1990).

[1] R.S. Manthy, 1978. *Natural Resource Commodities – A Century of Statistics*. The Johns Hopkins University Press, Baltimore (MD).

[2] A.H. Ulrich, *U.S. Timber Production, Trade, Consumption, and Price Statistics, 1950–1986*. USDA Miscellaneous Publications 1460, Washington (DC), 81 pp.

Interindustry technology flow

Prospects for technological change in forest products are heavily shaped by (1) commitment of resources to research and development (R&D) within the private and public institutions that comprise the forest products industry and its suppliers; and (2) developments in industries that are remote from forest products. For example, the forest products sector has made considerable use of sophisticated electronics components, including computers, lasers, and computerized axial tomography scanners (on an experimental basis). Many industries depend upon other sectors of the economy for the expansion of their technological capabilities. In the United States, five sectors account for more than 75 percent of total R&D: aircraft and missiles, chemicals and allied products, electrical machinery, nonelectrical machinery, and motor vehicles. Moreover, even within these sectors, many of the most important new technologies are acquired from outside. For example, the aircraft and missiles sector accounts for the largest amount of total R&D spending of any industrial sector. Yet, that industry is a massive importer of computer technologies from other sectors. Although aircraft and forest products may seem to be very remote from one another, both have greatly benefitted from metallurgical improvements and electronic and computer innovations.

Perhaps of greater relevance to the forest products industry has been the experience of another "traditional" industry that has been regarded as technologically conservative – the clothing industry. The clothing industry is also being shaped by the importation of high technologies. Computers have taken over many manual operations (e.g. the use of robots) and are used to monitor the manufacturing process.[3] For several decades, the chemical industry has been expanding the range of synthetic fibers, which are now a more important input into the clothing industry, in dollar terms, than are natural fibers. In addition, the clothing industry is absorbing a number of innovations from electronics and laser technology.

In a study of the interindustry flow of new technologies, Scherer[4] revealed the sources of recent innovations in the forest products industry (table 12.1). He developed a technology flow matrix for the United States economy for the year 1974, based upon company-financed R&D expenditures (that is, excluding inventions from government and university laboratories). By combining data on R&D expenditures with patent information on anticipated uses of inventions, Scherer constructed a matrix showing the

[3] *The New York Times*, American textiles lead a high-tech world industry. October 6, 1986, Section A: 18 (col. 4).
[4] F.M. Scherer, "Inter-Industry Technology Flows in the United States," *Research Policy*, 11 (1982), pp. 227–245.

Table 12.1. *Research and development flow for 1974*

	Cost	
Type of technology	Lumber and wood products	Papermill products
	($ million, U.S.	
Total own-industry R&D	72.6	202.3
Process[a]	64.2	86.4
Products coming from other industries[b]	66.9	119.6
Products going to other industries[c]	7.9	74.7
Final consumer products[d]	2.8	73.3

Notes:
[a] Own-industry R&D embodied in equipment used by the industry. [b] Other-industry R&D embodied in equipment purchased by forest products industries. [c] Own-industry R&D embodied in equipment used mainly by other industries. [d] Own-industry R&D embodied in final consumer products.
Source: F.M. Scherer, "Inter-industry Technology Flows in the US," *Research Policy*, 1982, 11:227–245.

"exchanges" of new technologies among industries. He found that the forest products industry was heavily dependent upon outside sources of technological change. In contrast, the computer and farm machinery industries were large-scale technology exporters. Lumber and wood products firms were identified as the main users of $67 million of R&D performed in other industries and $64 million of R&D performed inside the industry (1974 dollars). For the pulp-and-paper sector, the figures were $120 million and $86 million, respectively.

In addition, many important forest product innovations have originated abroad, especially in Scandinavia and Germany. Significant innovations may come from Japan in the future. Several countries have been increasing their financial support for forestry research more rapidly than the United States.[5]

The significance of external sources of technological change needs to be understood. At the very least, an enlarged monitoring activity should examine new directions and developments in other industries and countries for their potential relevance for forest products. The forest products industry might benefit from institutional innovations that would make such monitoring and evaluation more systematic and explicit or more readily available to the industry as a whole. A step was taken in this direction in

[5] H. Gregersen, J. Haygreen, S. Sindelar, and P. Jakes, "U.S. Gains from Foreign Forestry Research," *Journal of Forestry*, 82 (2), pp. 21–26.

1982, at a meeting of corporate R&D managers to discuss future technological developments,[6] but much more is needed in this area.

In *Wood Use: U.S. Competitiveness and Technology*,[7] the Office of Technology Assessment (OTA) offered the following reasons for the low level of R&D expenditures by the forest products industry: (1) the industry is mature in the sense that wood products are well developed and have been used in essentially the same form for a long time; and (2) wood products are not high technology and, therefore, are not likely to be subject to revolutionary technological breakthroughs in their manufacture and use.

Such reasoning is parochial and unconvincing. The world is full of old, "mature" industries and products that have been completely revitalized by "revolutionary technological breakthroughs," as suggested by the adoption of robots, synthetic fibers, and lasers in the textile industry – surely a mature industry. Agriculture and medicine are also mature industries, and yet they have both been transformed by revolutionary technological breakthroughs within the past fifty years.

Improving the monitoring and searching activities at the interfaces between forest products and high-technology industries and between domestic and foreign industries may facilitate forecasting as well as the transfer of valuable technologies in the years ahead. As we will discuss, the problem in the forest products industry is not maturity. Rather, many of the industry's difficulties in achieving technological improvements stem from the heterogeneity of raw materials and the wide variety of requirements for finished wood products. Moreover, the adoption of new technologies is often precluded by economic considerations.

Response to raw-material scarcity

The direction of technological change in the forest products industry, as elsewhere, is not a purely random or exogenous phenomenon, even though the industry may be affected by events that originate entirely outside the industry. Rather, technological change is influenced by the changing structure of costs of manufacturing (labor, capital, and raw materials) and the prices of competing products (plastics, steel, and concrete). Technological innovations in the forest products industry tend to have a strong labor-saving bias, suggesting that the industry tends to increase its competitiveness through improvements in labor productivity. We acknowledge that

[6] L.W. Tombaugh, and B.G. Macdonald, "The Next Twenty Years: Where will Technology lead?" in *New Forests for a Changing World: Proceedings 1983 Convention of the Society of American Foresters*, Society of American Foresters Pub. 84–03:579–586 1984 Bethesda (MD).

[7] U.S. Congress, *Wood Use: U.S. Competitiveness and Technology*, Office of Technology Assessment, Washington (DC) 1984, 2 vols.

labor and capital scarcity must be considered because they strongly influence technological change. However, many innovations unique to forest products have been triggered by raw material shortages. In this section, we focus on the influences of wood shortages on the development and adoption of technological innovations in the forest products industry.

The role of predictability of supply

In both the public and private sectors, research responds to expectations concerning future availability of raw materials. The forest products industry has a peculiar advantage in anticipating the future availability of one of its essential raw materials, timber.

Although certain trends in raw materials can be extrapolated into the future, projecting consequences of trends may be difficult. As the price of a raw material increases, a wide range of economic and social adjustments may then be called into play, such as simple conservation measures, changes in product design, and possible substitution of more abundant materials. Substituting more abundant materials for scarcer materials involves a range of technological changes that facilitate substitution or that simply reduce the need for the scarce material in the first place.

The recent technological history of forest products must be told in terms of how the increasing physical scarcity of timber, primarily the rising cost of large logs, has induced innovations that have facilitated the use of smaller logs and "inferior" timber sources. In the case of softwood timber (figure 12.1), an increasing output has been harvested from a relatively constant timber inventory. At the same time, the character of the inventory has changed (toward smaller trees), along with the character of finished products (less lumber, more panels, and more flakeboard).

Examples of major technological developments that were motivated by resource scarcity can be found in the structural panel and pulp-and-paper sectors. The basic ideas underlying new structural panels date back at least as far as the 1950s. The introduction and rapid acceptance of new structural panels in the 1970s and 1980s owed much to research and improved technological capabilities that could utilize low-cost hardwood resources. However, a powerful triggering mechanism was undoubtedly the sharp rise in the price of softwood veneer logs (figure 12.2), which placed plywood at a considerable cost disadvantage.[8] On the other hand, in the pulp-and-paper sector, fluctuations in the price of softwood pulpwood have played a less obvious role in developing pulping processes that expanded the variety of tree species used as raw materials. Instead, consistently lower prices for hardwood pulpwood, woodmill residue, and recycled paper contributed to

[8] J. Haygreen, H. Gregersen, A. Hyun, and P. Ince, Innovation and Productivity Change in the Structural Panel Industry. *Forest Products Journal*, 35 (10) (1985), pp. 32–38.

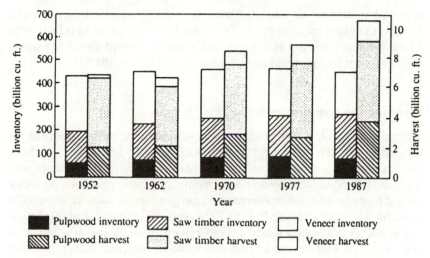

Fig. 12.1 Composition of inventory and harvest of softwood growing stock by size class from 1952 to 1987.

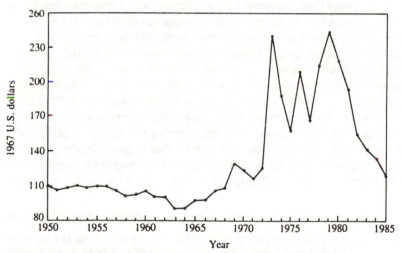

Fig. 12.2 Price of Douglas-fir veneer logs in western Washington and northwest Oregon from 1950 to 1985.

the introduction of processing techniques that could exploit these materials. The proportion of hardwood pulpwood grew from 15 percent in the early 1950s to 31 percent in 1986.[9,10] Wood residues from sawmills and

[9] U.S. Department of Commerce, *Current Industrial Reports – Pulp, Paper, and Board*. MA26A(77) Bureau of the Census, Washington (DC) 1977.
[10] U.S. Department of Commerce, *Current Industrial Reports – Pulp, Paper, and Board*, 1987 MA26A(87) Bureau of the Census, Washington (DC).

plywood mills now account for over 40 percent of woodpulp sources. Finally, the use of recycled paper rose from 12 million short tons in 1970 to 15 million short tons in 1981;[11] recycled paper comprised about 24 percent of fiber inputs in paper and paperboard production in 1987.[12]

Problems with projection models

Failing to take adjustment mechanisms into account was responsible for the naive "models of doom" energy forecasts of the 1970s.[13,14] Such models were based on narrow and unrealistic behavioral assumptions. They did not take into account how a regime of flexible prices would create strong incentives to utilize alternative energy sources, such as wood. The years immediately after the 1973 to 1974 Arab oil embargo and the drastic rise in energy prices gave rise to a rapid expansion in the use of wood as an energy source. This experience provides valuable evidence of the impressive speed with which the forest products industry and consumers can respond to a clear set of price signals.[15]

The lesson for the forest products industry is clear. Long-term extrapolations of increasing raw material scarcities are likely to be of no value – or worse, of negative value – unless they explicitly take into account the dynamics of technological changes induced by the scarcities themselves, as well as the nature of user responses to rising prices of inputs.

Historical observations are important in developing a framework for projecting technological change in the forest products industry. Econometric models have incorporated a wide range of empirical data on the pattern of timber utilization in the American economy.[16,17] These models make it possible to extrapolate the impact that changes in the growth of population, gross national products, and other economic variables will have on timber utilization. The question that needs to be considered here is

[11] U.S. Congress, *Wood Use: U.S. Competitiveness and Technology*. Office of Technology Assessment, Washington (DC), 1984 2 vols.

[12] W.E. Mies, D.A. Garcia, C.P. Espe, R. Galin, R.M. McGrath, N. DeKing, M.J. Ducey, M. Conrad, and J. Mikulenka, (eds.), *Pulp and Paper 1988 Fact Book*. Miller Freeman Publications Inc., San Francisco (CA), 1988 438 pp.

[13] J.W. Forrester, *World Dynamics*. Wright-Allen Press, Cambridge (MA) 1971.

[14] D.L. Meadows, J. Randers, and W. Behrens, *Limits to Growth*. Universe Books, New York, 1972 205 pp.

[15] U.S. Congress, *Wood Use: U.S. Competitiveness and Technology*.

[16] D.M. Adams, and R.W. Haynes, *The 1980 Softwood Timber Assessment Market Model: Structure, Projections, and Policy Simulations*. Forest Science Monograph 22, Society of American Foresters, Washington (DC), 64 pp. Supplement to Forest Science 26(3) 1980.

[17] W.L.M. McKillop, *Supply and Demand for Forest Products – An Econometric Study*. University of California Agricultural Experimental Sta., Berkeley (CA). *Hilgardia* 38(1), (1967), pp. 1–132.

how useful such models are at projecting the impact of technological change.[18]

The essential point is that econometric models, even conceptually and technically sophisticated models, often take information about technologies or technological change as exogenously given and then predict the consequences upon timber markets. However, models can simulate the behavior of technological change endogenously. For example, the United States Department of Agriculture (USDA) Forest Service, Forest Products Laboratory (FPL), Pulpwood Model,[19] based on a linear programming model by Gilless and Buongiorno,[20] estimates technological change as an endogenous process. This model defines current and future technological processes that make various grades of paper and paperboard by specifying wood or fiber input requirements and non-fiber costs for each process. As the model operates, future processes, which represent new technologies, can be adopted. Their adoption is partly determined by regional market price equilibria for wood and recycled fiber estimated by the model.

With the exception of the FPL Pulpwood Model and the International Institute of Applied Systems Analysis model,[21] forest products industry models generally do not address technological change as an endogenous behavioral phenomenon. That is, how will different sets of changes in market conditions generate different patterns of technological change in the industry?

The work of Hayami and Ruttan[22] and Binswanger and Ruttan[23] on induced innovation in agriculture also provides an approach to technological change that might well be replicated in the forest products industry. In fact, the induced-innovation hypothesis has been tested in agriculture and other fields,[24] and it is surprising that this approach has not yet been fully tested (as far as we know) in the case of forest products.

[18] A. Plantinga, W. Lange, and K. Skog, *Capacity Change in the Forest Products Industry: An Evaluation of Modeling Approaches*, in Proceedings of the Forest Sector Modeling Symposium SIMS, Swedish Agricultural University, Uppsala (Sweden) 1989.

[19] J.L. Howard, P.J. Ince, I. Durbak, and W.J. Lange, "Modeling Technology change and fiber consumption in the U.S. pulp and paper industry" in *Proceedings 1988 Southern Forest Economics Workshop*. ed. Robert Abt, University of Florida, School of Forest Resources and Conservation, Orlando (FL), 1988 pp. 211–219.

[20] J.K. Gilless, and J. Buongiorno, *PAPYRUS: A Model of the North American Pulp and Paper Industry*. Forest Science Monograph 8 Society of American Foresters, Bethesda (MD), 37 pp. Supplement to *Forest Science*, (1987) 33(1).

[21] M. Kallio, D.P. Dystra, and C.S. Binkley (eds.), *The Global Forest Sector: An Analytical Perspective*. John Wiley and Sons, Chichester, 1987, 706 pp.

[22] Y. Hayami, and V.W. Ruttan, *The Agricultural Development: An International Perspective*. Johns Hopkins University Press, Baltimore (MD), 1985, 506 pp.

[23] H. Binswanger, and V.W. Ruttan, *Induced Innovation*. The Johns Hopkins University Press, Baltimore (MD), 1978, 413 pp.

[24] C.G. Thirtle and V.W. Ruttan, *The Role of Demand and Supply in the Generation and Diffusion of Technical Change*, Harwood Academic Publishers, New York, 1987, 173 pp.

Economic performance of innovations

Looking at the reasons for past technological change calls attention to a central point of this chapter: decisions to develop and adopt new technologies are ultimately based on economic and not purely technological considerations. Even though new technologies possess attractive features or reduce the cost of a specific material, the technologies are often not economically superior because all associated costs have not been considered.[25]

Benefits associated with new technologies are frequently overstated, and the best improvements in the field rarely match what has been reported under ideal laboratory conditions. For example, best opening face (BOF) sawing, a computer program that selects the best first-cut in logs to make lumber, was developed by the FPL in the early 1970s. The Office of Technology Assessment reported that under laboratory conditions, BOF yields 6 to 90 percent more lumber from 5- to 20-inch logs and averages 21 percent more lumber recovery than conventional sawing.[26] However, the disparity in performance between ideal laboratory conditions and sawmills is considerable. The sense that some irrational lag is occurring in the adoption of BOF is greatly diminished when the evaluation of actual performance in sawmills shows an average increase of a mere 4 percent, not ≥ 20 percent, compared to conventional sawing.[27] As long as this disparity remains large, reticence in adopting new technology should not be dismissed as adoption lags or slow rates of diffusion.

Similar considerations lend understanding to the apparently delayed adoption of some other major innovations in the forest products industry (e.g. oriented strandboard (OSB) and waferboard, which were technically available in the 1950s,but were not widely adopted commercially until the 1970s). When all costs are taken into account, seemingly superior technologies may be adopted slowly at first because they do not decisively reduce costs. Radically new technologies usually represent clusters of new characteristics, some positive and some negative. The innovation, therefore, involves a sorting-out process, in which negative characteristics are reduced while positive ones are enhanced. In many cases, this situation gives rise to a long and costly development period.

Often, new technologies cannot be introduced without costly new manufacturing equipment. Therefore, the economics of adoption needs to be analyzed in terms of the present costs and discounted future financial returns of an investment process. Composites such as parallel-laminated veneer (PLV) and Com-Ply are attractive products because they make it

[25] USDA Forest Service, *The Outlook for Timber in the United States.* USDA Forest Resource Report 20, Washington (DC), 1974, 367 pp.
[26] U.S. Congress, *Wood Use.*   [27] *Ibid.*

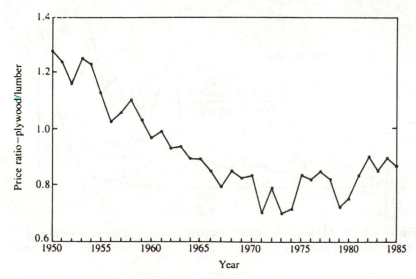

Fig. 12.3 Prices of softwood plywood and lumber in Douglas-fir region from 1950 to 1985.

possible to use lower-quality materials, hardwoods, and smaller logs. However, the expensive processing equipment required cannot be readily retrofitted into existing sawmills. Introducing such equipment is much more likely to be associated with replacing depreciated equipment at existing sawmills or establishing new mills. Either action would require the right stumpage market conditions, improved prospects for the adoption of composite products, and access to financing on acceptable terms; moreover, either action would probably be taken infrequently or be delayed.[28]

Many new technologies that have promised to save material have also required additional, and offsetting, doses of complementary inputs. Thus, promising new mechanical pulping technologies, which hold out the prospect of higher yields, are also burdened with the requirement of higher energy costs.[29] On the other hand, the diffusion of new technologies has been accelerated when the associated complementary inputs have been positive from an economic point of view. The rate at which plywood was adopted over lumber was rapid for two reasons: the employment of plywood on construction sites proved to be labor saving, and the price of plywood had declined sharply relative to the price of lumber (figure 12.3).[30]

[28] *Ibid.*
[29] M. Kallio, D.P. Dystra, and C.S. Binkley (eds.), *The Global Forest Sector: An Analytical Perspective.* John Wiley and Sons, Chichester, 1987, 706 pp.
[30] M. Clawson, "Forests in the Long Sweep of American History" *Science*, 204 (1979), pp. 1168–1174.

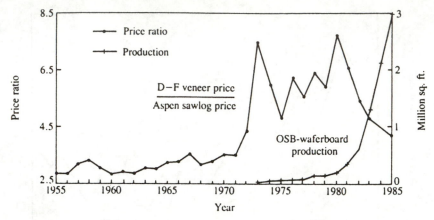

Fig. 12.4 Price of Douglas-fir veneer compared to price of aspen sawlogs and OSB-waferboard production from 1955 to 1985. Note: some data were estimated.

What is at issue is more than just a matter of eliminating "bugs." New technologies always represent clusters of characteristics, so the industry must cope with the more fundamental matter of optimizing those characteristics, suppressing some and enhancing others, while minimizing risk and uncertainty.

In the forest products industry, one particular institutional feature may be significant in shaping the timing of the decision to adopt new technology. In the present division of research labor, the initial research is done in the public sector by institutions such as FPL, regional Forest Service research stations, and state universities. But commercial success ordinarily goes beyond what can reasonably be attained by a public agency: fine-tuning the product design and characteristics to the specific needs of specialized categories of users, as well as improving process and machinery for which the public sector has only a modest capability. The final push must come from the private sector and must therefore await the stimulus of changing prices or costs that ordinarily shape the decision to adopt. A fitting example is the implementation of the OSB-waferboard technology in the early 1980s. This technology had been available since the 1950s but became a viable option only after softwood veneer log prices rose dramatically relative to aspen prices in the late 1970s. The rapid adoption of OSB-waferboard followed a sharp relative increase in veneer-log prices (figure 12.4).

In examining the adoption of new technologies, we need to consider the trajectory of slow and gradual improvement beyond the crude condition that usually characterizes the early stage of new technologies. A huge volume of literature systematically ignores this particular point. Some sociologists and economists tend to search for the evidence of first use of some new technology and then treat the subsequent delay in wider adoption as evidence of an irrational lag or excessive conservatism on the part of potential adopters. A more complicated history needs to be examined. The decision to adopt technology should be explored in the comparative context of alternative technologies. Particular focus should be placed on the progress of reducing costs, improving performance, and expanding confidence in the performance of the new technology, as well as on the systematic modification of the technology to accommodate the diverse range of needs of a heterogeneous user population.[31]

A somewhat perplexing and significant aspect of the slow adoption of a new technology is revealed in the use of wood trusses, which were originally designed for roof framing, were later designed for flooring, and were recently designed for entire houses. In the United States today, conventional roof trusses are used for most new woodframe houses, whereas "truss frames" (wood trusses that provide framing for the whole house) are just beginning to be used. Truss frames were originally developed in Germany approximately 150 years ago. The technique was introduced to the United States in the 1950s, but it has not received widespread acceptance, which is surprising in view of the large number of benefits claimed for truss framing. One source claims that truss frames eliminate the need for interior supports and require 30 percent less structural framing lumber than conventional construction.[32] Another source estimates a 20 percent saving in the amount of wood.[33]

An important feature is the uncertain economic impact of truss framing. Although an OTA table of the benefits of truss framing lists labor savings as the first item, the accompanying text is ambiguous. It states, "The truss frame system and panel assemblies often are simpler and faster to erect on site and may save labor."[34] The lack of clarity over associated labor costs probably reflects differences among designs of houses and differences in calculating associated labor costs. Because labor costs are considerably greater than material costs, uncertainty over the precise level of labor-cost differences could readily swamp the purported benefit of an associated reduction in material costs.

A considerable degree of uncertainty over the economic benefit of truss framing has persisted because of the cost of labor. The "conservatism" of

---

[31] N. Rosenberg, *Inside the Black Box: Technology and Economics*, Cambridge University Press, Cambridge, 1982, 304 pp.   [32] U.S. Congress, *Wood Use*.
[33] USDA Forest Service, *An Analysis of the Timber Situation in the United States, 1952–2030*. USDA Forest Resource Report, Review Draft, Part I, Washington (DC), 1987.
[34] U.S. Congress, *Wood Use*.

various agents in the building industry is easily invoked in discussions of these matters. But an appropriately conservative, even skeptical, approach may be justified when the economic benefits from new technology are surrounded by a wide band of uncertainty.

The adoption rate of new technologies in the forest products sector needs to be understood in terms of the overall economic impact of the technologies and not based on a one-dimensional interpretation of a specific effect. Economic evaluations are extremely difficult to make and the eventual outcomes are often counterintuitive. This is because genuine improvements in one part of the system give rise to less obvious but offsetting costs in other parts: for example, a deterioration in product quality, the need for a higher cost manufacturing process, more labor input, or a new design configuration to accommodate the use of a new material. Moreover, a pervasive factor complicates authoritative evaluation of new technologies. As time passes, technologies themselves pass along trajectories of performance and cost changes that may radically alter their economic efficiency. In most industries, the first generation of new technologies is typically primitive when compared to the characteristics of subsequent generations at later stages of maturity. Although this feature is shared with other industries, it may assume greater importance in the forest products industry as a result of interaction with the other sources of uncertainty and difficulties of information acquisition central to the industry.

Problems with a heterogeneous raw material

This section focuses on a distinctive characteristic of the forest products industry – the natural heterogeneity of its essential raw material, wood. If the industry is not unique, it is at least at the extreme end of a spectrum of possibilities with respect to variability or heterogeneity in physical characteristics of its primary raw material. This heterogeneity is based on the fact that wood is an organic material with a remarkable degree of natural diversity.

Such heterogeneity immensely complicates the process by which useful knowledge is accumulated and diffused within the forest products industry. Whereas research results on aluminum, iron and steel, pharmaceuticals, and electronics have the potential for some immediately wider application or even codification, and therefore for usefulness in other contexts, the results of forest products research are circumscribed by the nature of wood. The behavior of wood is highly variable from one species to another and also from one location in the log to another. The number of variables is truly immense. Consider, for example, the natural variation in wood density among species, an important feature of wood from a structural standpoint. For various species of pine, specific gravity varies from 35 to 60 lb./ft.³ (oven-dry). In addition, the coefficient of variation for specific gravity within each species is approximately 10 percent.[35]

This heterogeneity leads to a subtle interaction among many variables that generally takes a long time to sort out, whether new technology is being developed for construction or for pulping and papermaking. Technological problems are often too subtle and multivariate for scientific methodology to offer generalized results. The inherent subtlety of the information (acquisition process in forest products, not the mature state of the industry) accounts for many of the difficulties in bringing scientific methodology more effectively to bear upon technological problems. For example, an astonishing number of elementary facts about wood are not yet established with any kind of quantitative precision, such as the chemical structure of lignin and the response of wood to various forms of chemical or biological treatment.

Problems in wood drying

Consider a seemingly simple problem in forest products technology: optimal conditions for kiln-drying of wood. Over the past thirty years, wood drying has come to depend less on traditional air-drying and more on kiln-drying. The advantage of kiln-drying is a shorter drying time, which lowers the throughput time in the lumber production process. This advantage is particularly important for the recently developed technology of high-temperature drying, which varies greatly in effectiveness depending on tree species. Of interest is the fact that the energy requirements per unit of output seem to be lower in high-temperature kiln-drying than in normal-temperature kiln-drying. The shorter turnaround drying time allows greater flexibility in filling orders in a timely fashion and can potentially reduce capital costs of the kiln per unit of output. Shorter turnaround time also lowers the cost of holding wood while it is being dried. The final moisture content of kiln-dried wood is lower and more predictable as well as independent of ambient temperature and relative humidity. In many cases, firms use low-temperature kiln-drying and dehumidification to predry wood and then finish the drying process in a kiln at higher temperatures. While the cost per unit of drying wood is of course higher in kiln-drying than in air-drying, apparently the difference is justified by other considerations not included in the usual cost figures.[36] Just how sensitive

[35] USDA Forest Service, *Wood Handbook: Wood as an Engineering Material*, Agricultural Handbook 72, Washington (DC), 466 p.
[36] G. Wengert, and M. White, "Lumber Drying Cost Comparisons," *Timber Processing Industry* 4(1) (1979) pp. 12–14,32.

the optimal use procedure of kiln-drying is to such factors as the price of energy, capital, and labor would be interesting to know. Unfortunately, but not surprisingly, adequate data are not available for answering these questions.

Wood drying may appear to be a simple and straightforward process, but it is a deceptively tricky affair. The optimal drying procedure depends on a large number of variables such as species, season, geographic location, whether the tree was grown in a forest or on a plantation,[37] size of pile, composition of pile, and precise manner of stacking the wood. Furthermore, softwoods are more amenable to high-temperature drying than hardwoods. Hardwoods respond in numerous ways to high-temperature drying applications depending on species.[38]

Extensive experimentation is presently the only way to determine the optimal high-temperature drying procedure for each species under a large combination of circumstances.

Problems in developing a theoretical framework

Research activities in forest products are seldom guided by an overall theoretical framework that is applicable in all cases. Individual experiments are often of limited usefulness. For example, one cannot confidently take data from a small experimental kiln and extrapolate them to a commercial kiln because of the effects of pile size and composition on drying rate.

The scientific information necessary for technological innovation can be obtained. However, each small bit of information typically has to be acquired at a slow pace and at a high cost. Once acquired, information cannot always be used readily in other contexts involving different species, subspecies, or locations.

A major thrust of technological change in the forest products industry has been to overcome, or at least reduce, the effects of heterogeneity. Many innovations have involved taking a diversity of low-quality timber resources and converting them into products with lumber-type or plywood-type characteristics. Recent developments in structural panel products serve as examples, including waferboard and OSB. In the pulp-and-paper sector, note the increasing recourse to hardwoods and former waste materials. Of course, the obstacles posed by material heterogeneity are compounded by the extreme heterogeneity of the final product, which reflects, in turn, the diversity of final consumer needs.

---

[37] M.Y. Cech, and D.R. Huffman, "High-Temp Drying, Split-Pith Sawing Reduce Red Pine Degrade," *Canadian Forest Industry*, 92(8) (1972), pp. 28–33.

[38] S.R. Boone, "An Introduction to High-Temperature Drying: Past Research Efforts and Definition of Terms and Procedures." in *Proceedings of the Symposium on High-Temperature Drying of Hardwoods*, New Albany (IN), 1979, pp. 1–9.

Problems with heterogeneous products

Every final product in the wood-based construction industry is to some degree unique, not only because of the specificity of production location and environment but also because of the special constraints imposed by varied market requirements. The heterogeneity of products, the multiplicity of raw wood material, and the typically long life of many wood products in the construction industry contribute to the unusually long period needed to sort out the impact of separate variables on product performance.

In evaluating new materials or new production techniques in an industry such as electronics, experimentation can usually determine the effects of new approaches, designs, or materials very quickly, and can make immediate adjustments and adaptations accordingly. In the construction industry, by contrast, many years of observation may be needed to evaluate how a new wood-based material can withstand the abuse of weather. Surprising results are common because varying environmental conditions (temperature, humidity, sunlight, ocean spray, industrial pollution) and the peculiar complexity and diversity of the wood product lead to subtle interactions that take a long time to understand. Conflicting observations and claims combine in ways that complicate the isolation of the separate contributions of variables. For example, time is critical in thermal-moisture interactions and affects the thermal properties of new materials and designs; such matters are inherently difficult to sort out. Inevitably, time-consuming testing imposes delays upon the decision to adopt new technologies.

The slowness with which essential information about new technologies accumulates in the forest products sector is not confined to construction. Similar problems are endemic in the pulp-and-paper sector, as well. Many years of study may be needed to clarify something as elementary as the energy requirements associated with a new pulping technology, partly because of heterogeneity among wood materials but also because of varied performance requirements of the pulp. In thermomechanical pulping, for example, problems of quality control (achieving acceptable levels of brightness) and problems associated with operating the refiners were encountered after the first commercial pressurized refining system for producing news-grade pulp was introduced in Eastern Canada in 1964. But far more surprising was that the industry was unable to sort out conflicting claims over energy requirements for almost a decade. One example is the claim that energy requirements for pressurized refining were significantly lower than those for refiner mechanical pulping (an older system).[39] Such

[39] D. Atack, "Technical Development of Mechanical and Chemimechanical Pulping Processes," *Svensk Paperstidning*, no. 16 (1985).

claims eventually proved to be spurious. Essential scientific knowledge for the success of new technologies seems to grow very slowly in the forest products industry.

In summary, major reasons for the slow adoption of some important new technologies in forest products are (1) the body of technologically relevant information is highly fragmented; (2) the stock of information relevant to any given use is expanded very slowly; (3) the feedback loops from use and experience are much less significant as diffusers of useful information than in other industries; and (4) over a wide range of productive uses, scientific theory, although valuable, cannot play a very effective role in providing information tailored to the particularities of local use conditions.

Conclusions

Several key factors influence the process of technological change in the forest products industry. That straightforward policy recommendations can be, or ought to be, drawn from our analysis is not obvious. For example, relevant information accumulated by the forest products industry and needed for technological improvements encounters difficulties to a degree not encountered in many other industries. It does not follow, however, that information-gathering activities beyond those already in place are desirable. The FPL, as presently constituted, already studies some peculiar problems of the wood products industry. Moreover, a network of federal and university wood utilization researchers addresses many problems caused by the heterogeneity of knowledge about solid-wood processing. Federal and state utilization specialists play a significant role in transferring technology by helping firms solve technical problems and by facilitating the feedback and diffusion of useful information derived from working with the problems of the industry. Given these peculiarities, however, additional resources devoted to research or information and technology transfer would not necessarily yield higher social returns in the forest products industry compared to other industries.

Certain observations in this chapter do carry implications for the manner in which research and information gathering ought to be conducted and the priority that ought to be accorded the following processes: (1) monitoring and evaluating the developments in other industries; (2) monitoring the developments in other countries; (3) focusing on the internal dynamics of technological change; and (4) studying the economics of adoption and diffusion of new technologies in the forest products industry.

More systematic attention needs to be given to monitoring and evaluating developments in other industries that may be relevant to the forest products industry. At present, some attention seems to be given but on an individual and haphazard basis.

External monitoring should include more attention to ongoing developments in other countries as well as in other domestic industries. Several countries have been increasing their financial support for forestry research more rapidly than the United States. Imported technologies promise to play an even more important role in forestry-based activities in the future.

More attention needs to be devoted to understanding the internal dynamics of technological change, as opposed to constructing econometric models that simply spell out implications of historical trends. In particular, attempts to determine the future adequacy of timber resource supplies need to examine the internal behavioral mechanisms that influence the adoption of new technology within the industry, including trends in all major factors of production (such as raw materials, labor, and capital).

Studies of the economics of technology adoption and diffusion within the forest products industry should receive more attention. Much research has been devoted to identifying potential performance improvements of new technologies, especially their wood-saving consequences, without systematically considering the costs of implementing these new technologies. The impression has often been given that new and technologically superior innovations have been sitting on the shelf because of some innate (or regulation-induced) "conservatism" in industry decision-makers. A closer examination of such shelved technologies often reveals perfectly sound economic reasons for postponing adoption of the technology, reasons embedded in low levels of expected profitability.[40] Thus, for the forest products industry, like other industries, the decision to adopt new technologies is inescapably an investment decision. Consequently, the same economic variables that are ordinarily consulted in such decisions need to be examined to justify past decisions and to guide future decisions to adopt new forest product technologies.

[40] J.L. Bowyer, S. Suo, K. Skog, and V.L. Morton, *Predicting the Rate of Timber Utilization Innovations*, Final Report USFS-FPL/University of Minnesota, Cooperative Research Project, Contract USDA-FP-85-0748, 1987, 51 pp. (plus appendices).

13 Scientific instrumentation and university research

Introduction

The purpose of this chapter is to examine certain roles played by American research universities in the development of an important category of technology: scientific instruments. In the years since the Second World War the research universities performed much more complex functions than can be summarized in the statement that they served as the main centers for the performance of basic research, although that is obviously fundamental.[1] In addition, within the university context, and in connection with the performance of basic research, there took place a complex interplay between scientific and technological forces that led to other potentially significant outcomes. Obviously, the immediate increments to knowledge resulting from basic research itself are, sometimes, of the greatest economic significance. However, I will suggest that there have been paths of influence and causation that have not yet been systematically identified or examined, much less measured. I will further suggest that the emergence and diffusion of new technologies of instrumentation (as well as new research methodologies) are central and neglected consequences of university basic research. As a result, the eventual economic impact of basic research, taking place in a

This chapter is reprinted, with small changes, from *Research Policy*, 21 (1992), pp. 381–390. I acknowledge the great benefit derived from conversations with Harvey Brooks. Valuable comments were also received from Marvin Chodorow, Sir Aaron Klug, W.E. Steinmueller, and an anonymous referee of *Research Policy*. The financial support for the research on which this chapter is based was provided by the Technology and Economic Growth Program of the Stanford University Center for Economic Policy Research.

[1] For example, although it will not be discussed, the research universities also performed a great deal of applied research across the whole range of engineering disciplines, as well as in metallurgy and materials science, in medicine and pharmacy, and in agriculture. It may be added that the overemphasis upon the contributions of American universities should be attributed, not to chauvinism, but to the author's comparative ignorance of developments elsewhere.

particular academic discipline, has commonly expressed itself through the medium of new instrumentation technologies and the subsequent life histories of these new technologies. This chapter attempts to provide some preliminary mapping of such lines of influence.

What follows, then, is obviously exploratory and not definitive. Nevertheless, if its central conclusion is correct, this chapter points to the importance of a more thorough examination of the role played by university research as the source of a highly influential category of modern technology: instruments of observation and measurement. Moreover if this role is eventually judged to be highly significant, it would appear that the economic benefits of university research are being substantially underestimated.

The importance of scientific instruments

Scientific instruments may be usefully regarded as the capital goods of the research industry. That is to say, the conduct of scientific research generally requires some antecedent investment in specific equipment for purposes of enhancing the ability to observe and measure specific categories of natural phenomena. Moreover, much of the scientific instrumentation that is now in existence had its historical origins in the conduct of basic research – specifically, in the attempt to advance the frontier of scientific knowledge through an expansion in observational or experimental capabilities. In this sense, a central part of the "output" of the university research enterprise has been much more than just new theories explaining some aspects of the structure of the universe, or additional data confirming or modifying existing theories. A further output (or by-product) has been more powerful and versatile techniques of instrumentation including, in many cases, the ability to observe or measure phenomena that were previously not observable or measurable at all. New instrumentation has thus often been an unintentional and, to a surprising extent, even an unacknowledged, product of university research.

A common denominator among a wide range of scientific instruments is that they were initially designed in response to some very specific, narrowly defined requirement of research in a particular discipline. However, after their successful development, it became apparent that the instrument had useful applications in some other scientific realm – whether basic or applied – often requiring substantial modification or redesign. The analogy with more conventional capital goods should be apparent here. Machine tools originally designed to meet the specific requirements of textile or locomotive or musket manufacturers were later transferred to manufacturers of sewing machines, bicycles, typewriters, and automobiles. Such transfers have been numerous and diverse.[2] Similarly, scientific instruments designed to improve technical capability or to solve one set of research problems have often turned out to have applications in disciplines and technology sectors far from those where they originated.

The most spectacular of such transfers has involved the computer. Computers are, of course, the scientific instrument *par excellence*; their origins can be traced to research conducted in several countries, although the research context from which they originally sprang is now largely forgotten. In the past thirty years, computers have become indispensable wherever extensive calculations are made – which is to say everywhere in the scientific world. The demand for greater calculating capability turned out to be enormous when the cost of computing was reduced by many orders of magnitude. The computer has made possible many kinds of research activities that would have been simply impossible if computational costs and capabilities had remained frozen at the levels which prevailed at the outbreak of the Second World War. Moreover, much of the progress in research capability in the past couple of decades has occurred by linking other new scientific instruments to the computer. This includes computer control of a wide range of experiments that could hardly have been undertaken in its absence. In addition, the availability of powerful computers has opened up the possibility of large-scale simulation of physical and biological processes.

At the same time, the computer has spread into uses in business, government, medical care, and private households which are extremely remote from its scientific points of origin, and certainly very far from the specific purposes that dominated the thinking of the pioneers of computing. A quick stroll, for example, through the intensive care unit of any major hospital will disclose a number of essential technologies that are directly dependent upon the computer for the continuous monitoring of vital signs: blood pressure, respiratory rate, pulse rate, and cardiac rhythm.

A common denominator among many of the pioneers in developing the computer – Howard Aiken at Harvard, John Atanasoff at Iowa State University, Konrad Zuse in the German aircraft industry, and John P. Eckert, Jr. and John W. Mauchly at the University of Pennsylvania – is that their contributions resulted from the fact that they were confronted by extremely tedious and time-consuming computational requirements in their research work, typically involving solutions to large systems of

---

[2] See Nathan Rosenberg, "Technological Change in the Machine Tool Industry, 1840–1910," *Journal of Economic History* (December 1963). Reprinted as chapter 1 in Nathan Rosenberg, *Perspectives on Technology*, Cambridge University Press, Cambridge, 1976.

differential equations.[3] Interest in useful applications of this capability outside the sphere of research (including military R&D during the Second World War) was, for a long time, limited or non-existent.[4]

The diffusion and impact of scientific instrumentation

The computer has been, of course, strictly *sui generis*. No other scientific instrument has had anything like its immensely diverse range of applications. Nevertheless, a detailed history of the development of instrumentation in the twentieth century would probably reveal an inventive process similarly dominated by the requirements of academic research. The subsequent diffusion paths of this instrumentation have been highly complex, but there are three aspects that need to be stressed.

Diffusion across disciplines

Instrumentation and techniques have moved from one scientific discipline to another in ways that have been very consequential for the progress of science. In fact, it can be argued that a serious understanding of the progress of individual disciplines is often unattainable in the absence of an examination of how different areas of science have influenced one another. Moreover, this understanding is frequently tied closely to the development, the timing, and the mode of transfer of scientific instruments among disciplines. The flow appears to have been particularly heavy from physics to chemistry, as well as from both physics and chemistry to biology, to clinical medicine, and ultimately, to health-care delivery.[5] There has also been a significant flow from chemistry to physics, and in recent years from applied physics and electrical engineering to health care. The transistor revolution was a direct outgrowth of the expansion of solid-state physics, but the success of that revolution was in turn heavily dependent upon further developments in chemistry and metallurgy which made available

---

[3] See David Ritchie, *The Computer Pioneers*, Simon & Schuster, New York, 1986.

[4] For a further discussion of the inability to foresee the economic consequences of the computer see chapter 11. See also Paul Ceruzzi, "An Unforeseen Revolution: Computers and Expectations, 1935–1985," in Joseph J. Corn (ed.), *Imagining Tomorrow*, MIT Press, Cambridge (MA), 1986, pp. 188–201.

[5] The National Research Council Physics Survey Committee noted that "Many physical techniques have become so fully integrated into biological research that their origin in physics is forgotten until some underlying physical advance in the method provides a reminder; recent examples include various spectroscopies, electron microscopy, X-ray crystallography, and nuclear resonance." *Scientific Interfaces and Technological Applications*, Physics Through the 1990s, National Academy Press, Washington (DC), 1986, pp. 27–28.

materials of a sufficiently high degree of purity and crystallinity. It would be most interesting to understand better than we do at present why the traffic is so heavy in some disciplinary directions but so light in others.[6]

One relevant point, however, is clear. The availability of new or improved instrumentation or experimental techniques in one academic discipline has been a frequent cause of interdisciplinary collaboration. In some cases, it has involved the migration of scientists from one field to another, such as those physicists from the Cavendish Laboratories in Cambridge who played a major role in the emergence of molecular biology. This amounted to interdisciplinary research in the special sense that individuals trained in one discipline crossed traditional scientific boundary lines and brought the intellectual tools, concepts, and experimental methods of their field to the assistance of another. There have been a number of other instances where the availability of novel instrumentation has been crucial to the establishment of new disciplines, as in the cases of geophysics, computational physics, and artificial intelligence.

The story of the migration of scientific instruments from their points of origin to their utilization in other disciplines is an underresearched topic meriting several monographs, at the very least. It is interesting to note that much of the transfer from physics to other disciplines, as already suggested, has involved the migration of labor as well as capital, for example, PhD's in physics have changed or transferred fields in greater numbers than PhD's in other disciplines. This point was emphasized by the United States National Research Council's Physics Survey Committee which reported in 1986:

Much of the outward mobility of physics PhD's has been into engineering and interdisciplinary areas such as geophysics, materials research, and biophysics; but PhD physicists also work in areas ranging from chemistry to the biosciences. Some of this mobility occurred within academe where physicists teach and conduct basic research in related science and engineering departments. Most of it, however, occurred in the industrial sphere where applications of physics research move easily across disciplinary barriers.[7]

The transfer of scientific instrumentation from one field to another has been an intrinsic part of the history of scientific research for several decades. The electron microscope, for which a Nobel Prize in Physics was awarded several years ago, was rapidly adopted throughout the entire range of the biological as well as the physical sciences. Particle accelerators, which were originally devised to examine the structure of the atomic nucleus, eventually exercised a major impact on medical research and treatment through

---

[6] *Ibid.*, p. 54.
[7] *An Overview*, Physics Through the 1990s, National Academy Press, Washington (DC), 1986, p. 99.

their role in producing radioisotopes. Isotope tracer techniques have been of fundamental importance in both medical diagnostics and biological research. Nuclear magnetic resonance (NMR) is a classic instance of a tool of pure science developed by physicists at Harvard and Stanford Universities, in order to measure the magnetic moments of atomic nuclei – an innovation for which, again, the creators received the Nobel Prize in Physics. The technique quickly became a fundamental tool in analytical chemistry. More recently, the technology has been transferred to the biological sciences and the realm of medicine, where magnetic resonance imaging has become invaluable in clinical diagnosis:

Whole-body scanning by NMR provides sectional images of the human body of remarkable clarity and with none of the potential hazards of X-ray scanning. There is now discussion that NMR may one day allow doctors to observe human metabolism without surgical procedure, moving us one step closer to the possibility of knifeless biopsy.[8]

NMR is far from unique as a technique that originated purely as a scientific research tool and was subsequently introduced into medical diagnostics. Computerized X-ray transmission tomography (CT), which was developed in the 1970s (primarily in the United Kingdom), is widely regarded as the most significant single step forward in medical imaging during the twentieth century. Together with ultrasonics, widely used by cardiologists and obstetricians, there is now an impressive array of relatively non-invasive diagnostic technologies (high-frequency ultrasound is similarly acquiring an important therapeutic application in the fragmentation of kidney stones through the use of lithotripters). The National Research Council Physics Survey Committee was thus able to conclude that:

The record clearly shows that most innovation in medical instrumentation since the turn of the century, even that of the past few decades, has come from the universities and medical schools and not from the medical-device industry.[9]

Diffusion from the academic laboratory to industry

The transfer of instrumentation from one field of science to another, or from basic to applied problems, is only a part of the story of the eventual impact of instruments originating in university laboratories. Instrumentation developed by academic scientists has, in the post Second World War years, also moved in massive amounts into many areas of industrial technology. Indeed, much of the equipment, perhaps most, that one sees

[8] *Scientific Interfaces*, Physics Through the 1990s, p. 86.
[9] *An Overview*, Physics Through the 1990s, p. 256.

today in an up-to-date electronics manufacturing plant had its origin in the university research laboratory. In this sense, scientific instruments are now effectively indistinguishable from industrial capital goods. Consider the following:

a. Ion implantation originated as a technique of basic scientific research in the field of high-energy particle physics. Its origin lay in the early work in particle physics which flowed from the recognition that magnetic and electric fields could be used to impart energy to particles. Methods of charging, accelerating, and directing these ion beams were developed in order to elucidate theories of physics. As the frontier of very large-scale integration created a need for controlling the deposition of impurities on semiconductor devices with ever-higher degrees of precision, ion-implantation techniques were transferred to the semiconductor industry. It now constitutes the preferred technique of deposition in integrated circuit technology.[10]

b. It is conceivable that the transfer of ion-implantation techniques from the research laboratory to the semiconductor industry may be partially duplicated with the use of synchrotron radiation sources, which already offer several potentially useful techniques for improving the manufacture of integrated circuits. In the late 1970s, synchrotron radiation moved from merely being an annoying side effect in experimental high-energy physics to assume a more positive role in condensed-matter physics and biology. As the current methods of X-ray lithography approach their limits in the realm of submicron lithography, the instrumentation of synchrotron radiation is becoming directly applicable to the manufacturing requirements of integrated circuits. This could have significant consequences for international competition in electronics. As matters now stand, Japanese firms, organized in consortia, have already moved vigorously into this new technology, with more than ten synchrotron storage rings under development for use in manufacturing integrated circuits. On the other hand, although the United States has many such rings for research purposes, IBM is the only American firm that is currently building a synchrotron storage ring for commercial use. This venture into X-ray radiation sources represents a high-risk activity. Not only is IBM's emerging technology extremely complex and expensive, but alternative and cheaper circuit-etching technologies may be available by the mid 1990s, when IBM's new method is expected to become sufficiently mature to enter production.

c. The most important recent advance in semiconductor processing is phase-shifted lithography. This technique is an application of interferometry that allows higher resolution by interacting two beams of

---

[10] *Scientific Interfaces*, Physics Through the 1990s, chapter 8.

monochromatic light in order to produce precise patterns on a chip. Although this particular application is new, interferometers have been an important scientific instrument since the early part of the twentieth century. In fact, the interferometer had been invented in the 1880s by A.A. Michelson, America's first Nobel Prize winner, in order to test the classical Newtonian concept of absolute motion.

d. The scanning electron microscope, a scientific research tool of great sophistication, has migrated from its university origins, initially as a research tool at Cambridge University, to the world of manufacturing technology. It has become an indispensable measurement tool in microelectronics fabrication, where the elements of memory chips are now at a scale that are too small to be resolved with optical microscopes.

The semiconductor industry is hardly unique in its experience of transferring research instrumentation, as opposed to transferring knowledge derived from research, from the university laboratory to the factory floor. Similar statements could be made about the advanced technology of industrial process control, robotic sensing, and a variety of other more specialized instrumentation applications. Also in a similar category are: the diffusion of techniques for the production, measurement, and maintenance of high vacuums in larger and larger volumes; the transfer of cryogenic techniques from laboratory to large-scale industrial use (as in booster rockets); and industrial-scale superconducting magnets which had their origins in experimental physics. The common denominator running through and connecting all these experiences is that instrumentation developed in the pursuit of scientific knowledge eventually had direct applications within the manufacturing process. Consequently, they constitute benefits of basic research activity which are separate and distinct from those flowing from pure scientific knowledge and the eventual applications of that knowledge.

Diffusion from industry to the wider research community

There is a further dimension to the connection between laboratory instrumentation and commercialization which deserves recognition. Many instrumentation technologies originating in university laboratories have eventually been taken up and exploited by profit-making firms. This has typically resulted in standardized off-the-shelf equipment which provides improved performance and versatility at a much-reduced cost. The result is that the instrumentation diffuses rapidly throughout both industry and the wider university research community. This process has vastly expanded the size of the industrial and research populations to which the instrumentation was accessible.

One essential aspect of this expansion in use has been modification of design so that instruments can be employed by people with lower levels of training. Often, in fact, it has proven worthwhile to redesign to *lower* performance ceilings in order to permit the substitution of automatic control for control by a highly trained operator.[11] Thus, the ultimate benefits have flowed not only to the industrial world, but in some considerable measure back to a much larger scientific research community whose members have been provided with greater access to necessary instrumentation.

In this respect, an important and insufficiently appreciated aspect of the high level of performance of American science has been the emergence of a strong scientific instruments industry in the United States. The entrepreneurial efforts of this industry, including the fruitfulness of its interactions with university researchers, who were frequently both the designers and the users of the innovation, have been of immense value to the scientific community.[12] Firms have had a strong incentive to find new markets for existing instruments and thereby to expand the population of users, who often turned out to be other scientists.

The benefits resulting from the successful commercialization of new scientific technologies are more than a matter of individual instruments. Rather, the migration of scientific instruments to industry has been matched by a reverse flow of fabrication and design skills that have vastly expanded the capacity of university scientists to conduct research. This is perhaps most apparent in the ways in which micro-fabrication technologies have made possible the conduct of new fundamental research in fields such as condensed-matter physics:

The ability to produce structures on a nanometer scale has facilitated recent investigations into such areas as conduction electron localization, non-equilibrium superconductivity, and ballistic electron motions. Microscience is becoming an area of increasing activity in solid-state research laboratories. Indeed, one of the major reasons for which the National Science Foundation established a National Submicron Facility in the late 1970s was to help to make this impressive microfabrication technology available to scientists for fundamental research.[13]

In short, the interplay between universities and private industry in the development of new and improved techniques of instrumentation has clearly been and will probably continue to be a symbiotic one.

[11] A high-resolution electron microscope of Japanese design was installed at Cambridge University in 1990. The earlier high-resolution electron microscope, built by the Cambridge engineering and physics faculty in the 1970s, remained capable of attaining higher levels of performance than its automatically controlled successor, but only in the hands of a skilled faculty member. (I am grateful to Dr. W.C. Nixon of Peterhouse College, Cambridge, for his guided tour of this facility and his patient explanation.)

[12] Eric von Hippel has paid particular attention to the dominant role played by users in the scientific instruments industry. See Eric von Hippel, "Users as Innovators," chapter 2, *The Sources of Innovation*, MIT Press, Cambridge (MA), 1987.

[13] *Scientific Interfaces*, Physics Through the 1990s, p. 141.

The role of instrumentation in shaping science and technology

So far, the discussion has focused on ways in which novel instrumentation has been initiated and generated by the requirements of basic research. The main avenues along which the influence of new instruments has been diffused have also been identified. It is now appropriate to call attention to another set of influences that run from technology "upstream" to basic science, and which similarly have been badly neglected.

Two key points need to be made. First, a new instrument, once available, usually requires further development, including sometimes basic research, in order to improve its performance. Second, these new lines of research, triggered initially by the needs of instrumentation, often subsequently acquire a dynamic and significance of their own.

Examples here are: the computer in its 1946 form, as the ENIAC at the University of Pennsylvania; the first transistor in its 1947 form at Bell Labs.; and the first ruby laser in 1960. In each case, the new technology had very poor performance characteristics. The ENIAC was a gigantic and clumsy apparatus, more than 100 feet long, with approximately 18,000 vacuum tubes that consumed over 100 kW of electricity. The transistor which, among other things, eventually transformed the computer by eliminating its dependence upon vacuum tubes, was itself initially unreliable and sometimes behaved in unpredictable ways. The laser was, even until quite late, regarded more as a scientific curiosity than as a technological innovation. The patent attorneys at Bell Labs. were at first reluctant even to apply for a patent on the grounds that there was no apparent application in the communications industry.

A common feature of new instruments, then, is that their initial performance levels are poor and/or unpredictable. They may also require components or materials which possess characteristics not presently available or available only at very high cost. Sometimes, their apparent potential can be realized only if a particular scientific or technical bottleneck is overcome. In most cases, the availability of a new instrument (or technique) has therefore given rise to intense research activity stimulated by the need to improve its performance, to develop some ancillary technology, or to identify a cheaper or more reliable material base. The transistor coupled with the evident potential of semiconductors resulted in an explosion of research in solid-state physics and the physics of surface phenomena in the late 1940s and 1950s. The number of basic publications in semiconductor physics rose from less than twenty-five per annum before 1948 to over 600 per annum by the mid 1950s.[14] In the early 1950s, as the transistor experienced a widening range of applications, serious reliability problems

[14] C. Herring, "The Significance of the Transistor Discovery for Physics," Bell Telephone Laboratories, unpublished manuscript, no date.

emerged. The defects were eventually traced to surface phenomena and, consequently, a great deal of basic research needed to be undertaken. In the end, the effort to solve these reliability problems in the performance of transistor components led to much fundamental new knowledge in the area of surface physics.

The development of the laser suggested, among other things, the possibility of using optical fibres for transmission purposes. This resulted in a burgeoning of research in the field of optics, a scientific subdiscipline which had been a relatively quiet intellectual backwater until that time. The growth of activity in the discipline was thus generated, not by forces internal to the field of optics, but by a radically altered assessment of the potential opportunities for laser-based technologies. Moreover, different kinds of lasers gave rise to different categories of fundamental research. As Brooks has noted, "While the solid-state laser gave a new lease on life to the study of insulators and of the optical properties of solids, the gas laser resuscitated the moribund subject of atomic spectroscopy and gas-discharge physics."[15]

The conclusion which can be drawn is that, in the years since the Second World War, a succession of new technological capabilities in instrumentation has played a major role in shaping the agenda of research in universities and elsewhere. These connections have not been well recognized, in part for reasons that are inherent in the nature of scientific research. Questions which are initially raised by some particular observation or performance anomaly in a special context have a way of raising new questions of much greater generality. Further questions or implications are eventually raised as a result of findings of further research and, consequently, still further questions of a more fundamental nature are posed. In a very serious sense, the new questions take on a life of their own as they are pursued far beyond the requirements of the technologies that initially gave rise to them. Thus, the need for highly perfect crystals in semiconductor technology produced an immense stimulus to classical crystal physics and chemistry. Although Shockley had been very interested in dislocations in the late 1940s, the great expansion in such interest and the emergence of a science of imperfections in crystals in the 1950s owed very much to the growing needs of semiconductors.[16] Moreover, the working materials in the early experiments tended to be silicon and germanium

[15] Harvey Brooks, "Physics and the Polity," *Science* (26 April, 1968), p. 399.
[16] Shockley was one of the editors of the volume, *Imperfections in Nearly Perfect Crystals*, financed by the Office of Naval Research. This book was a landmark in the emergence of the new discipline of imperfections. Although published in 1952, its contents were based on a symposium conducted in October 1950. See W.B. Shockley, J.H. Holloman, R. Maurer, and F. Seitz (eds.), *Imperfections in Nearly Perfect Crystals*, John Wiley, New York, 1952.

simply because industrial requirements had already led to methods of crystal growth and purification for these materials that were far more advanced than for other substances. The semiconductors also turned out to be excellent materials for observing individual dislocations and their electronic effects. Ultimately, scientific study which had been powerfully stimulated by the attempt to improve the performance of transistors in a variety of electronic devices led to a new approach to the subject of dislocations, emerging eventually as a theory of great power and generality, in no way restricted to the concern with transistor effects or the class of semiconductor materials that gave rise to the research in the first place.

The instrumentation requirements of university research have thus had consequences far beyond those that are indicated by thinking of them simply as an expanding class of devices that are useful for observation and measurement. Furthermore, they have played more pervasive, if less visible roles which include making a direct impact upon industrial capabilities, on the one hand, and stimulating more fundamental research, on the other. This even includes a role of great importance in redefining and expanding the agenda of fundamental university research in both scientific and technical disciplines.

It is possible to go a step further. It follows from what has been said that the rate of progress, and the timing of progress, in individual scientific disciplines may be shaped, to a considerable degree, by the transfer of instruments, experimental techniques, and concepts from one scientific discipline to another. But the timing of these transfers, and the circumstances that are conducive to them, have not yet been studied, as far as I know, in a very systematic way, and are not, as a result, very well understood. It is therefore possible that more research along these lines may powerfully illuminate the course of scientific progress in the twentieth century. And, needless to say, the scope of such research must be international.

Conclusions

It seems natural at this point to pose the question: what were the consequences of the role played by the research university in the development of scientific instruments, as it has been characterized here, upon the operation of the economy? Such a question necessarily poses the counterfactual: how would the performance of the economy have differed in the absence of the university's research capability?

One possible response is to conclude that all the instrumentation technologies would eventually have been developed anyway, but that they would have taken longer to develop. The economic contribution of the research community is therefore to be measured by how much sooner those capabilities were acquired as a result of university research, and what the economic value was to society of having each capability X years sooner.

An alternative and less facile response would be that the presence of the university research capability shaped not only the rate of technological change but also its direction and therefore its qualitative outcome as well. I lean strongly toward this latter response. I have already indicated some of the ways in which a powerful university research community has altered the shapes of these instruments and influenced the ways in which they were utilized. America's distinctive leadership in the experimental, as compared to the purely theoretical, sciences in the post Second World War years was surely closely connected to the country's outstanding instrumentation capabilities. In addition, however, the presence of this community has meant that new instruments have not merely improved the effectiveness of existing research at basic and applied levels. Rather, they have also been responsible for formulating new questions at the level of fundamental and applied research that would otherwise not have been posed or explored. In the field of medicine, where it is frequently observed that diagnostic capabilities have outrun the possibilities of therapeutic intervention, it is almost certainly true that improved diagnostic capabilities have exercised a powerful influence upon the search for more effective therapies and have also posed further research questions of a fundamental nature.[17]

It is far from obvious how one should go about dealing with the counterfactual world that these observations imply. The university context in which much scientific instrumentation originated also provided a high degree of resonance and amplification for these innovations. Had they originated or experienced their development in a purely commercial context, it is doubtful that the environment would have provided the great stimulus to further research, and to the opening up of entirely new research fields, which actually occurred. But, since so much new instrumentation arose precisely because university researchers were allowed to pursue

[17] "While the modern imaging modalities afforded by advances in physics have contributed significantly to diagnostic accuracy and to the monitoring of the condition and comfort of patients during the diagnostic phase in a cost-effective manner, there is a question concerning the effect of these advanced-technology diagnostic methods on outcome. Diagnostic capabilities in the areas of cancers, cardiovascular disease, and metabolic diseases appear to have outstripped therapeutic capabilities. However, the same sophisticated new diagnostic tools afford the means to follow and evaluate therapeutic modalities. Thus, the rapid advances in noninvasive diagnostic methods of the past decade are showing signs of bringing advances in therapy in the next." *Scientific Interfaces*, Physics Through the 1990s, pp. 254–255. For further discussion of the subtleties of the interactions between diagnostic capability and therapeutic intervention, as well as the more general question of the nature of the interactions between basic and applied research, see J.H. Comroe, Jr. and R.D. Dripps, "Scientific Basis for the Support of Biomedical Science," *Science* (9 April 1976).

fundamental questions that offered no apparent prospects of financial payoffs, it is difficult to take seriously a counterfactual that suggests that the same instrumentation would eventually have been developed in a purely commercial context.

Thus, the deeper counterfactual is not how much later these same instruments would have emerged had they been developed entirely by private industry. The deeper counterfactual is how the university origin influenced the features that were given prominence and those that were suppressed. Ultimately, one has to ask the question whether certain instrumentation would have been developed at all.

But there are two final and different counterfactuals that one might pose as well: how much would the basic research thrust of the university science community have been impoverished if it had been deprived, not just of the scientific instruments that have been referred to in this chapter, but of the stimulus to further research that was provided by the attempt to improve the performance of these instruments, once they appeared in their earliest, primitive forms? And finally, in view of the various impacts, upon the larger economy, of instrumentation that originated in the university context, what has been the social rate of return to society's investment in such instrumentation? Although there have been readily identifiable forces that have powerfully influenced the demand for scientific instruments – for example, the requirements of the military and the needs of the health-care system – another highly influential component of demand has been the requirements of scientific research, as conducted within the university community. Moreover, it is also suggested that this scientific research community undertook radical innovative initiatives that led, in many cases, to the eventual supplying of its own internal demand and, in the process, provided large external benefits as well.

Index

Abegglen, James 131
Abramovitz, Moses 45
adoption of innovations 111
    decision calculation 255–256
    forest products 240–244
    rates 69–70, 71
    telecommunications 225–226
aeronautical engineering 19
Aiken, Howard 230, 252
aluminum smelting 186–187
American innovations
    colonial period 109–110
    imitation 121
    nineteenth century *see* American
        nineteenth-century innovation
American nineteenth-century innovation
    109–120
    agricultural machinery 116
    capital-goods sector 117–118
    demand 112–115
    import of technology 109, 115
    interchangeable components 110, 115,
        118
    labor scarcity 117–118
    land ownership 114–115
    market characteristics 112–113
    mass production 116–117
    mechanization 119
    population growth 113
    resources abundance 111, 112, 113, 114,
        116, 117
    specialized machines 110, 112–113
    standardization 110, 113, 118
    supply 115–120
    United States system of manufacture
        110–111, 112, 116, 119
American Telephone and Telegraph *see*
    AT&T
American universities 149–150
    interface with industrial world 149–150

aniline dyes 144
apprenticeships 30
asymptotic perturbation theory 155
AT&T 209
    breakup 227, 228
    communications satellite 224, 226
    Long Lines 22, 217, 224
    Picturephone 229
    research 215, 218
Atanasoff, John 252
Automated Operator Services 208, 212

Babbage, Charles 24–46
    calculating engine 25–26, 39–41
    copying 26
    division of labor 25, 27–31, 37–38
    division of mental labor 39–40
    dynamic comparative advantage of
        machinery 37–38
    economies of scale 41–43
    factory visits 26
    influence on Marx 29, 36–37, 43–45
    innovation-process difficulties 33–35
    manufacturers and makers 27
    manufacturing processes description 25
    mass production 26
    technological obsolescence 34–35
    testing of new machinery 35–37
backward linkages 76
bandwagon effect 73
bankruptcy of innovators 36–37, 96, 130
Bardeen, John 217, 218
Becker, Gary 30
Bell, Alexander Graham 209, 210–211, 219
Bell Labs. 20, 152, 155
    lasers 219: patenting 3, 223, 259
    telecommunications research 215
transistor discovery 22, 212, 217, 218–219
Bell System, divestiture 227
Bessemer process 19–20

264

energy efficiency 166, 169
Binswanger, H. 239
biotechnology industry 147
Blaug, Mark 25
"blindsided" 149
Boston Consulting Group 195
bourgeoisie 89, 90
Brattain, Walter 217, 218
Brooks, Harvey 122
Buongiorno, J. 239
Business Cycles (Schumpeter) 60

cable television 214–215
calculating engine 25–26, 39–41
capitalism
    application of science 91
    cutting losses 95
    decision-making: decentralization 98–99;
        multiple sources 93–95
    distinctive features 95–97
    dynamic nature 51
    entrepreneurs 55, 66n11
    evolutionary nature 51, 60
    experimentation encouraged 97
    growth of productivity 90
    industrialization incentive 92
    innovation within 92–95
    large firms 99–100
    long waves and 65
    market pressures 90–91
    Marx on 88–92, 96
    organisational diversity 99–100
    overseas markets 89
    path dependency 60–61
    risk 95: reduction measures 96–97
    scientific and technological progress and
        59
    self-destruction 55
    socialism after 91–92
    stationary 49
    vulnerability of innovator 36–37, 96, 130
Capitalism, Socialism and Democracy
    (Schumpeter) 47, 51, 52, 60
carbon taxes 166–167
Carnegie Foundation 151
Carothers, W.H. 146
Carter, President Jimmy 180
Carty, J.J. 221
causality, long waves 63n4, 64–68, 83
Cavendish Laboratories 254
Center for Integrated Systems (Stanford)
    151
Center for Renewable Resources 181
central planning 95
    annual quotas 103
    autonomy and 98–99

consumer neglect 102–103
economies of scale 103–106, 107
inertia 95
short-term goals 102
slowness to cut losses 95
socialism and 101–103
Chandler, Alfred 106
change *see* innovations; technological
    change
Charpie Report 82n32
chemical engineering, new discipline
    creation 18, 146, 198
chemical processing
    chemical engineering discipline 18, 146,
        198
    commercialization 190–191, 198
    competitive process in 196
    economies of scale 198–200
    expenditure on R&D 190, 192–193
    Haber/Bosch process 194, 195
    historical perspective 191
    innovations 190–202: improvements and
        modifications 195–196, 197;
        Schumpeterian 195, 196
    learning curves 195–197, 201
    long-lived assets 197
    markets 200
    natural-resource endowments 191
    path dependence 194
    research 190–193
    specialized engineering firms (SEFs),
        200–202
Chinese Great Leap Forward 105–106
Citizens' Band radios 203
Clark, J. 67
clothing industry 233
clustering of innovations 66–68, 69, 73–74,
    75, 78
    cyclical nature 78–82
    recurrence 78–82
    stagnation of depression periods 80–83
coal 176–177
color television
    premature standardization 206–207
    receivers 129
Columbia University 152
commercialization 18, 128–129, 146
    chemical processing 190–191, 198
    new discipline creation 18–19
    telecommunications 203
communications media 22
    see also telecommunications
communications satellite 224, 226
Communist Manifesto, The (Marx and
    Engels) 87, 89, 90, 91
competition 51, 52

innovation and 52
obsolescence and 35
complementary metal oxide semiconductors
    technology (CMOS) 137
computer-aided tomography scanner 156
computerized X-ray transmission
    tomography (CT) 255
computers 17, 252–253
    inability to perceive consequences 220
    transfer between specialities 154
consumer electronics
    Japan 136–137
    Japan and United States compared
        131–133
    laser printers 138
    successive improvements 130–131, 132,
        133
consumer preferences 1, 56–59
    economic assumptions 11
    endogenous 57, 58
    identification of needs 5
    innovations and 57–58
    neglected by central planning 102–103
    Schumpeter on 56–57
Coy, George 210
craft traditions 91, 119–120
Crick, Francis 155
cryogenic techniques 257

data processing 204–205
decision-making
    accumulation of information 93–95, 147
    centralized *see* central planning
    decentralization 98–99
    heterogeneity of human input 95
    multiple sources 93–95
    rational 53–56
    sequential 93–94
    under uncertainty 54
Delbruck, Max 155
depressions
    clustering of innovations 80–83
    R&D expenditure 82
deskilling 44
development
    costs 140
    design and construction of plant 144–145
    domination in R&D 2, 13
    "downstream" 127, 202
    economic considerations 145
    expenditures on 2
    exploitation ability 18
    frequent revision or redirection 94–95
    importance of 14
    improvements and modifications 14–15,

126–127, 130–131, 132, 133, 195–196,
    197: incremental improvements 135,
    136–137
new discipline creation 18–19
pilot plants 145–146
recycle problems 145–146
testing 13–14, 34, 35–37, 141
see also research and development
    (R&D)
diffusion of innovations 68–69
    different paths 74
    education and training 72
    infrastructure costs 71
    interindustry flow 76–78
    production costs 69
    rates 69–70, 71
    related technologies 73–74
    substitute innovations 71, 72
    time lag 68, 69, 70
    unrelated industries 77
    unrelated technologies 72
division of labor 25
    Babbage 27–31, 37–38
    deskilling 44
    inventions and 31, 32
    Marx 43
    mental 39–40
DNA discovery 148
drying of wood 245–246
Du Pont Laboratories 146, 152
Dunkerley, Joy 178

East India Company 98
Eastman Kodak 152
Eckert, John P., Jr. 252
economic experimentation 87–108
    autonomy 98–99
    encouraged in capitalism 97
    freedom to conduct 98–99
    governmental control 98–99
    market test 97–98
    Marx on history of capitalism 88–92
economic theory
    application to technological change
        5–6
    competition 51, 52
    equilibrium 48–49, 50
    incomplete information 5
    information costs 11, 12–13
    liberation of performance by innovation
        17–19
    maximizing behavior 11
    neo-classical 5–6: Schumpeter rejection
        47, 49, 56
    uncertainty 10, 14
    Walras' view 48–49

Economic Theory in Retrospect (Blaug) 25
economies of scale
   Babbage 41–42
   central planning and 103–106
   chemical processing 198–200
   Marx 42–43
   Mill 42–43
   socialism 107
   waste utilization 42
Edison Effect 142
educational system 72
electric power 172, 181, 185–187
electronic microscope 156, 254, 257
energy-efficient technologies 161–189
   alternative sources 166, 188
   buildings 163–164
   carbon taxes 166–167
   consequences of efficiency 165–167
   cost of capital 164
   electricity 169, 185–187
   energy consumption by country 162
   energy intensity 167–168, 172, 173
   energy required per unit of output 167
   energy sources 168, 170–171
   energy-use patterns: change 184–185;
      life-cycle accounting 185–188
   environmental impacts 165
   flexibility in requirements 172–174
   form of delivery 169, 187
   fundamental issues 161–165
   future prospects 183–189
   historical perspective 167–172
   implementation 162–165
   long time horizons 163–164, 188
   long-lived capital assets 163–164
   nuclear power 188
   petroleum 172
   policies 180–183
   population density and geography 174
   possible payoffs 165
   pricing 177–178, 179, 182, 183
   resource availability and utilization
      174–177
   subsidies 181
   substitutions: of capital and labor for
      163; of energy inputs 163, 184, 185
   synthetic fuels 188
   taxes 182
   transportation 174
   uncertainties 188
Engineering Research Centers 151
entrepreneurs 55, 66n11
epochal innovations 76n24
equilibrium analysis 48–49, 50
Exxon Research and Engineering Company
   151

factor prices 69
factor substitution 5, 13
feudalism 88, 89–90
fiber optics 21, 148, 208, 223–226, 260
   advantages 223–224
   foreseeing consequences 3
   long time horizon 224–225
   telephone system 4, 208, 223–226
Fishlow, Albert 114
food prices 114
forest products 232–249
   adoption of innovations 240–244
   best opening face (BOF) 240
   capital costs 240–241
   Com-Ply 240–241
   drying of wood 245–246
   economic performance of innovations
      240–244
   energy source 238
   Forest Products Laboratory 239, 248
   Forest Service research stations 242
   heterogeneity of products 247–248
   heterogeneity of raw materials 235,
      244–245, 246
   imported innovations 234–235
   interindustry technology flow 233–235
   labor costs 243
   laboratory and sawmill performance
      disparity 240
   oriented strandboard (OSB) 240, 242
   parallel-laminated veneer (PLV) 240–241
   plywood 241
   projection models 238–239
   public-sector research 242
   pulp and paper sector 236, 237–238,
      247–248
   raw materials: heterogeneity 235,
      244–245, 246; scarcity 235–236;
      substitution 237
   research and development 233–235:
      public sector 242
   supply prediction 236–238
   theoretical framework 246
   utilization specialists 248
   waferboard 240, 242
   wood trusses and truss frames 243–244
   woodworking: mass production 117;
      United States resource abundance 116
forward linkages 76
Freeman, C. 67
Frischtak, Claudio 62–84

Gamow, George 155
General Electric 152
giant firms 100
   chemical processing 198–200

research 106
  socialism and 103–105, 106
Gilchrist–Thomas basic lining 19
Gilless, J.K. 239
Gosban 107
Gosplan 107
government involvement
  autonomy and control 98–99
  telecommunications 227–228
Great Leap Forward (China) 105–106
green revolution 148
Guggenheim Fund 151

Haber/Bosch process 194, 195
handicraft *see* craft traditions
Hauptman, Herbert 154
Hayami, Y. 239
Herschbach, Dudley 154
High-Definition Television (HDTV)
  206–207
high-technology industries 140
  interdisciplinary research 147–149
history, economic interpretation 59–61
History of Economic Analysis (Schumpeter)
  24, 60, 61
Hoechst AG 151
Hubbard, Gardiner 219
Hubbard, Graham Greene 210
Hudson's Bay Company, 98

IBM 20, 152, 220
imitation 53
  Japanese 122, 125
import of technology 121–138, 234
  American nineteenth-century innovation
    109, 115
  forest products 234–235
  socialism and 101
improvements 14–15, 71–72, 126–127
  chemical processing 195–196, 197
  mass production 130–131, 132, 133
  successive 135, 136–137
Ince, Peter 232–249
industrial research laboratories 20, 106,
  141–142, 152–153
industrialization
  energy resources 174
  Marx on capitalism and 88–92
  United States energy abundance 174–177
industry, isolation of science from 107–108
information
  accumulation 93–95, 147
  costs of acquisition 5–6, 11, 12–13, 23
  decisions taken sequentially 93–94
  disclosure 150

economic theory and 5–6
  exchange 120–130
  incomplete 5
  knowledge of options 11
  scientific and technological knowledge
    11–12
information theory 21–22, 155
  channel capacity 155
innovations
  adoption *see* adoption of innovations
  Babbage and difficulties with 33–35
  backward linkages 76
  capitalism and 92–95
  chemical processing *see* chemical
    processing
  clusters *see* clustering of innovations
  competition and 52
  complementary inventions 4
  consumer taste and 57–58
  cyclical nature 78–82
  definition of major innovation 15
  diffusion *see* diffusion of innovations
  discontinuous leap 16, 17–18
  endogenous nature 58
  epochal 76n24
  exploitation ability 18
  export 38
  failure to foresee consequences 3–5
  forest products industry 233, 234, 235
  forward linkages 76
  imitation 53
  imported *see* import of technology
  incremental improvements 135, 136–137
  investment and 73–74
  lag between invention and 68, 69
  lateral effects 76n22
  liberation of economy from past 17–18
  long waves *see* long waves
  market power and 52
  Marx and 92
  monopoly power and 52–53
  nineteenth century *see* American
    nineteenth-century innovation
  path dependency 15, 16, 17–18
  process 136
  product 136
  production costs 69, 71
  rational decision-making and 53–56
  Schumpeter on 50–51
  subsequent 15
  substitute 71, 72
  testing requirement 13–14, 34, 35–37, 141
  uncertainty of outcome 92–93, 95
  unrelated industries 77
  unrelated technologies 72
  United States *see* American innovations

see also technological change and
    individual innovations, e.g. fibre optics;
    lasers
innovators
    bankruptcy 36–37, 96, 130
    dynamic comparative advantage 37–38
    risk 130
instrumentation 16–17, 250–263
    basic research and 250–251
    computer 252–253
    computerized X-ray transmission
        tomography (CT) 255
    cryogenic techniques 257
    diffusion: academic laboratory to
        industry 255–257; across disciplines
        253–255; industry to wider research
        community 257–258
    electron microscope 156, 254, 257
    importance 251–253
    improvements in observational
        capabilities 17
    inferior initial performance 259
    ion-implantation 156, 256
    isotope tracer techniques 255
    lasers 259, 260
    nuclear magnetic resonance (NMR) 255
    off-the-shelf equipment 257–258
    particle accelerators 156, 254
    as production tool 156–157
    role in shaping science and technology
        259–261
    synchrotron radiation 256
    transfers to other technologies 251–252
    ultrasonic 255
    X-ray lithography 256
insurance 96, 97
Integrated Services Digital Network
    (ISDN) 209, 214
interchangeability of components 110, 115,
    118
interdisciplinary research 147–149
interindustry technology flow 233–235
International Rice Research Institute 148
inventions 111
    determinants of: Adam Smith 31;
        Babbage 31–33
    exogenous nature 58
    time lag before innovation 68, 69
ion-implantation 156, 256
isotope tracer techniques 255

Japan
    color television 129
    commercialization 128–129
    consumer electronics 131–133, 136–137
    exports to United States 122–123, 124
    imitation 122, 125
    incremental improvements 135, 136–137
    industrial targeting 121
    information exchange 129–130
    mass production 135
    personnel 129–130
    photolithography 134, 136
    price 133, 135
    radios 129
    RAM 134–135
    reliability 133, 135
    research 134, 153
    robotics 128
    subsidies 121
    system complexity 123, 125
    transistors 132
job tenure in Japan 129n15

Karle, Jerome 154
Kash, Don 180–181
Kelly, Mervin 217–218
Kihara, Nobotoshi 131
Kondratiev, N.D. 63, 64, 65
    see also long waves
Kuznets, S. 45

labor
    apprenticeships 30
    dexterity 30, 31
    division see division of labor
    piecework 30
    purchase of bundles 28, 29
Landau, Ralph 190–202
laser printers 138
lasers 219, 225
    development 260
    foreseeing consequences 3
    interdisciplinary research 147
    patenting 3, 223, 259
    research and development of 143–144
learning by doing 30, 195, 201
learning by using 196–197, 211
learning curves 36
    chemical processing 195–197, 201
Lee, Yuan 154
limited liability 96
lithography
    phase-shifted 256–257
    photolithography 134, 136
    X-ray 256
Little, Arthur D. 146
long cycles see long waves
Long Lines 22, 217, 224
long waves 62–84
    bandwagon effect 73
    capitalism 65

causality 63n4, 64–68, 83
cyclical nature of innovations 78–82
economic logic 64
economy-wide repercussions 75–78
education and training 72
historical necessity 78–79
identification and dating of inventions
    and innovations 80
innovations 63, 65, 66
Kondratiev 63
neighborhoods of equilibrium 66–67
price cycles 62, 63
recurrence 78–82
related technologies 73–74
saturation notion 80, 81
Schumpeter 66–67
substitute innovations 71, 72
time lag between invention and
    innovation 68, 69
timing 68–75
unrelated technologies 72

Mansfield, Edwin 128
Mao, Chairman 105
Marconi, Guglielmo 213, 214, 220
market tests 97–98
market viability 1
marketable shares 96–97
Marshallian industry boundaries 77
Martin, James 225
Marx, Karl 9, 87
    bankruptcy of innovators 36–37
    on capitalism 88–92, 96, 97
    division of labor 43
    economic interpretation of history 59–61
    economies of scale 42–43, 104
    influence of Babbage on 29, 36–37, 43–45
    risk 96, 97
    Schumpeter and 58–60, 61
mass production 130–131, 133, 135
    American nineteenth-century innovation
        116–117
    Babbage on 26
materials science 149
Mauchly, John W. 252
Maudslay, Henry 33
mauve, synthesis of 144
medicine, interdisciplinary research
    147–148
Mensch, Gerhard 80–81, 82, 83
metallurgy
    electricity use 186
    origins 20
Michelson interferometer 257
Microwave Communications Inc. 224

Mill, John Stuart
    Babbage and 25, 43
    economies of scale 42–43
Mincer, Jacob 30
Minister of International Trade and
    Industry (Japan) 121
MIT (Massachusetts Institute of
    Technology) 146, 152, 218
    Whitehead Institute 151
modifications *see* development,
    improvements and modifications
monopoly 52–53
Muscovy Company 98

National Research Council 191
National Research Council Physics Survey
    Committee 255
National Science Foundation 151, 258
National Submicron Facility 258
natural gas 172
neo-classical economics
    applicability to technological change 5–6
    Schumpeter rejection 47, 49, 56
Nixon, President Richard 180
Nobel Prizes 20, 142, 154, 156, 218, 254,
    257
nuclear magnetic resonance (NMR) 255
nuclear physics, interdisciplinary research
    147
nuclear power 188

obsolescence 34–35
*On the Economy of Machinery and
    Manufactures* (Babbage) 24–25
on-the-shelf technologies 13–14
optics 21
organizational diversity, capitalism and
    99–100
overseas markets 89

particle accelerators 156, 254
path dependence
    chemical processing 194
    disruption by scientific research 17–18
    innovations 15, 16, 17–18
    technological change 9–23
    telecommunications 205–207
Perkin's synthesis of mauve 144
petroleum 172
    United States abundance 191, 194
petroleum sources 176, 177
pharmaceuticals
    interdisciplinary research 148
    transfer between specialities 154
photolithography 134, 136
physics, transfer of concepts to other

disciplines 154–155
Picturephone 229–230
piecework 30
pilot plants 145–146
Plantinga, Andrew 232–249
Polanyi, John 154
polymerization 146–147, 190–191
Prandtl, Ludwig 155
price-cycle 62, 63
Principles of Political Economy (Mill) 25, 43
process design 2–3
process innovation 136
product concepts, new 18
product design 1, 2–3
product innovation 136
product standardization 110, 113
production costs 69, 71
Productivity and Technical Change (Salter)
    12
Prony, Monsieur 39–40
public sector
    cutting losses 95
    see also government involvement
pulp-and-paper sector 236, 237–238,
    247–248
Purdue University 152

radio
    entertainment devices 214, 220
    ship-to-shore communication 213, 220
    systems in 213–215
Radio Corporation of America (RCA) 220
rate-of-return regulation 225–226
rational decision-making 53–56
rationality 53–54, 58
reaction dynamic 154
rejuvenation of mature industries 70–71n17
research and development (R&D)
    agenda formulation 19–21
    American university system 149
    budgets 142–143
    chemical processing 190–191, 192–193
    commercialization 143–144, 146: value of
        findings 149, 150
    corporate funding 215, 216
    dependency on technological change
        19–21
    design and construction of plant 144–145
    development component domination 2,
        13
    disclosure of information 150
    discontinuous leap 16, 17–18
    disruption of path dependency 17–18
    economic impact of basic research
        250–251
    expenditure 13, 142–143, 151–152,

190–191, 192–193: during depressions
    82; federal funding 150
forest products 233–235, 242
high-technology industries 140, 147–149
impact of science on technology 142–144
impact of technology on science 140–142
industrial research labs 20, 106, 141–142,
    152–153
industry and: industrial applications 2–3,
    107–108; interface 149–150; isolation
    from production 107–108; private
    industry 152–153, 157–158; solving
    industrial problems 141
institutional implications 149–151
instrumentation as production tool
    156–157
interdisciplinary research 147–149
Japan 134, 153
large firms 106
laser 143–144
predictive basis 140–141
public sector 242
recycle problem 145–146
research frontier 143
research policy 139–158
scale up 2–3
science/technology interactions 140
shaped by what gone before 15–16
telecommunications *see*
    telecommunications research and
    development
time lags 143
transfer: between specialities 153–156;
    144–147
resources
    chemical industry and 191
    energy sources in United States 174–177
    petroleum in United States 191, 194
    United States 111–114, 116–117,
        174–177, 191, 194
Richardson, Owen 142
risk 95
    central planning and aversion 102
    insurance 96, 97
    limited liability 96
    reduction in capitalism 96–97
    stock markets 96
robotics 128
Rockefeller Foundation 151
Rural Electrification Administration 181
Ruttan, V.W. 239
Rycroft, Robert 180–181

Salter, W.E.G. 12
Sanders, Thomas 209, 210
Sarnoff, David 220

saturation 80, 81
scale, economies of *see* economies of scale
Scherer, F.M. 233
Schmookler, Jacob 45
Schumpeter, Joseph 9, 456, 47–61
  Babbage and 24
  business cycles 66–67
  competition 51, 52
  consumer preference 56–57
  decision-making under uncertainty 54
  endogenous forces 58
  epochal innovations 76n24
  long waves 66–67
  Marx and 58–60, 61
  monopoly power 52, 53
  rationality 53–54
  rejection of neo-classical theory 47, 49,
    56
  resource allocation 56
  self-destruction of capitalism 55
Schurr, Sam 167
Science Policy Research Unit 150
scientific instruments *see* instrumentation
sectoral studies *see individual technologies,*
    e.g. chemical processing; energy-
    efficient technologies;
    telecommunications
semiconductors 132, 259, 260–261
  see also transistors
Shannon, Claude 22, 155
ship-to-shore communications 213, 220
Shockley, William 217–218, 260
Siemens' open-hearth furnace 19
Skog, Kenneth 232–249
Smith, Adam 25, 27–28, 28–29, 30, 112
  division of labor and inventions 31
socialism
  after fall of capitalism 91–92
  annual quotas 103
  bureaucracy 104
  bypassing capitalism stage 92
  central planning 101–103
  collective farms 104
  economies of scale 103–107
  experimentation hostility 100–101, 103
  giantism 103–105
  Gosban 107
  Gosplan 107
  Great Leap Forward (China) 105–106
  incentive lacking 103
  isolation of science from industry
    107–108
  problems of 100–108
  risk aversion 102
  short-term goals 102
  technology importation 101

Soete, L. 67
solid-state physics 20–21, 218
  see also transistors
Solow, Robert 45
Solow–Swan paradigm 62
Sony Medical Electronics 148
Sony Walkman 5
specialized engineering firms (SEFs)
    200–202
  advantages accruing to 200–201
  role 201–202
Sprint 224
stagnation
  clustering of innovations 80–83
  R&D expenditure 82
Stalemate in Technology (Mensch) 80
Stalk, George 131
standardization 110, 113, 118
  craft traditions and 119–120
  premature, in telecommunications
    206–207, 225
steam power 175
steel industry 19–20
Steinmueller, W. Edward 121–138
stock markets 96
superconductivity 18
synthetic fuels 188
systems engineering 211–212
Szilard, Leo 155

technological change
  Babbage and determinants of 31–33
  commercialization *see* commercialization
  determinants 3, 31–33
  economic-theory application 5–6, 23
  endogenous 23, 66
  exogenous 23
  factor substitution 5, 13
  gluts 32–33
  history 10
  import *see* import of technology
  misreading from neoclassical perspective
    23
  outside sources 234
    see also import of technology
  path-dependent aspects 9–23
  research-agenda shaping 19–21
  science and 16
  "soft determinism" 15–16
  uncertainty 10
  see also innovations
technological obsolescence 34–35
technological options 11–12
telecommunications 21–22, 203–231
  adoption-decision calculations 225–226
  capital-equipment replacement 209

channel capacity 155
Citizens' Band radios 203
commercialization 203
consequences of innovation 3
data processing 204–205
definitions 204–205
evaluation of options 205–206
facsimile machines 204, 205
fiber optics *see* fiber optics
government involvement 227–228
historical analysis 203–204
ISDN 209, 214
learning curve 211
Long Lines 22, 217, 224
Modified Final Judgement 227
networks 204, 207
one-way communication 213, 214
path dependence 205–207
Picturephone 229–230
point to point 210, 211, 213
policy implications 226–229
premature standardization 206–207
public network 228
research *see* telecommunications research
   and development
satellites 224, 226
ship-to-shore 213, 220
social variables 203
standards 225
systemness 207–215, 221, 222
systems engineering 211–212
systems in radio and television 213–215
telephone system *see* telephone system
uncertainty of future 206–207
unique features 205
telecommunications research and
   development 215–216
basic research 206–209
corporate funding 215, 216
inability to perceive consequences
   219–223
uncertainty of outcome 217
telegraphy 219, 221, 222
telephone system 21, 208
   Automated Operator Services 208, 212
   car phones 224
   central switching 210, 211
   centralized switching 222
   Customer Premise Equipment 208
   direct long-distance dialing 212
   electronic mail transmission 208
   electronic switching 208
   fibre optics 4, 208, 223–226
   ISDN 208–209, 214
   leasing agents 210, 222
   long lines 22, 217, 224

point to point 210, 211
poor quality initially 222
systemness 208–212
systems engineering 211–212
Touchtone 212
universal service 208, 211
Voice Mail 208
see also telecommunications
television
   cable 214–215
   colour: premature standardization
      207–207; receivers 129
   home-shopping capability 214–215
   systems in 213–215
Temin, Peter 228
Tennessee Valley Authority 181
testing activities 13–14, 34, 35–37, 141
Theory of Economic Development, The
   (Schumpeter) 48
Thomson, J.J. 142
Thoreau, Henry 231
Townes, Charles 223
training 72
transistors 20–21, 22, 225, 259, 260–261
   discovery 212, 217, 218–219
   failure to appreciate consequences
      221–222
   Japan 132
Trotsky, Leon 65n8
truss framing 243–244

ultrasonics 255
uncertainties
   decision-making under 54
   economic analysis 14
   energy sources 188
   energy-efficient technologies 183–189
   innovation and 92–93, 95
   technological change and 10
unit operations 146
United States
   imports from Japan 122–123, 124
   innovations *see* American innovations
   resources 111–114, 116–117, 174–177,
      191, 194
   United States system of manufacture *see*
      American nineteenth-century
      innovation

Vail, Theodore 211
video recorders 131–133
Voice Mail 208

Walras' economics 48–50
   circular flow 49–50
waste utilization 42, 104, 145–146

water power 175
Watson, Thomas, Sr. 220
Wealth of Nations (Smith) 30n11–n12,
    32
Whitehead Institute 151

Wilkins, Maurice 155
wood trusses 243–244
woodworking *see* forest products

Zuse, Konrad 252